MINECRAFT™

NEW YORK

ONLINE SAFETY FOR YOUNGER FANS

Spending time online is great fun! Here are a few simple rules to help younger fans stay safe and keep the Internet a great place to spend time:
- Never give out your real name—don't use it as your username.
- Never give out any of your personal details.
- Never tell anybody which school you go to or how old you are.
- Never tell anybody your password except a parent or a guardian.
- Be aware that you must be 13 or over to create an account on many sites. Always check the site policy and ask a parent or guardian for permission before registering.
- Always tell a parent or guardian if something is worrying you.

Copyright © 2021 by Mojang AB. All Rights Reserved. Minecraft, the MINECRAFT logo and the MOJANG STUDIOS logo are trademarks of the Microsoft group of companies..

Published in the United States by Del Rey, an imprint of Random House, a division of Penguin Random House LLC, New York.

DEL REY is a registered trademark and the CIRCLE colophon is a trademark of Penguin Random House LLC.

Originally published in hardcover in the United Kingdom by Farshore, an imprint of HarperCollinsPublishers. This book is an original creation by Farshore.

ISBN 978-0-593-35590-9
Ebook ISBN 978-0-593-35591-6

Printed in China on acid-free paper

Written by Craig Jelley

Illustrations by Ryan Marsh

randomhousebooks.com

2 4 6 8 9 7 5 3 1

First US Edition

Design by John Stuckey and Andrea Philpots
Additional design by Jessica Coomber, Joe Bolder, Ian Pollard, Anthony Duke and Matt Burgess

Special thanks to Sherin Kwan, Alex Wiltshire, Milo Bengtsson, Agnes Larsson and everyone at Mojang Studios.

MINECRAFT™
BLOCKOPEDIA

UPDATED EDITION

CONTENTS

SECTION 3: REFINED BLOCKS

SECTION 4: UTILITY BLOCKS

USING THIS BOOK

STAT BLOCK

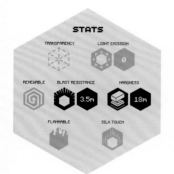

STATS

TRANSPARENCY · LIGHT EMISSION
RENEWABLE · BLAST RESISTANCE · HARDNESS
FLAMMABLE · SILK TOUCH

This handy little hexagon contains the essential details about a block so that you can see at a glance how it compares to others. Each stat has its own special icon so that you can easily see a block's most important features.

FOUND BOX

FOUND:
At the bottom of every world

This box gives you a simple snapshot of where you can find this block, whether it is hidden in certain biomes or structures or you need to craft it.

RECIPES

Talking of crafting, if it is possible to craft a block, then it will have a recipe showing the ingredients you can use to make it or its variants. Sometimes it will show smelting recipes instead.

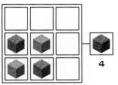

COARSE DIRT RECIPE   DEEPSLATE RECIPE

SEE ALSO TAB

This collection of images and numbers are references to other pages. They're a way of finding out more about a block by its relationship with other blocks, for instance, if it's used in a crafting recipe, or if they generate together.

TRANSPARENCY

OPAQUE   SEMI-   TRANSPARENT
           TRANSPARENT

Demonstrates whether a block is transparent, opaque or somewhere in between. Transparency in Minecraft isn't just whether you can see through a block; it also determines whether certain blocks can be placed on it, whether light travels through it and much more.

LIGHT EMISSION

This stat shows whether or not a block emits light, and if it does, how bright that light is, up to a maximum of 15.

RENEWABLE

RENEWABLE   NOT
               RENEWABLE

If a block is renewable, it means that you can create endless supplies of them. Some blocks only appear in limited quantities upon world generation.

BLAST RESISTANCE

3.5m

This explains how resilient blocks are to explosions. A higher blast resistance means it can withstand bigger explosions, such as those from fireballs and TNT.

HARDNESS

18m

This dictates how tough the block is, which can affect the strength of the tool you need to mine it, as well as how long it will take.

FLAMMABLE

FLAMMABLE   NOT
              FLAMMABLE

Flammable blocks are those that may catch alight and burn to nothing if exposed to adjacent fire blocks. Some blocks can be ignited by lava, too.

SILK TOUCH

SILK TOUCH MAKES   NO
BLOCK DROP   EFFECT

A block mined with the Silk Touch enchantment will drop itself instead of its usual items, and is the only way to collect some blocks. This icon demonstrates whether you need to collect a block with this method.

BLOCKS, SO MANY BLOCKS ...

... and every single one comes with its own unique purpose in the world of Minecraft. And together, they can make magic! I still remember how excited I was when I first played Minecraft, many years ago, and I realized how creative I could be with its blocks.

Even today, as the Vanilla Minecraft Game Director, the blocks still inspire me, just as they inspire our community to craft the most amazing creations. Seeing what players do with our blocks is always a delight for us Minecraft developers. We design each one to be detailed enough to have a clear function in the world, but simple enough so you can use it for anything you want. A big dripleaf can be a pretty table, a dead bush can be the trunk of a beautiful miniature tree and honeycomb can be the fanciest tapestry in a grand castle.

I, and many others, have spent quite a lot of time trying to understand why Minecraft seems to be loved by so many all over the world. One of the answers, I believe, is the blocks themselves. Their simplicity — both when it comes to removing and placing them and in the way they look — makes it easy for you to create something beautiful. You quickly understand how to interact with and shape your world, and soon you realize the endless number of opportunities this gives you! Your Minecraft world truly becomes your own. To be able to inspire our players to have fun and to express themselves in their own creative way is one thing I love so much about Minecraft.

Being easy to learn doesn't mean it's easy to master — that's another beautiful strength of Minecraft. There are fantastically advanced redstone contraptions, masterpiece creative builds, huge role-playing servers, extraordinarily fun minigames ... All these are built out of our simple, yet loveable, blocks. It takes an enormous amount of skill and creativity to craft these builds. I love how our players, from all parts of the world, of all ages, identities and ethnicities, can play in many kinds of ways and all find joy and delight in Minecraft. I feel so incredibly privileged that we, in an amazing collaboration with our community and everyone here at Mojang Studios, have the opportunity to work on a game that provides happiness to so many. I love how our game of blocks, adventures, creativity, and an appropriate dose of ridiculousness actually can (and should!) make the world a better place.

I hope you will enjoy reading this book and become an expert in Minecraft's blocks! Thank you so much for playing, and I hope you will continue to enjoy Minecraft for many, many more years. This book, and this game, are for you <3

AGNES LARSSON
VANILLA MINECRAFT GAME DIRECTOR

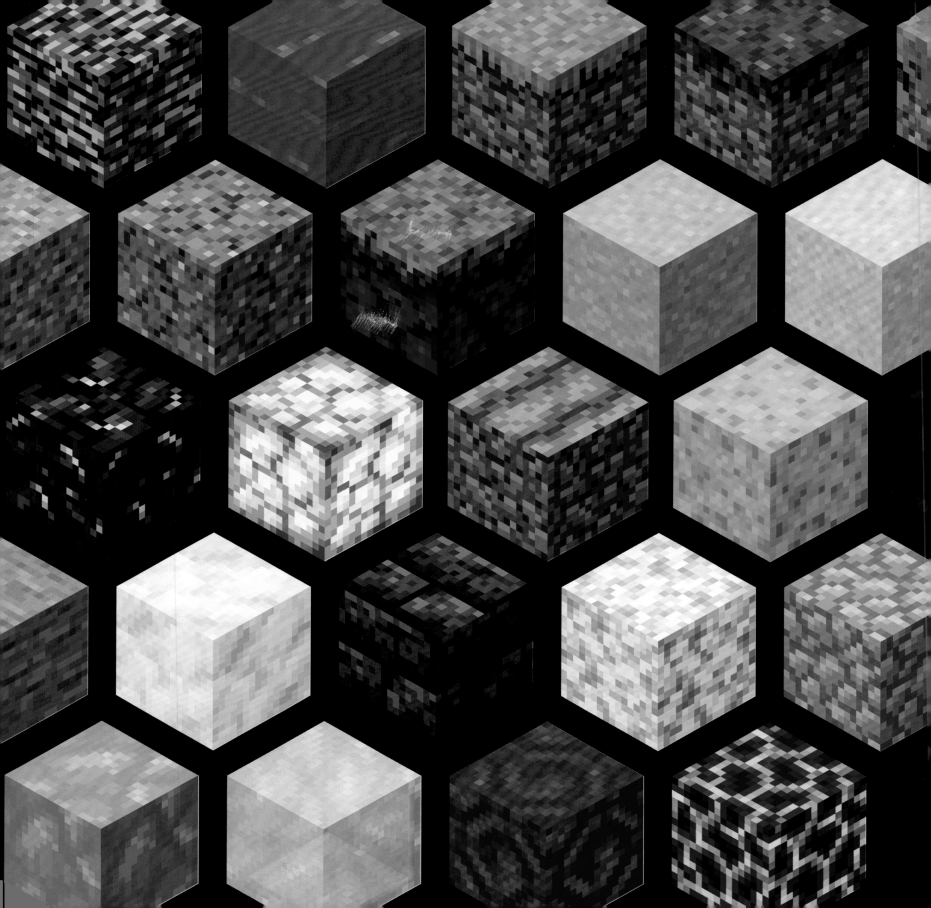

WORLD BLOCKS

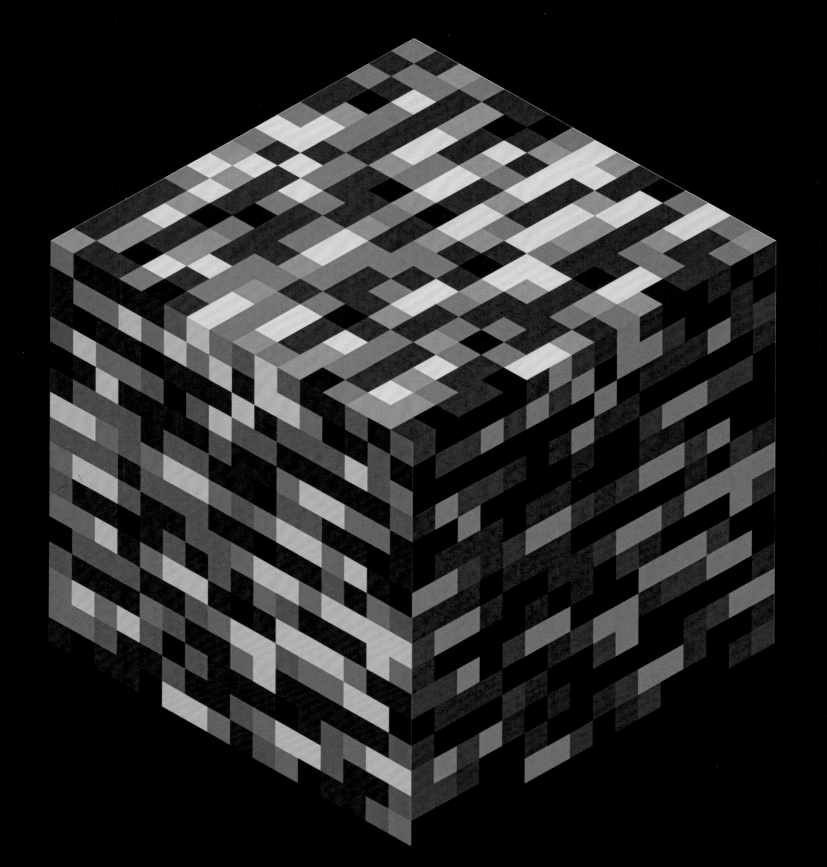

BEDROCK

FOUND:
Bottom of the Overworld, top and bottom of the Nether

A mysterious block that separates players from the endless void, bedrock is the foundation of the entire world. For that reason alone, it's fortunate that it's unbreakable, with an astronomically high blast resistance and hardness.

STATS

TRANSPARENCY	LIGHT EMISSION
	0

RENEWABLE	BLAST RESISTANCE	HARDNESS
	3.6m	18m

FLAMMABLE	SILK TOUCH

BEHAVIOR
While it's almost impossible to acquire bedrock, it does have its uses. If you encounter bedrock in the End, you can set a fire on it that will burn indefinitely, just like netherrack. Of course, as well as being impossible to destroy, it's also impossible to move with pistons.

GENERATION
The bottom five layers of any generated Overworld are comprised of bedrock, although there can be gaps in some layers. In the Nether, it populates the top and bottom four layers of the dimension. In the End, bedrock is found as part of End gateway and exit portal structures.

WORLD'S END
During early development of the game, there was a sea of lava beneath the lowest level of bedrock. Bedrock is available in the Creative inventory, so you can make use of it if you're not in Survival mode. The multi-platform edition of Minecraft is named Bedrock Edition, after this block.

13

14

AIR

One of the most important blocks in Minecraft is air. It occupies all spaces where there isn't a block present, but is transparent so you can still see the other blocks! It allows movement through it and players can avoid suffocating or drowning if they can get their head into an air block.

STATS

TRANSPARENCY	LIGHT EMISSION
	0

RENEWABLE	BLAST RESISTANCE	HARDNESS
	0	0

FLAMMABLE	SILK TOUCH

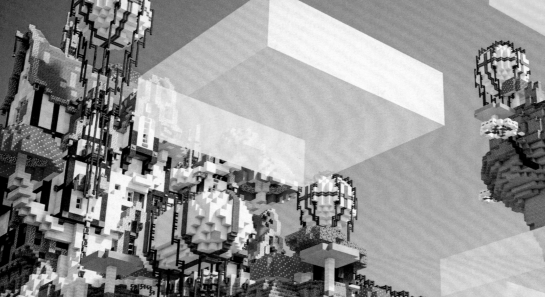

GENERATION
Air blocks are created whenever another block is removed from a block space. Conversely, air is destroyed whenever a block is placed to occupy a space. It can't be explicitly placed in the world as it can't be collected as an item.

ABSENCE OF BLOCKS
Air can't be collected by any normal method and is therefore unavailable in inventories. In the early days of Minecraft, air wasn't classified as a block at all – it was only during The Update That Changed the World that it achieved block classification.

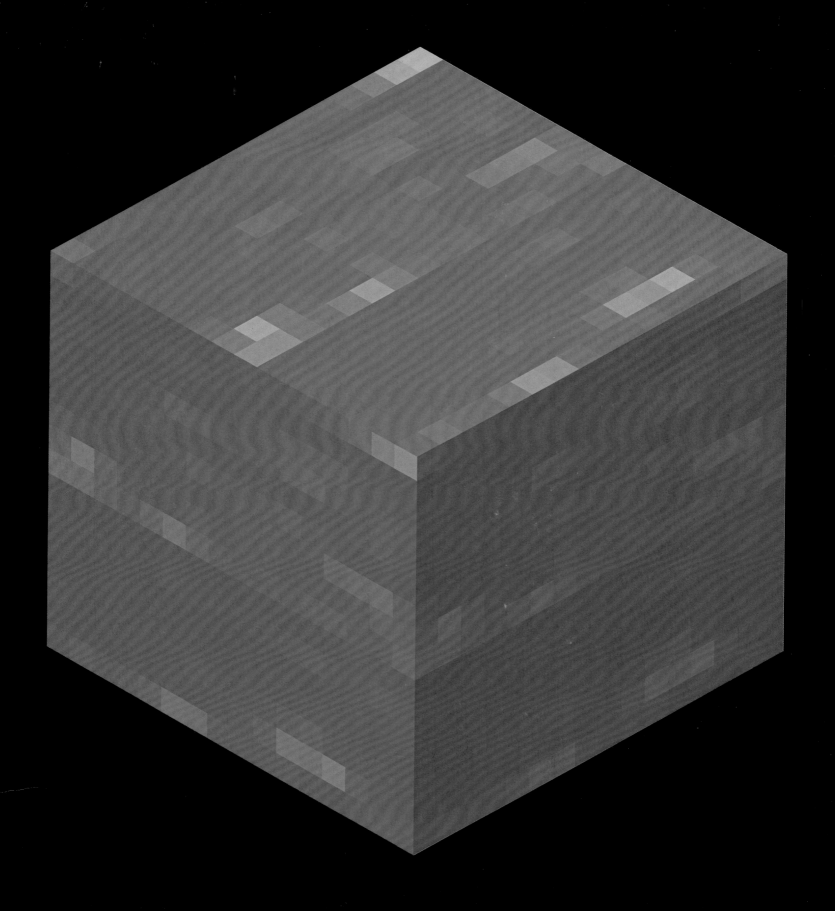

WATER

FOUND:
All Overworld biomes

A most ubiquitous liquid, water is found in bodies great and small, from oceans to desert wells. Water will flow from its source to fill nearby air blocks and can sometimes even break solid blocks. Luckily, players and many mobs are able to swim through water with ease.

STATS

TRANSPARENCY		LIGHT EMISSION
		0

RENEWABLE	BLAST RESISTANCE	HARDNESS
	100	0

FLAMMABLE	SILK TOUCH

BEHAVIOR
All water originates from a water source block. As it flows, it replaces air blocks up to 8 blocks horizontally from the source and downward infinitely until it reaches a solid block. The flow from the source block creates a current that can carry mobs and players away from the source.

GENERATION
Water will only generate in the Overworld, in lakes, oceans, rivers and springs. It can also form a part of certain structures such as villages and woodland mansions. The appearance of water varies depending on the biome it generates in. For instance, water in deserts has a greenish hue.

FONT OF LIFE
Water reduces the level of a light source by a single point, meaning it's dimmer underwater. Water that comes into contact with lava will turn into a block of either cobblestone, stone or obsidian. Water can be collected in a bucket and poured into a cauldron, which is the only way to store water in the Nether.

GRASS BLOCK

FOUND:
All Overworld biomes

One of the first two blocks to be added to Minecraft, the grass block is a common sight across the Overworld, thanks to its tendency to spread to adjacent dirt blocks. However, grass blocks can also turn to dirt if the light level is too dim, or they're covered by an opaque block.

STATS

TRANSPARENCY	LIGHT EMISSION
	0

RENEWABLE	BLAST RESISTANCE	HARDNESS
	0.6	0.6

FLAMMABLE	SILK TOUCH

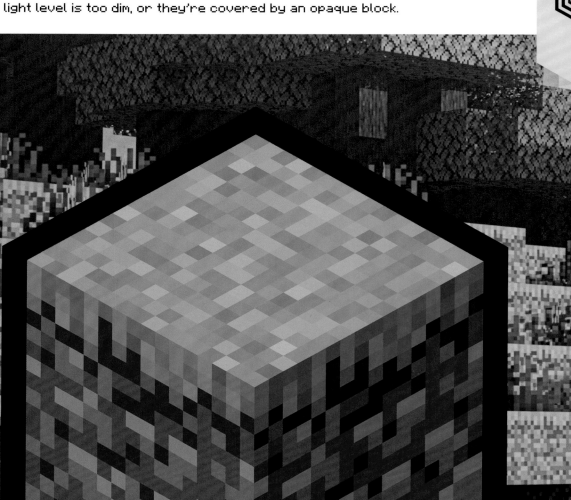

COMMON GROUND

Grass blocks generate in most biomes and have different textures in each one. They can spread grass to nearby dirt blocks if the light level is above 4 and there are no solid blocks above the dirt. Adding bone meal to grass blocks will cause grass or ferns to grow in the block space above it. They drop dirt when destroyed without Silk Touch.

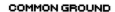

22   84

PODZOL

Podzol is a ground block native to the giant tree taiga and bamboo jungle biomes. Trees, flowers and mushrooms can grow in its ashy soil. It was added to Minecraft as a variation of the dirt block, but has since become a block in its own right.

STATS

TRANSPARENCY	LIGHT EMISSION
	0

RENEWABLE	BLAST RESISTANCE	HARDNESS
	0.5	0.5

FLAMMABLE	SILK TOUCH

FERTILE GROUND

Podzol has a special capacity to grow mushrooms at any light level, just like mycelium. However, unlike mycelium, you can plant saplings, flowers and sugar cane on this block, too. Large spruce trees also turn the grass blocks near its roots into podzol.

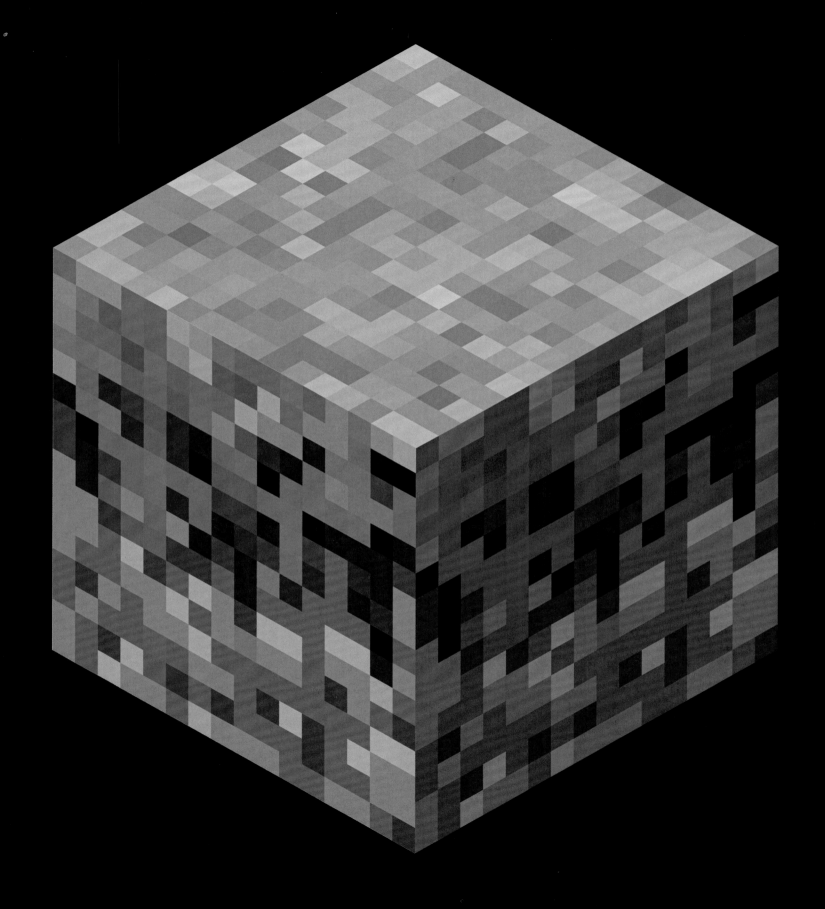

MYCELIUM

A ground block that generates only in the mushroom fields biome, mycelium is perfectly suited for the growth of fungi huge and small, at any light level. It isn't as versatile as other dirt blocks, so flowers, trees and other types of flora will be unable to take root in it.

STATS

TRANSPARENCY	LIGHT EMISSION
	0

RENEWABLE	BLAST RESISTANCE	HARDNESS
	0.5	0.6

FLAMMABLE	SILK TOUCH

BEHAVIOR

Mycelium can spread to adjacent dirt blocks if the light level above the mycelium is more than 9, and more than 4 over the dirt block. It will revert to dirt if an opaque block is placed over it, much like a grass block will. Mycelium is notable for the spore particles it emits from the top of the block.

GENERATION

Mushroom fields is one of the rarest biomes, which makes mycelium one of the rarer ground blocks, too. Because it covers the top layer of the entire biome, you're sure to have a plentiful supply of mycelium if you can find one...and have a Silk Touch–enchanted tool to harvest the block with.

FUNGI FRIEND

Mycelium can also support crimson and warped fungi, but they won't grow into the giant versions found in the Nether. To grow normal huge mushrooms in mycelium, you need a 3-block radius around the mushroom and at least 7 air blocks above it.

101 | 126

...RT

...eneath the surface in any Overworld biome and you will likely hit an ...ndance of dirt blocks. Many plants can be grown in dirt, from bamboo to ...t berry bushes, or alternatively, you can hoe it to transform it into the ...e versatile farmland block.

STATS

TRANSPARENCY	LIGHT EMISSION
	0

RENEWABLE	BLAST RESISTANCE	HARDNESS
	0.5	0.5

FLAMMABLE	SILK TOUCH

COARSE DIRT

TURNED LAND

Mycelium and grass blocks can both spread into dirt if the light level above the dirt is over 9 or 4 respectively. Dirt is one of the only ground blocks that drops itself without requiring a Silk Touch–enchanted tool. Many ground blocks, such as podzol and mycelium, will drop dirt as an item when mined without Silk Touch.

COARSE DIRT

Unlike normal dirt, grass and mycelium can't spread to coarse dirt. However, you can turn it into normal dirt using a hoe. It's often found in the less forgiving biomes of the badlands and savanna.

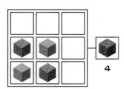

4

COARSE DIRT RECIPE

FARMLAND

Unsurprisingly, farmland is one of the best blocks for growing crops. As well as the plants that dirt can support, farmland also allows you to plant seeds for pumpkins, potatoes and more. Farmland can be created by tilling grass blocks, dirt paths or dirt with a hoe.

STATS

TRANSPARENCY	LIGHT EMISSION
	0

RENEWABLE	BLAST RESISTANCE	HARDNESS
	0.6	0.6

FLAMMABLE	SILK TOUCH

CROPS GALORE

Farmland naturally generates in villages, where beetroot, carrots, wheat, pumpkins, melons and potatoes are found growing in it. It is dry when it's created, but needs to be hydrated for crops to grow and avoid turning back into dirt. Blocks up to 4 spaces away from water will remain hydrated.

 22 104 106 108 110

DIRT PATH

Commonly found crisscrossing villages to create walkways, dirt paths are very similar to grass blocks. They're primarily used as decorative blocks, but villagers also use them to find routes through their hometown. You can make a dirt path by using a shovel on a grass block.

STATS

TRANSPARENCY	LIGHT EMISSION
	0

RENEWABLE	BLAST RESISTANCE	HARDNESS
	0.65	0.65

FLAMMABLE	SILK TOUCH

MADE FOR WALKING
Dirt paths are slightly shorter than a normal grass block, which means that you're unable to place some items on them, such as torches. They have a similar look to grass blocks in warm biomes. They will turn to dirt if a solid block is placed over them and will only drop dirt when broken.

GRAVEL

Unlike most ground blocks, gravel is affected by gravity and will fall if there's no solid block beneath it. You'll find it in underground veins in the Overworld and the Nether, so beware when mining overhead. You can use it to craft concrete powder and coarse dirt.

STATS

TRANSPARENCY	LIGHT EMISSION
	0

RENEWABLE	BLAST RESISTANCE	HARDNESS
	0.6	0.6

FLAMMABLE	SILK TOUCH

LOOSE ROCKS
Like most blocks that are susceptible to the pull of gravity, gravel will suffocate players and mobs if it falls on their heads. It might come as a surprise then that you can still grow a single plant on gravel – bamboo will flourish when placed on the block.

 26   96

SAND

Found all over desert biomes, sand is a block that falls when no solid block is underneath it, and will suffocate any player or mob it lands on. It's surprisingly productive, and you can use it in recipes for TNT, concrete powder and sandstone. It can also be smelted in order to create glass.

STATS

TRANSPARENCY	LIGHT EMISSION
	0

RENEWABLE	BLAST RESISTANCE	HARDNESS
	0.5	0.5

FLAMMABLE	SILK TOUCH

RED SAND

BEACHFRONT BLOCK

As well as generating in desert biomes, sand can also be found under lakes, oceans and other bodies of water in many biomes. The red sand variant is found in the badlands biome. It can be used to create red sandstone, or stand in for sand when crafting TNT, but not concrete powder.

 42 188 276

CLAY

FOUND:
At the bottom
of rivers, lakes
and swamps

Clay is most often found under shallow bodies of water like lakes and rivers, but also abundantly in swamps. When it's destroyed, it will drop clay balls, which can be crafted back into clay blocks. The quickest way of mining clay is to shovel it, but it's weak enough that your hands will also work.

STATS

TRANSPARENCY	LIGHT EMISSION
	0

RENEWABLE	BLAST RESISTANCE	HARDNESS
	0.6	0.6

FLAMMABLE	SILK TOUCH

MODEL BLOCK

If you place a block of clay in a furnace, you can smelt it into terracotta, which is a hardened clay that you can color with dyes. During the early days of Minecraft, it was possible to summon an Ender Dragon in the End dimension by building a creeper head made out of clay!

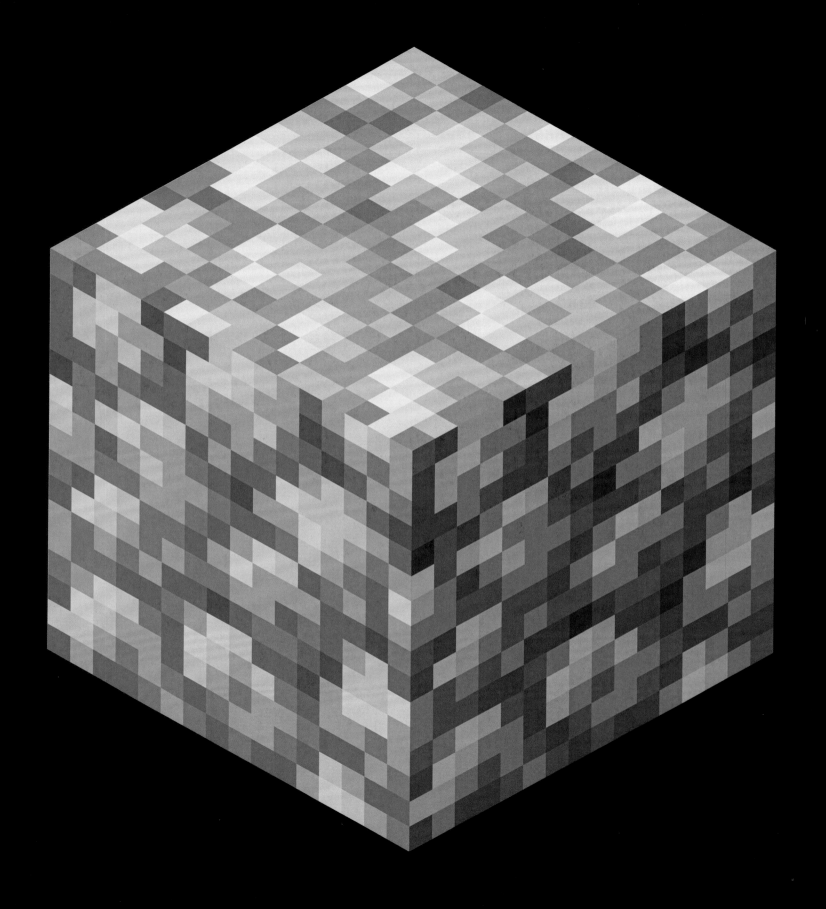

COBBLESTONE

FOUND:
All Overworld biomes

One of the most familiar blocks in Minecraft, cobblestone was one of the first two blocks to be added to the game. It drops when you mine stone and has plenty of uses in crafting: you can use it in recipes for tools and weapons, redstone mechanisms and various decorative blocks.

STATS

TRANSPARENCY	LIGHT EMISSION
	0

RENEWABLE	BLAST RESISTANCE	HARDNESS
	6	2

FLAMMABLE	SILK TOUCH

MOSSY COBBLESTONE

MOSSY COBBLESTONE

A variant of cobblestone with moss growing through the cracks, mossy cobblestone is common in dank dungeons, jungle temples, pillager outposts and some villages. It has identical properties to cobblestone, and can also be made by crafting cobblestone with vines or a moss block.

BEHAVIOR

You will only be able to mine cobblestone if you use a pickaxe. It has a decent blast resistance that can sustain some explosive damage, such as from ghast fireballs. Silverfish take a liking to cobblestone, as well as other stone blocks, and will burrow into it, turning it into an infested block.

GENERATION

Cobblestone generates naturally in structures around the world, including underwater temples and strongholds. It also forms when flows of lava and water meet on the same horizontal plane. It's most commonly seen in Overworld villages, where the buildings are all formed with cobblestone, though desert villages use sandstone instead.

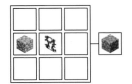

MOSSY COBBLESTONE RECIPE

 44   168   172   232

STONE

Often found under layers of grass or dirt, stone accounts for the
majority of blocks found underground. As for cobblestone, silverfish
can enter stone and turn it into an infested block. Cobblestone will be
dropped if you destroy stone without a Silk Touch–enchanted tool.

STATS

TRANSPARENCY	LIGHT EMISSION
	0

RENEWABLE	BLAST RESISTANCE	HARDNESS
	6	1.5

FLAMMABLE	SILK TOUCH

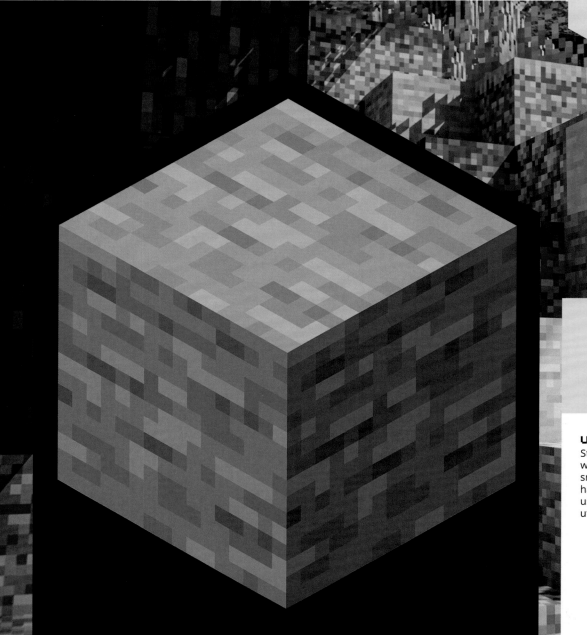

SMOOTH STONE

UBIQUITOUS BLOCK

Stone is also created when lava flows on top of
water. You can smelt cobblestone into stone, and
smelt stone into its smooth stone variant, which
has the same properties as stone. Stone can be
used to craft slabs, stairs, stone bricks and some
utility blocks like the stonecutter.

SMOOTH STONE
SMELTING RECIPE

 16   48   168   172   255

DIORITE

Diorite is a white, pockmarked variant of stone that can be found in every Overworld biome. It occurs in mineral veins below the surface, in the same fashion that mineral ores do. Diorite can also be found around coral reefs, where it often replaces coral blocks in reef formations.

STATS

TRANSPARENCY	LIGHT EMISSION 0
RENEWABLE	BLAST RESISTANCE 6	HARDNESS 1.5
FLAMMABLE	SILK TOUCH

POLISHED DIORITE

QUARTZ-INFUSED

Diorite is crafted with cobblestone and Nether quartz, which makes it a relatively expensive stone. A block of diorite can be crafted with a block of cobblestone to make andesite, or a Nether quartz to make granite. Diorite is also used in recipes for polished diorite and diorite slabs, stairs and walls.

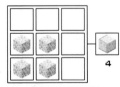

POLISHED DIORITE
RECIPE

 32 33 148

ANDESITE

STATS

TRANSPARENCY	LIGHT EMISSION
	0

RENEWABLE	BLAST RESISTANCE	HARDNESS
	6	1.5

FLAMMABLE	SILK TOUCH

Andesite generates in mineral veins and as part of coral reefs, in a similar manner to diorite. It can also be found in some buildings of snowy tundra villages. Polished andesite is found in many rooms of woodland mansions and also in the basements of igloos.

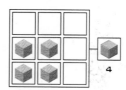

POLISHED ANDESITE

VERSATILE MATERIAL

Polished andesite is obtained by crafting together four blocks of andesite. You can also trade with stone mason villagers to get the polished variant. Andesite can be used to craft walls, and both variants can be used to create slabs and stairs.

4

POLISHED
ANDESITE RECIPE

GRANITE

The reddish grains of the granite block generate in mineral veins and as part of coral reefs, though armorers in desert villages also use the block to build part of their houses. If you're diving down to the bottom of the sea, you might also spot polished granite as part of the ocean ruins structure.

STATS

TRANSPARENCY	LIGHT EMISSION
	0

RENEWABLE	BLAST RESISTANCE	HARDNESS
	6	1.5

FLAMMABLE	SILK TOUCH

POLISHED GRANITE

SOLID TRADE

Granite can be used to craft a similar range of decorative blocks to andesite, and you can also trade for it by talking to masons. To save on resources, a single block of granite can be used on a stonecutter to make shaped granite blocks. The same can be done with andesite and diorite, too.

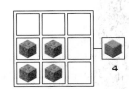

POLISHED
GRANITE RECIPE

30   31

DEEPSLATE

If you go far enough underground, you'll eventually reach the inky black of the deep dark biome, where deepslate replaces any stone block below level 0. Within the depths of this claustrophobic biome, any ores that try to replace deepslate will even turn into deepslate ore variants.

STATS

TRANSPARENCY	LIGHT EMISSION
	0

RENEWABLE	BLAST RESISTANCE	HARDNESS
	6	3

FLAMMABLE	SILK TOUCH

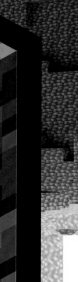

LAYER OF STRENGTH
Deepslate is one of the strongest stone blocks, equaled only by End stone, though it is slightly less effective against explosions. You can destroy the block with any pickaxe, but it will drop cobbled deepslate unless the tool is enchanted with Silk Touch. If you don't have Silk Touch, you can smelt cobbled deepslate into deepslate anyway.

DEEPSLATE RECIPE

 30 37 70 134

COBBLED DEEPSLATE

The normal drop when you destroy deepslate, cobbled deepslate is a multi-purpose block used in several recipes. It can replace cobblestone to make furnaces, brewing stands and stone tools. It can even be crafted into its own slabs, stairs and walls, which can also be formed on a stonecutter.

STATS

TRANSPARENCY	LIGHT EMISSION
	0

RENEWABLE	BLAST RESISTANCE	HARDNESS
	6	3.5

FLAMMABLE	SILK TOUCH

POLISHED DEEPSLATE CHISELED DEEPSLATE

DARK COBBLES

The two unique blocks that cobbled deepslate can make are chiseled deepslate and polished deepslate, both of which are primarily used for decoration. The polished variant shares the same beveled edges as polished andesite and diorite, while the chiseled version has an ominous face on each side ...

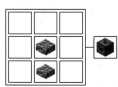

POLISHED DEEPSLATE RECIPE

CHISELED DEEPSLATE RECIPE

 28 31 32 165 176

SMOOTH BASALT

FOUND:
As the outer crust of amethyst geodes

The dark volcanic form of smooth basalt forms the outermost layer of amethyst geodes that appear underground, surrounding layers of calcite and the precious gem itself. It's possible for cracks to form in the smooth basalt and calcite layers, which allow a window to the amethyst inside.

STATS

TRANSPARENCY	LIGHT EMISSION
	0

RENEWABLE	BLAST RESISTANCE	HARDNESS
	4.2	1.25

FLAMMABLE	SILK TOUCH

PROTECTIVE BLOCK

The geodes that smooth basalts generate in are found right down to the bedrock layer and can even replace bedrock! Smooth basalt's dark and patchy texture makes it a popular choice for gothic and medieval builds. It doesn't have any use as a crafting material, but you can make it in a furnace by smelting basalt found in the Nether.

SMOOTH BASALT RECIPE

JFF

ght look like a stone, but tuff appears in mineral veins, just like
ond, gold and other ores. These mineral veins can be found under
iomes but most frequently in the deep dark biome. They look similar
obblestone and are equally strong, both against tools and blasts.

STATS

TRANSPARENCY	LIGHT EMISSION
	0

RENEWABLE	BLAST RESISTANCE	HARDNESS
	6	1.5

FLAMMABLE	SILK TOUCH

TUFF ENUFF
Tuff can generate in place of many ground blocks, like stone, granite and deepslate. Although it appears only in mineral veins, the veins can consist of more than 160 separate blocks of tuff, making them one of the biggest mineral veins in Minecraft. All ores found in tuff will become deepslate ores.

 28   34   134

ALCITE

rising the middle layer of amethyst geodes that generate in the world, calcite has the weakest composition of the geode blocks. You mine the chalky white block easily with a pickaxe, but will drop nothing u use any other tool.

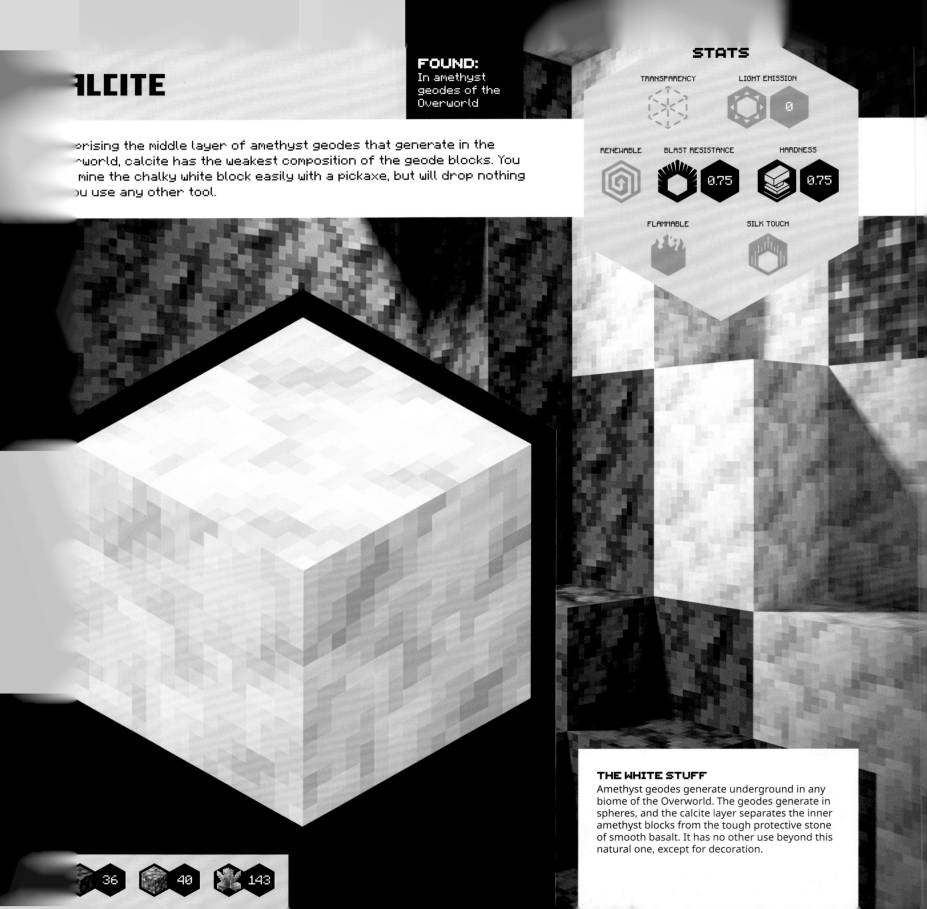

STATS

TRANSPARENCY	LIGHT EMISSION
	0

RENEWABLE	BLAST RESISTANCE	HARDNESS
	0.75	0.75

FLAMMABLE	SILK TOUCH

THE WHITE STUFF
Amethyst geodes generate underground in any biome of the Overworld. The geodes generate in spheres, and the calcite layer separates the inner amethyst blocks from the tough protective stone of smooth basalt. It has no other use beyond this natural one, except for decoration.

BUDDING AMETHYST

FOUND:
In amethyst geodes of the Overworld

If you clear away the outer layers of amethyst geodes, you'll see dazzling purple stones within. One of them is budding amethyst, where the delicate amethyst clusters emerge from and grow in stages. It's impossible to collect the block, even with Silk Touch–enchanted tools.

STATS

TRANSPARENCY	LIGHT EMISSION
	0

RENEWABLE	BLAST RESISTANCE	HARDNESS
	1.5	1.5

FLAMMABLE	SILK TOUCH

BLOSSOMING PRISM
Budding amethysts have a 20% chance to add a bud, or increase a bud's size, with each game tick. As well as being unable to be collected, it's impossible to move with pistons, and will break when pushed, so you can collect amethyst shards only from within amethyst geodes.

39

 36 37 143

LOCK OF AMETHYST

FOUND: In amethyst geodes of the Overworld

block of amethyst appears in the center of amethyst geodes along with ding amethyst. It's the only concentrated mineral block that generates rally in the world. Its shimmering purple exterior makes it a popular pration, and it also makes a chiming sound when you step on it!

STATS

TRANSPARENCY	LIGHT EMISSION
	0

RENEWABLE	BLAST RESISTANCE	HARDNESS
	1.5	1.5

FLAMMABLE	SILK TOUCH

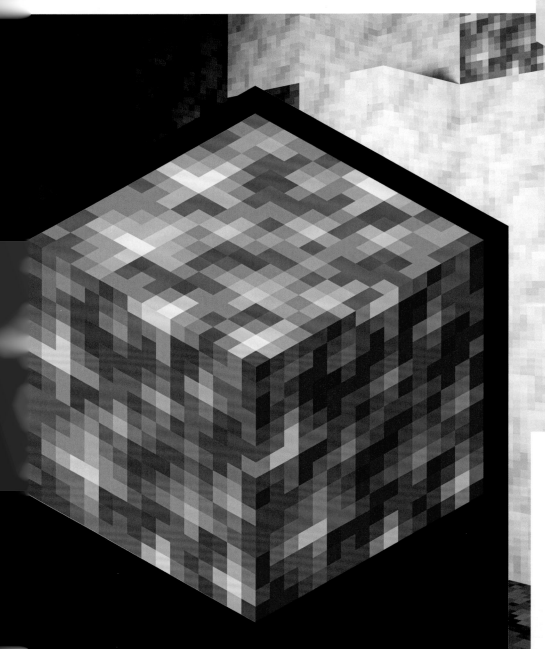

PURPLE HAZE

You must mine a block of amethyst with an iron pickaxe or stronger to collect it, otherwise it drops nothing. Unlike most other mineral blocks, you can't turn the block of amethyst back into its resource blocks, so you're unable to use it as a storage block for excess amethyst shards.

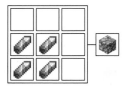

BLOCK OF AMETHYST RECIPE

DRIPSTONE BLOCK

STATS

TRANSPARENCY	LIGHT EMISSION
	0

RENEWABLE	BLAST RESISTANCE	HARDNESS
	1	1.5

FLAMMABLE	SILK TOUCH

Between the stalagmites and stalactites of dripstone caves, you'll find the more ordinary dripstone block, which has a similar texture to the pointed dripstones around it. It has the same hardness as stone, but its blast resistance is low, more so even than pointed dripstone!

GENERATION

Dripstone blocks generate as part of dripstone caves, where they can be seen in the cave walls. They also form dripstone clusters – columns of dripstone that reach from the floor to the ceiling of a cave. You can mine dripstone blocks with any kind of pickaxe.

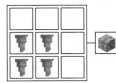

DRIPSTONE BLOCK RECIPE

 30   74

SANDSTONE

Compressed beneath layers of sand you'll find blocks of tougher sandstone. However, it still has a lower hardness than other stones, which means it's quicker to mine. Sandstone and its variants also feature heavily in desert wells, desert temples and desert villages.

STATS

TRANSPARENCY	LIGHT EMISSION
	0

RENEWABLE	BLAST RESISTANCE	HARDNESS
	0.8	0.8

FLAMMABLE	SILK TOUCH

CHISELED SANDSTONE	CUT SANDSTONE	SMOOTH SANDSTONE

MULTI-PURPOSE

The interesting designs of sandstone and its variants make it popular in decoration. Sandstone can be crafted into slabs, stairs and walls or smelted into the stronger smooth sandstone variant. Chiseled and cut sandstone can be crafted with sandstone or its slabs, or cut on a stonecutter.

CUT SANDSTONE RECIPE

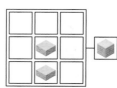

CHISELED SANDSTONE RECIPE

 26   174

RED SANDSTONE

Unlike sandstone, red sandstone doesn't generate under sand, though it does occur naturally in badlands villages, where it appears as part of the foundations of buildings. Like sandstone, red sandstone and its variants have intricate patterns that make them a common decorative choice.

STATS

TRANSPARENCY

LIGHT EMISSION

0

RENEWABLE

BLAST RESISTANCE
0.8

HARDNESS
0.8

FLAMMABLE

SILK TOUCH

CHISELED RED SANDSTONE

CUT RED SANDSTONE

SMOOTH RED SANDSTONE

BADLANDS SAND

The easiest way to obtain red sandstone is by crafting it with 4 blocks of red sand. Red sandstone and its variants share the same properties as its sandstone counterparts. Smooth red sandstone, as well as smooth sandstone, has a similar hardness and blast resistance to cobblestone, but all other variants are weaker in both respects.

SMOOTH RED SANDSTONE

INFESTED BLOCKS

They might seem innocent enough, but these infested blocks hide a rather irritating secret. Once you break one of them, it will release its annoying inhabitant – a silverfish that has made the block its home. They can be found in strongholds, igloos and woodland mansions.

STATS

TRANSPARENCY	LIGHT EMISSION
	0

RENEWABLE	BLAST RESISTANCE	HARDNESS
	0.75	0

FLAMMABLE	SILK TOUCH

INFESTED STONE

INFESTED STONE BRICKS

INFESTED CRACKED STONE BRICKS

INFESTED MOSSY STONE BRICKS

INFESTED CHISELED STONE BRICKS

INFESTED DEEPSLATE

HIDDEN PESTS

If an infested block is broken and the silverfish that drops out isn't defeated in a single hit, then all infested blocks in the nearby area will break and spawn more silverfish, all of which are aggressive to the player. The blocks themselves are indistinguishable from their counterparts, except they break in half the time to take you by surprise!

 28   30   166

PRISMARINE

Prismarine blocks are the main material that ocean monuments are made from. Dark prismarine is slightly more scarce as it's only found inside the treasure rooms within monuments; otherwise their differences are purely aesthetic, as they share identical stats.

STATS

TRANSPARENCY

LIGHT EMISSION
0

RENEWABLE

BLAST RESISTANCE
6

HARDNESS
1.5

FLAMMABLE

SILK TOUCH

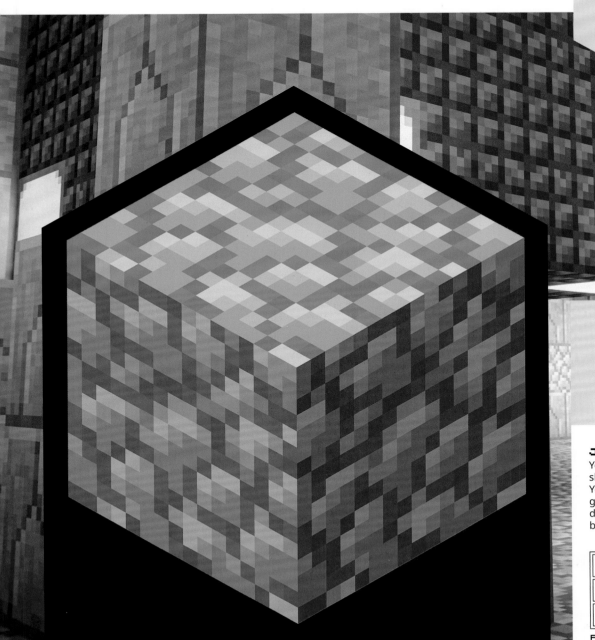

PRISMARINE BRICKS   DARK PRISMARINE

JEWEL OF THE OCEAN MONUMENT

You can craft prismarine bricks using 9 prismarine shards instead of the 4 used to craft prismarine. You can get the shards by defeating either type of guardian. Prismarine is a sought-after decoration due to its animated texture, which alternates between blues, greens and purples.

PRISMARINE RECIPE

DARK PRISMARINE RECIPE

45

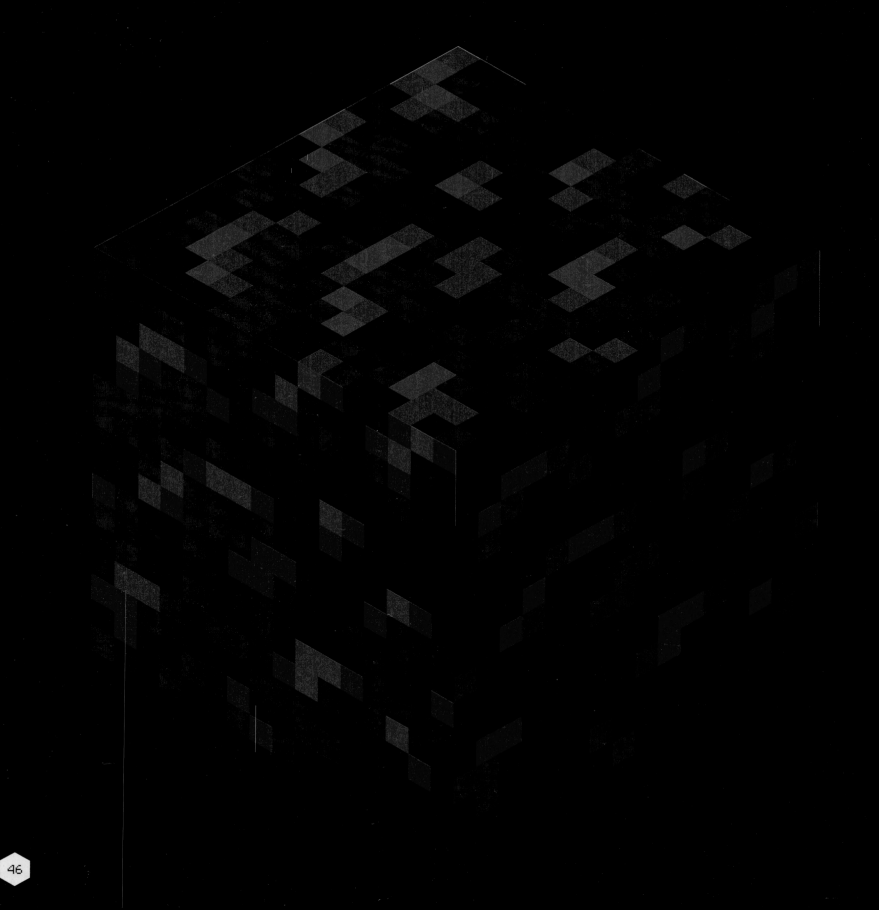

OBSIDIAN

One of the strongest blocks in Minecraft, obsidian is found in the End, or is created in the Overworld by water that flows onto lava. Its hardness means it can only be mined with the strongest pickaxes – diamond or netherite – and it can withstand any explosion, even from the Wither!

STATS

TRANSPARENCY	LIGHT EMISSION 0
RENEWABLE	BLAST RESISTANCE 1200	HARDNESS 50
FLAMMABLE	SILK TOUCH

BEHAVIOR
The most obvious use of obsidian is for building blast-resistant structures, something commonly seen in Survival mode and PvP servers. The other use for obsidian is to create Nether portals. These portals must be at least a 4x5 formation of obsidian, which is then ignited to reach the Nether.

GENERATION
Obsidian generates naturally in the End in pillar formations, or as part of End ships; and in the Nether in bastion remnants and Nether fortresses. In the Overworld, it is found in ruined portals and woodland mansions. When water flows onto lava it will create a block of obsidian.

MYSTICAL MATERIAL
Obsidian is also used in recipes for other super-powerful blocks. Combined with glass and a Nether star, it can create a beacon, which, in the right formation, can bestow a player with incredible buffs. You also need obsidian to craft an enchanting table, as well as Ender chests.

59 222 240 261

LAVA

Flowing molten lava is a common sight in the Overworld, sometimes in caves or pooled above ground, as well as in the Nether. It has a bright glow and can set flammable blocks on fire if they're close enough. It flows like water and can spread four blocks horizontally and downward infinitely in the Overworld.

STATS

TRANSPARENCY	LIGHT EMISSION
	15

RENEWABLE	BLAST RESISTANCE	HARDNESS
	100	0

FLAMMABLE	SILK TOUCH

SEARING STREAM

Lava will flow faster and farther in the Nether than it does in the Overworld. It's impossible to collect lava as an item, but it can be scooped up in a bucket and placed in a cauldron. Any player and most mobs that come into contact with lava will take fire damage for a few seconds, even after contact. Items dropped in lava are also destroyed, unless they're made of netherite.

 16 46 242

MAGMA BLOCK

A close cousin of lava is the magma block, a static, fiery block that causes damage to any mob or player that walks over it, even if the block is underwater. It can be found in ruined portals, bastion remnants and basalt deltas in the Nether, and on ocean floors in the Overworld. It won't destroy items as lava does.

TRANSPARENCY	LIGHT EMISSION	RENEWABLE
	3	
BLAST RESISTANCE	HARDNESS	FLAMMABLE	SILK TOUCH
0.5	0.5		

BUBBLE COLUMN

FOUND:
Underwater

When magma blocks generate underwater, their heat turns water above them into bubble columns, which pull players who enter them down. A similar phenomenon occurs with soul sand, though these bubbles will push players up. Players can swim through bubble columns to replenish their air supply underwater.

TRANSPARENCY	LIGHT EMISSION	RENEWABLE
	0	
BLAST RESISTANCE	HARDNESS	FLAMMABLE	SILK TOUCH
100	0		

FIRE

A force of Minecraft nature that can lay waste to many blocks, fire is a sight to behold. Of course, such wild flames can also be a powerful light source. Fire can be caused by lava within range of flammable blocks, lightning stikes, or by a player using a flint and steel or a fire charge.

STATS

TRANSPARENCY	LIGHT EMISSION
	15

RENEWABLE	BLAST RESISTANCE	HARDNESS
	0	0

FLAMMABLE	SILK TOUCH

FLAMING NUISANCE

Fire will cause damage to players and many mobs, but deals less damage than lava. Fire damage will continue even after the victim has left the fire. Fire can spread into an air block in any direction as long as the air block is adjacent to a flammable block. Fire generates naturally in the Nether, too. Of course, fire can't be collected as an item.

ICE

If you step onto ice, you'll notice that your speed increases slightly, and it's hard to stop and control your movement, because it's a very slippery block. It tops frozen lakes, rivers and oceans in snowy and cold biomes and melts in direct light, though it will often freeze again if the light fades.

STATS

TRANSPARENCY	LIGHT EMISSION
	0

RENEWABLE	BLAST RESISTANCE	HARDNESS
	0.5	 0.5

FLAMMABLE	SILK TOUCH

GENTLY DOES IT

Ice can't be obtained as an item without using Silk Touch. If ice is destroyed without the enchantment, it will turn into a block of water. Ice also generates as part of the structure in igloos, ice spikes and icebergs.

 16   52

PACKED ICE

STATS

TRANSPARENCY

LIGHT EMISSION 0

RENEWABLE

BLAST RESISTANCE 0.5

HARDNESS 0.5

FLAMMABLE

SILK TOUCH

Whereas an ice block is translucent and will melt, packed ice won't let light through and resists melting when exposed to the sun. It's a little slipperier than normal ice and a much rarer find, appearing only in igloos, ice spikes, snow-capped peaks biomes and snowy tundra villages.

ICE CUBE
Packed ice won't turn to water when it's mined, as normal ice does, but you will need a Silk Touch–enchanted tool to collect it. You can craft it using 9 blocks of normal ice and, in turn, 9 packed ice blocks make a blue ice block.

PACKED ICE RECIPE

BLUE ICE

Blue ice has more in common with packed ice than the regular ice block. It's the slipperiest of the three blocks, which means that walking is faster on blue ice than any other block in Minecraft. You'll often find it on the underside of icebergs, or forming large arches in snowy tundras.

STATS

TRANSPARENCY	LIGHT EMISSION
	4

RENEWABLE	BLAST RESISTANCE	HARDNESS
	2.8	2.8

FLAMMABLE	SILK TOUCH

LIGHT RESISTANCE
Blue ice will disappear when destroyed instead of turning into water, though it's resistant to the melting effect of light. Blocks placed on blue ice (or other ice blocks) will inherit the slippery nature of the block. If lava flows beside blue ice and over soul soil, it will transform into basalt.

BLUE ICE RECIPE

 51   54

FROSTED ICE

Unlike other ice blocks in Minecraft, frosted ice is not generated naturally in any biome. It only appears when a player wearing boots enchanted with Frost Walker passes near a water block. It behaves in a similar way to ice in that it's slippery and will melt into water.

STATS

TRANSPARENCY

LIGHT EMISSION
0

RENEWABLE

BLAST RESISTANCE
0.5

HARDNESS
0.5

FLAMMABLE

SILK TOUCH

WATCH YOUR STEP
Frosted ice only exists for a few seconds before it reverts back into water, unless it's in a dark location. The texture of the block changes as it gets closer to expiration. You can also destroy frosted ice, but it will only turn into water. It's impossible to obtain frosted ice as an inventory item.

SNOW BLOCK

You'll typically find the snow block in wintry biomes, from the ice spikes to the snowy slopes, and you might also see it in walls of igloos and snowy tundra village houses. It's more resistant to light than ice and will drop snowballs when destroyed, unless you use Silk Touch to make it drop itself.

STATS

TRANSPARENCY	LIGHT EMISSION
	0

RENEWABLE	BLAST RESISTANCE	HARDNESS
	0.2	0.2

FLAMMABLE	SILK TOUCH

SNOW BUSINESS

You can stack two snow blocks and a carved pumpkin or jack-o'-lantern to summon a snow golem, which will pelt hostile mobs with snowballs, knocking them back, or damaging them in the case of blazes. You can craft three snow blocks to create snow layers.

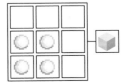

SNOW BLOCK RECIPE

 16   104

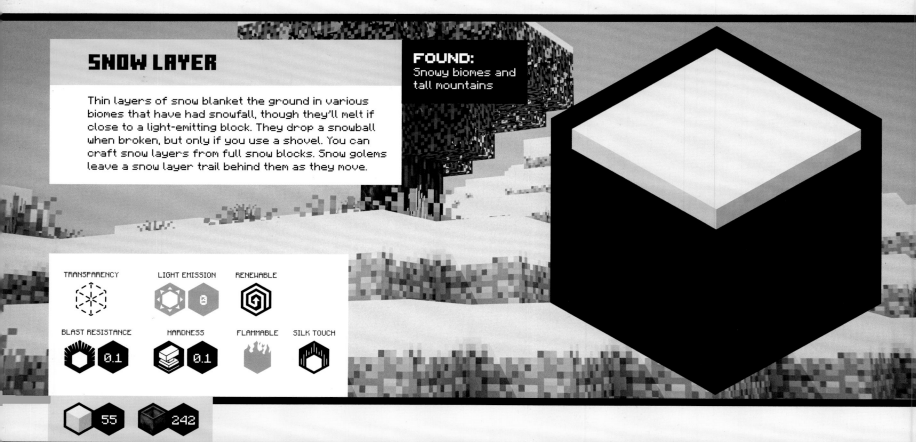

SNOW LAYER

Thin layers of snow blanket the ground in various biomes that have had snowfall, though they'll melt if close to a light-emitting block. They drop a snowball when broken, but only if you use a shovel. You can craft snow layers from full snow blocks. Snow golems leave a snow layer trail behind them as they move.

FOUND:
Snowy biomes and tall mountains

TRANSPARENCY	LIGHT EMISSION	RENEWABLE
	0	

BLAST RESISTANCE	HARDNESS	FLAMMABLE	SILK TOUCH
0.1	0.1		

55   242

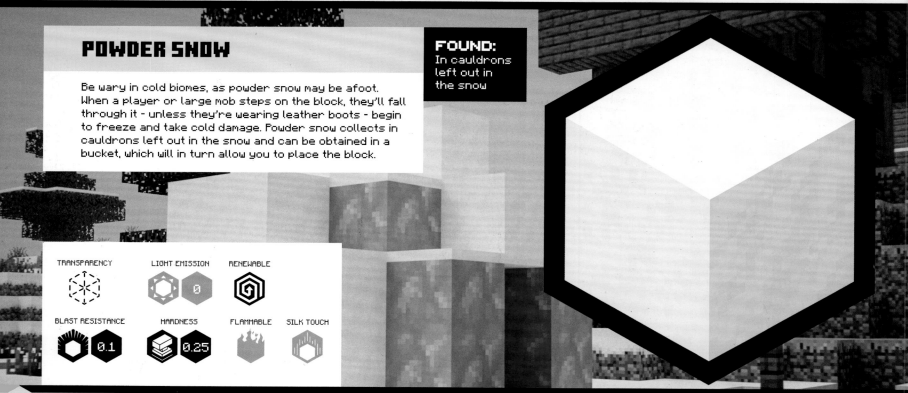

POWDER SNOW

Be wary in cold biomes, as powder snow may be afoot. When a player or large mob steps on the block, they'll fall through it – unless they're wearing leather boots – begin to freeze and take cold damage. Powder snow collects in cauldrons left out in the snow and can be obtained in a bucket, which will in turn allow you to place the block.

FOUND:
In cauldrons left out in the snow

TRANSPARENCY	LIGHT EMISSION	RENEWABLE
	0	

BLAST RESISTANCE	HARDNESS	FLAMMABLE	SILK TOUCH
0.1	0.25		

NETHER PORTAL BLOCK

FOUND:
In obsidian Nether portal frames

If you ignite an obsidian frame with fire, a swirling purple Nether portal will appear before you. The Nether portal block transports players between the Nether and the Overworld if they touch it. It emits ethereal purple particles and eerie howls as it swirls ominously.

STATS

TRANSPARENCY	LIGHT EMISSION
	11

RENEWABLE	BLAST RESISTANCE	HARDNESS
	0	∞

FLAMMABLE	SILK TOUCH

NEW DIMENSION
To summon a Nether portal, you'll need to build a 4x5 obsidian frame and light it with flint and steel or a fire charge. It allows players, mobs and items to travel back and forth between dimensions. Explosions will extinguish a Nether portal, so be wary of ghast fireballs!

END PORTAL FRAME

FOUND:
In strongholds
of the
Overworld

Though it appears to be an innocuous decorative block, the End portal frame is very powerful. Twelve of them generate in stronghold portal rooms. Some have eyes of Ender already socketed, while others are empty. If they all have an eye of Ender, the portal to the End will appear.

STATS

TRANSPARENCY	LIGHT EMISSION
	1

RENEWABLE	BLAST RESISTANCE	HARDNESS
	3.6m	∞

FLAMMABLE	SILK TOUCH

EYE OF ENDER

SOUL ENTRANCE

Strongholds generate across the Overworld, and mostly underground, so it's very hard to find End portal frames. However, you can throw eyes of Ender anywhere in the Overworld to lead you to a stronghold. The block is indestructible and impossible to add to your inventory.

END PORTAL BLOCK

FOUND:
Strongholds,
The End's first
island

The End portal block appears when you fill all the End portal frames with eyes of Ender, activating the End portal. It also generates when an exit portal is activated in the End. Like the Nether portal block, it's also impossible to obtain the End portal block in your inventory.

STATS

TRANSPARENCY	LIGHT EMISSION
	15

RENEWABLE	BLAST RESISTANCE	HARDNESS
	3.6m	∞

FLAMMABLE	SILK TOUCH

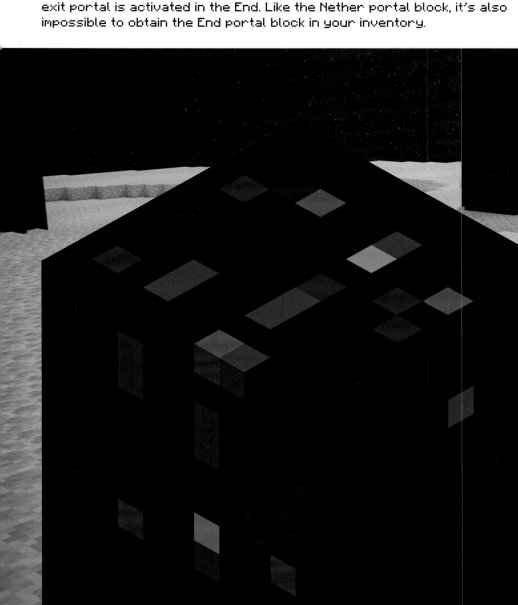

OMINOUS ENTRANCE
The End Portal Block gives off the maximum possible light when it's activated. Most mobs can travel freely through the End portal block, but you'll be pleased to know that the Ender Dragon is unable to pass through it. Players returning to the Overworld via the End portal will be taken to their spawn point.

59

END GATEWAY

You might be forgiven for thinking the End gateway is just a non-flat End portal block. It has the same texture, gives off the brightest light and transports players, after all. However, the End gateway transports players between the main island of the End to the outer islands.

STATS

TRANSPARENCY	LIGHT EMISSION	15
RENEWABLE	BLAST RESISTANCE 3.6m	HARDNESS ∞
FLAMMABLE	SILK TOUCH	

KEY TO THE END CITY

End gateway blocks generate as part of the End gateway structure, which consists of bedrock as well. It pulses with a beam of light from above and below when it activates, or when an entity passes through the End gateway, which is a useful reminder of its location.

 12 59

NYLIUM

The Nether doesn't seem like the most hospitable place for plant life, which makes nylium blocks all the more miraculous. These variants of netherrack can support roots and fungi – the crimson variety grows in crimson forests, while warped nylium appears in warped forest biomes.

STATS

TRANSPARENCY	LIGHT EMISSION
	0

RENEWABLE	BLAST RESISTANCE	HARDNESS
	1	0.4

FLAMMABLE	SILK TOUCH

WARPED NYLIUM

62	126	128

CRIMSON NYLIUM

NETHER LAND

Nylium will decay into netherrack if an opaque block is placed above it, though it won't change if lava or water flows over it. You can use bone meal on netherrack adjacent to nylium blocks to turn it into nylium. Using bone meal on a nylium block will generate corresponding vegetation – crimson roots and fungus will appear on crimson nylium, for instance. You can use bone meal on a fungus again to grow a giant fungus.

NETHERRACK

The majority of the Nether's visible terrain is composed of netherrack. Its cracked, dark red texture is reminiscent of cobblestone, but it has much lower hardness and blast resistance. Though not technically a flammable block, fire will burn atop netherrack indefinitely once ignited.

STATS

TRANSPARENCY	LIGHT EMISSION
	0

RENEWABLE	BLAST RESISTANCE	HARDNESS
	0.4	0.4

FLAMMABLE	SILK TOUCH

LOST TO TIME
Netherrack also forms the base for the ruined portal structures that form in the Nether and the Overworld. It drops itself as an item when mined, and nylium will also drop netherrack if mined without Silk Touch. Netherrack can also be smelted to form Nether bricks.

SHROOMLIGHT

When a huge fungus generates in the crimson or warped forests of the Nether, you will often find shroomlights dotting its canopy. These bioluminescent blocks emit the brightest light possible and grow on both huge warped and huge crimson fungi in their respective forest biomes.

STATS

TRANSPARENCY		LIGHT EMISSION

TRANSPARENCY	LIGHT EMISSION	
		15

RENEWABLE	BLAST RESISTANCE	HARDNESS
	1	1

FLAMMABLE	SILK TOUCH

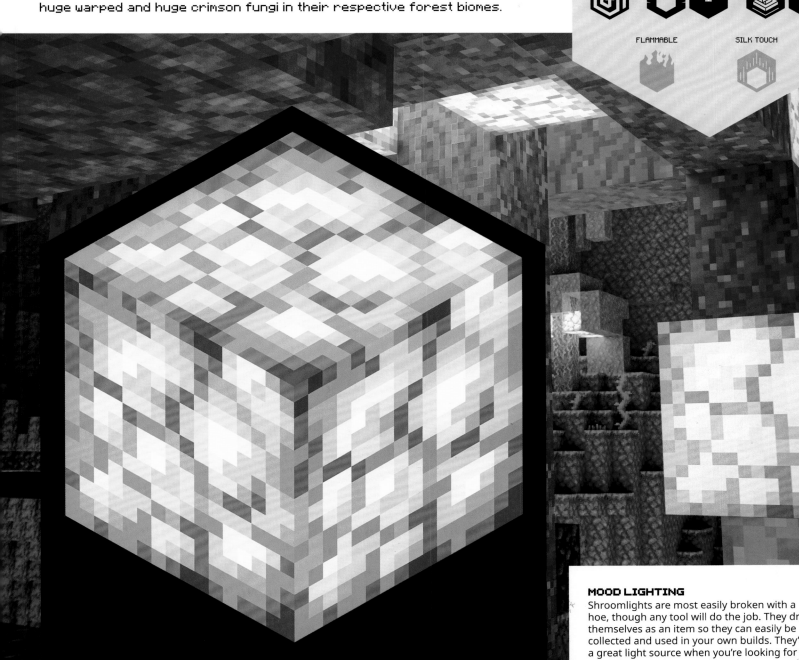

MOOD LIGHTING
Shroomlights are most easily broken with a hoe, though any tool will do the job. They drop themselves as an item so they can easily be collected and used in your own builds. They're a great light source when you're looking for something a little more alien.

 126   128

SOUL SAND

The creepy texture of soul sand is an indicator of its sinister effect. It slows the movement of any mob or player walking over it, and you can use it to construct the Wither boss mob. You can find it most easily in the soul sand valley, though it's prevalent in many Nether biomes.

STATS

TRANSPARENCY	LIGHT EMISSION
	0

RENEWABLE	BLAST RESISTANCE	HARDNESS
	0.5	0.5

FLAMMABLE	SILK TOUCH

WITHER CONSTRUCTION

HAUNTING EFFECTS

Soul sand is useful to brewers, as you can grow the common potion ingredient Nether wart on it. If a fire is lit on soul sand, it becomes soul fire, but the block also has an effect when in water: soul sand will create a bubble column that will lift players, mobs and items up through the water.

SOUL SOIL

STATS

TRANSPARENCY	LIGHT EMISSION
	0

RENEWABLE	BLAST RESISTANCE	HARDNESS
	0.5	0.5

FLAMMABLE	SILK TOUCH

Unlike soul sand, you can only find soul soil in the soul sand valley biome of the Nether. It doesn't slow down players and mobs like its sandy counterpart, but can be used as a replacement in construction of the Wither. Fires on soul soil will ignite into blue soul fire.

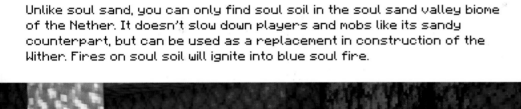

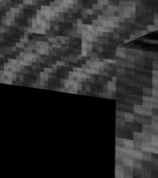

EERIE INGREDIENT

Soul soil can be used to create a few lighting options – the soul torch and soul campfire – although soul sand can also be used in its place. It's one of the main ingredients of basalt, too – lava that flows over soul soil while it's adjacent to blue ice will be turned into a basalt block.

BLACKSTONE

The Nether's answer to cobblestone, blackstone is a little weaker and a little darker, but otherwise identical. It is found frequently in the basalt deltas and in bastion remnant structures. You can use it in recipes for stone tools, furnaces and brewing stands instead of cobblestone.

STATS

TRANSPARENCY	LIGHT EMISSION
	0

RENEWABLE	BLAST RESISTANCE	HARDNESS
	6	1.5

FLAMMABLE	SILK TOUCH

POLISHED BLACKSTONE

CHISELED POLISHED BLACKSTONE

NETHER VERSATILITY

Blackstone can be used to craft polished blackstone, either by crafting or stonecutting, while chiseled polished blackstone, blackstone slabs and blackstone stairs can also be made on a stonecutter. The blackstone slabs and stairs both have a higher hardness than their source block, which is common for similar shaped blocks.

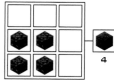

POLISHED BLACKSTONE RECIPE

POLISHED BLACKSTONE BRICKS

FOUND: Bastion remnants and ruined portals

The brick variants of blackstone are slightly rarer than the base polished blackstone block, as you'll only find them generating in bastion remnants and ruined portal structure. As they have identical characteristics to blackstone, they're primarily considered decorative blocks.

STATS

TRANSPARENCY	LIGHT EMISSION
	0

RENEWABLE	BLAST RESISTANCE	HARDNESS
	6	1.5

FLAMMABLE	SILK TOUCH

CRACKED POLISHED
BLACKSTONE BRICKS

NETHER CONSTRUCTION

Polished blackstone bricks can be created with four blocks of polished blackstone, and the cracked variant is made by further smelting the polished blackstone bricks. Stonecutting can be used to turn polished blackstone bricks into slabs, stairs and walls.

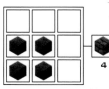

POLISHED BLACKSTONE
BRICKS RECIPE

GILDED BLACKSTONE

Among the dark blackstone and basalt of bastion remnants, you might see a twinkling of gold — that would be gilded blackstone. It has the chance to drop gold nuggets when you destroy it; otherwise it drops itself. It always drops itself if you use Silk Touch-enchanted tools.

STATS

TRANSPARENCY	LIGHT EMISSION
	0

RENEWABLE	BLAST RESISTANCE	HARDNESS
	6	1.5

FLAMMABLE	SILK TOUCH

PIGLINS X GOLD

If you destroy gilded blackstone, you'll cause nearby piglins to become hostile. They love the block so much that they'll often run toward it, stare at it for a while, then pick it up. Your best chance of finding gilded blackstone is within the chests of bastion remnants, or on the plinths that support the chests.

BASALT

FOUND:
Soul sand valley
and basalt delta
Nether biomes

The Nether's basalt delta biome is home to basalt and polished basalt, though you can also find them in basalt pillars, or as part of bastion remnants. Lava changes into basalt when it is flowing adjacent to blue ice, and over the top of soul sand, making it a renewable resource.

STATS

TRANSPARENCY	LIGHT EMISSION
	0

RENEWABLE	BLAST RESISTANCE	HARDNESS
	4.2	1.25

FLAMMABLE	SILK TOUCH

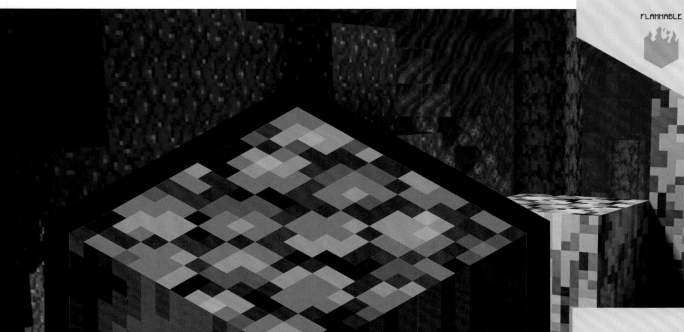

POLISHED BASALT

DUAL TEXTURES

Both variants have different textures on their horizontal and vertical faces, like logs, which makes them an obvious choice in decoration. Polished basalt can also be crafted with four basalt blocks. Both blocks drop themselves as an item when you mine them.

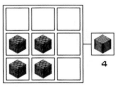

POLISHED BASALT
RECIPE

 48 53 80

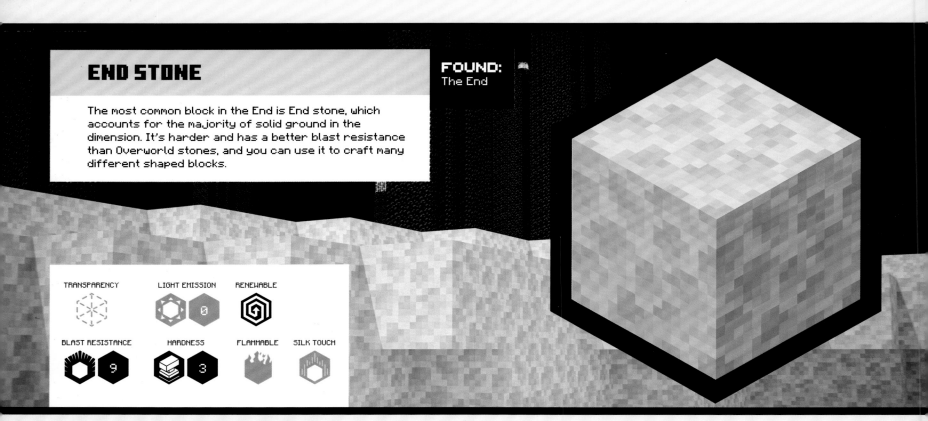

END STONE

FOUND:
The End

The most common block in the End is End stone, which accounts for the majority of solid ground in the dimension. It's harder and has a better blast resistance than Overworld stones, and you can use it to craft many different shaped blocks.

TRANSPARENCY	LIGHT EMISSION	RENEWABLE
	0	

BLAST RESISTANCE	HARDNESS	FLAMMABLE	SILK TOUCH
9	3		

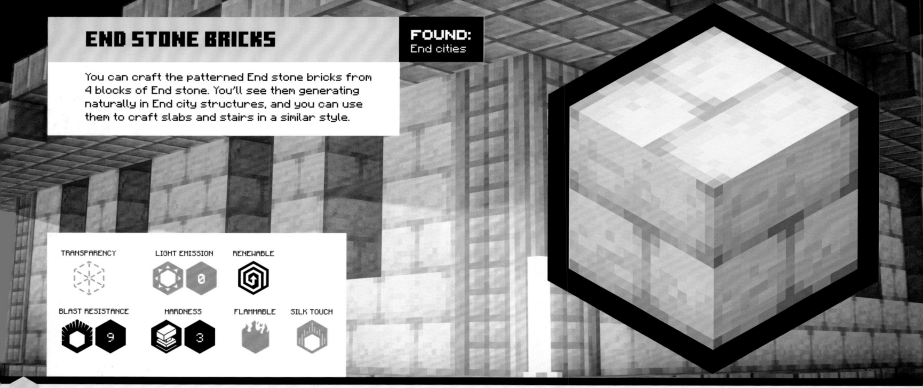

END STONE BRICKS

FOUND:
End cities

You can craft the patterned End stone bricks from 4 blocks of End stone. You'll see them generating naturally in End city structures, and you can use them to craft slabs and stairs in a similar style.

TRANSPARENCY	LIGHT EMISSION	RENEWABLE
	0	

BLAST RESISTANCE	HARDNESS	FLAMMABLE	SILK TOUCH
9	3		

END STONE BRICK SLAB

FOUND:
By crafting only

The half-height variant of End stone bricks is one of the strongest slabs in the game, both in terms of hardness and blast resistance. While the double slab looks to be the same physically as End stone itself, it is a distinct block in its own right.

TRANSPARENCY	LIGHT EMISSION	RENEWABLE
	0	

BLAST RESISTANCE	HARDNESS	FLAMMABLE	SILK TOUCH
9	3		

END STONE BRICK
DOUBLE SLAB

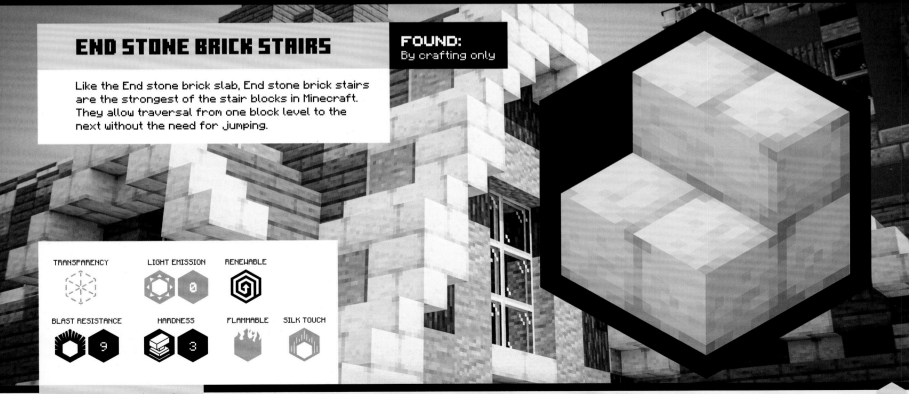

END STONE BRICK STAIRS

FOUND:
By crafting only

Like the End stone brick slab, End stone brick stairs are the strongest of the stair blocks in Minecraft. They allow traversal from one block level to the next without the need for jumping.

TRANSPARENCY	LIGHT EMISSION	RENEWABLE
	0	

BLAST RESISTANCE	HARDNESS	FLAMMABLE	SILK TOUCH
9	3		

SOUL FIRE

FOUND:
Soul sand valley
in the Nether

If you light a fire on soul sand or soul soil, it ignites into the searing blue flames of soul fire. Visitors to the Nether may also see naturally generated soul fire in the soul sand valley. It's slightly dimmer than normal fire but inflicts more damage per second to any who step on it.

STATS

TRANSPARENCY	LIGHT EMISSION	
		10

RENEWABLE	BLAST RESISTANCE		HARDNESS	
		0		0

FLAMMABLE	SILK TOUCH

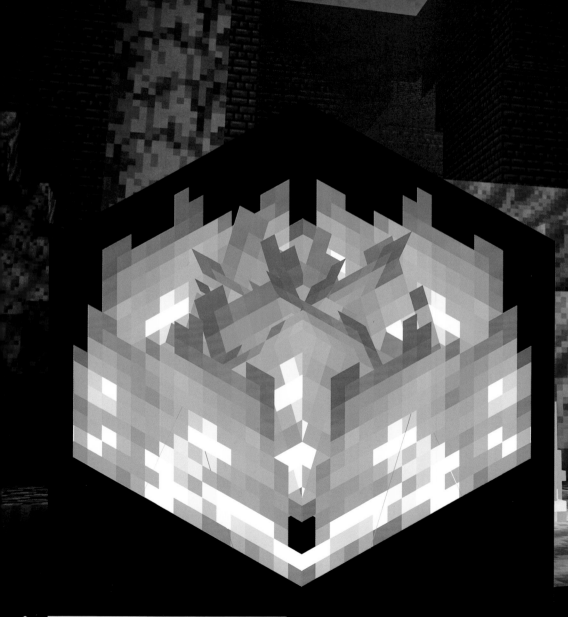

STABLE FIRE
Unlike its standard counterpart, soul fire doesn't spread, which means that you can safely place it next to flammable blocks without fear of an inferno. It can also withstand rainfall, unlike fire. Piglins and hoglins are scared of soul fire, despite living among the Nether's many infernos.

BONE BLOCK

Deep under desert and swamp biomes, you might come across fossils of long-extinct creatures, composed of bone blocks. The blocks have horizontal and vertical textures, so they can be placed directionally. They also generate in Nether fossil formations in the Nether.

STATS

TRANSPARENCY	LIGHT EMISSION
	0

RENEWABLE	BLAST RESISTANCE	HARDNESS
	2	2

FLAMMABLE	SILK TOUCH

ANCIENT FOSSILS
You can craft a bone block with 9 pieces of bone meal, and it's possible to craft the same amount of bone meal from a bone block, which makes bone blocks an efficient storage method for excess bone meal. Coal ore sometimes replaces bone blocks in fossil formations.

134

POINTED DRIPSTONE

Protruding from floors and ceilings of dripstone caves, pointed dripstone is the component block of stalagmites and stalactites. Stalactites are gravity-obeying and will cause damage to players and mobs underneath if they fall. A stalagmite will also cause damage to any player or mob that steps on one!

STATS

TRANSPARENCY	LIGHT EMISSION
	0

RENEWABLE	BLAST RESISTANCE	HARDNESS
	3	1.5

FLAMMABLE	SILK TOUCH

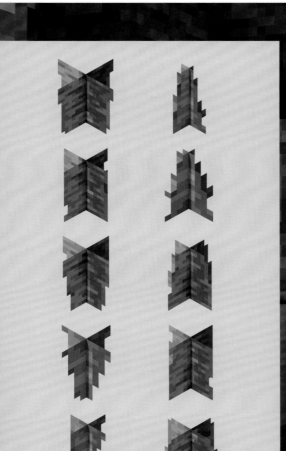

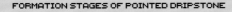
FORMATION STAGES OF POINTED DRIPSTONE

GENERATION
Pointed dripstone generates in dripstone caves on dripstone blocks, but you can also place it on floors to create stalagmites – the ones that stick up – or on ceilings to make stalactites, which are the ones that hang down.

BEHAVIOR
If one of the two blocks above a stalactite is a water source, the stalactite will drip and very slowly grow. If there's a solid block within the 11 blocks below, a stalagmite will begin to grow there. If a cauldron is within the 10 blocks below a dripping stalactite, the cauldron will gradually fill with water. Stalactites can also drip with lava if there's a lava source above, and fill a cauldron.

GOOD POINT WELL MADE
If you fall on a stalagmite, you'll take damage equivalent to falling from a height four times as high, which seems harsh for a block that can be broken with any tool! You can also use four pointed dripstones to craft a dripstone block.

 16 41 48 242

COBWEB

Found in the corners of many naturally generated structures — strongholds, igloos, mine shafts and woodland mansions — cobwebs can be a bit of an annoyance. They will slow players, mobs and items down as they pass through, and can even cushion them on long falls.

STATS

TRANSPARENCY	LIGHT EMISSION
	0

RENEWABLE	BLAST RESISTANCE	HARDNESS
	4	4

FLAMMABLE	SILK TOUCH

STRING THEORY
Cobwebs can be obtained using shears, or with a Silk Touch–enchanted sword. If destroyed by anything else, they will drop string. They're widely used in redstone mechanisms for their slowing properties, which are useful for many time-sensitive elements of contraptions.

SPONGE

The humble sponge is most famous for its water-absorbing properties. Ocean monuments often contain a room filled with around 30 sponges, which you can mine with any tool to make them drop themselves. Wet sponges can be smelted in a furnace to become sponges.

STATS

TRANSPARENCY	LIGHT EMISSION
	0

RENEWABLE	BLAST RESISTANCE	HARDNESS
	0.6	0.6

FLAMMABLE	SILK TOUCH

WET SPONGE

SUPER SOAKER-UPPER

When you place a dry sponge, it will soak up water around it and turn into a wet sponge. Wet sponges will instantly dry when placed in the Nether and dry biomes, too. A sponge can absorb 65 blocks of water before it is full, and can soak up water up to 7 blocks away.

PRODUCTIVE BLOCKS

LOGS

Six varieties of tree grow across the forests, mountains and plains of the Overworld: acacia, birch, dark oak, jungle, oak and spruce. Each yields its own variant of log, which has a unique style, from pale birch to darker spruce. The vertical faces of logs are different from the horizontal ones.

STATS

TRANSPARENCY		LIGHT EMISSION

0

RENEWABLE	BLAST RESISTANCE	HARDNESS

  2 2

FLAMMABLE	SILK TOUCH

BIRCH LOG

ACACIA LOG	DARK OAK LOG	JUNGLE LOG

OAK LOG	SPRUCE LOG

WOODWORKING

Dozens of crafted blocks can trace their roots back to logs. Most immediately, stripped logs can be created if you use an axe on a log placed in the world; wood, which you can craft with 4 matching logs; and wood planks, which you can make with just a single log.

SAPLINGS

From small saplings, mighty trees grow. Saplings are the seedlings of the great trees that dot the landscape. Most can rise from a single dirt block in the ground, though a dark oak needs at least four saplings in a 2x2 formation. Giant jungle and spruce trees can also be grown in this way.

STATS

TRANSPARENCY		LIGHT EMISSION
		0
RENEWABLE	BLAST RESISTANCE	HARDNESS
	0	0
FLAMMABLE		SILK TOUCH

BIRCH SAPLING

22   316

ACACIA SAPLING	DARK OAK SAPLING	JUNGLE SAPLING
OAK SAPLING	SPRUCE SAPLING	

SHOOTS AND LEAVES

Saplings need different amounts of space to flourish into trees, but giving a 5x5 space around them horizontally and keeping the air above them clear for at least 7 spaces will be enough. If your sapling isn't in a space that meets these criteria, you can quickly destroy it by hand and move it – even put it in a flower pot. though it won't grow!

LEAVES

STATS

TRANSPARENCY	LIGHT EMISSION
	0

RENEWABLE	BLAST RESISTANCE	HARDNESS
	0.2	0.2

FLAMMABLE	SILK TOUCH

The lush, verdant canopy of trees is made almost entirely of leaves. They're easy to destroy, even without a tool, but using shears is the only way they drop themselves as an item without using Silk Touch. Leaves are semi-transparent and reduce light as it passes through the block.

ACACIA LEAVES	DARK OAK LEAVES	JUNGLE LEAVES

OAK LEAVES	SPRUCE LEAVES

BIRCH LEAVES

LEAF DROP LOTTERY
Destroyed leaves have a chance to drop a number of different items, including saplings and sticks. Oak and dark oak leaves can additionally drop apples. Leaves, like wood itself, are very flammable and are excellent at spreading fire due to the number of leaves that spawn at once.

 80 81

VINE

Leaves aren't the only thing that adorn the branches of trees. You'll often see wafer-thin vines draped over them, too. You can only place vines on vertical block faces and you need shears to collect them. Players and mobs can use the vines as a foothold to climb, just like ladders.

STATS

TRANSPARENCY	LIGHT EMISSION
	0

RENEWABLE	BLAST RESISTANCE	HARDNESS
	0.2	0.2

FLAMMABLE	SILK TOUCH

NATURE'S CLIMBERS

Vines only generate in jungles and swamps, so you'll most often see them on jungle trees. Vines constantly attempt to spread, regardless of light level, and will succeed if the surrounding blocks are air or a solid block. They are used to craft mossy cobblestone and as a pattern on banners.

28	131	229	314

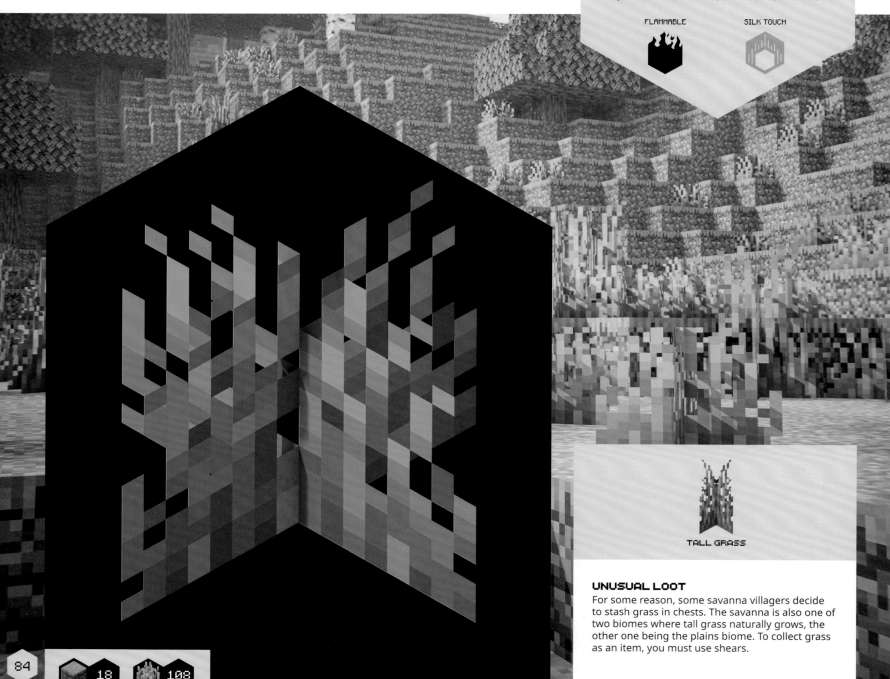

GRASS

A common sight in many biomes, grass and tall grass are transparent blocks that spawn on grass blocks. Their appearance changes based on the biome, but all can drop wheat seeds when you destroy them. They're superflammable and will burn away more quickly than any other block!

STATS

TRANSPARENCY

LIGHT EMISSION

0

RENEWABLE

BLAST RESISTANCE

0

HARDNESS

0

FLAMMABLE

SILK TOUCH

TALL GRASS

UNUSUAL LOOT

For some reason, some savanna villagers decide to stash grass in chests. The savanna is also one of two biomes where tall grass naturally grows, the other one being the plains biome. To collect grass as an item, you must use shears.

18   108

FERN

Like grass, ferns generate on ground blocks in jungle and taiga biomes, though large ferns only appear in taigas. They have a more extravagant aesthetic than grass, with big fanned leaves. You can collect them easily with shears, and they also often drop wheat seeds.

STATS

TRANSPARENCY

LIGHT EMISSION

0

RENEWABLE

BLAST RESISTANCE
0

HARDNESS
0

FLAMMABLE

SILK TOUCH

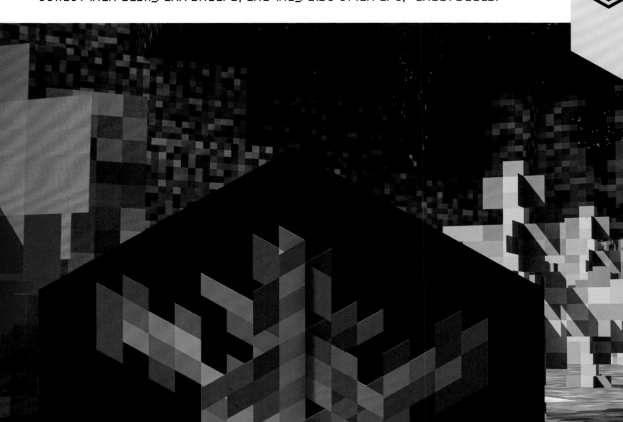

LARGE FERN

PLANT FOOD
You can use bone meal on ferns (and grass) to grow them into their larger variants. You can also find ferns in loot chests of taiga biomes, and some wandering traders will give you a fern in exchange for an emerald. Sounds like a bad deal ...

 18 108

85

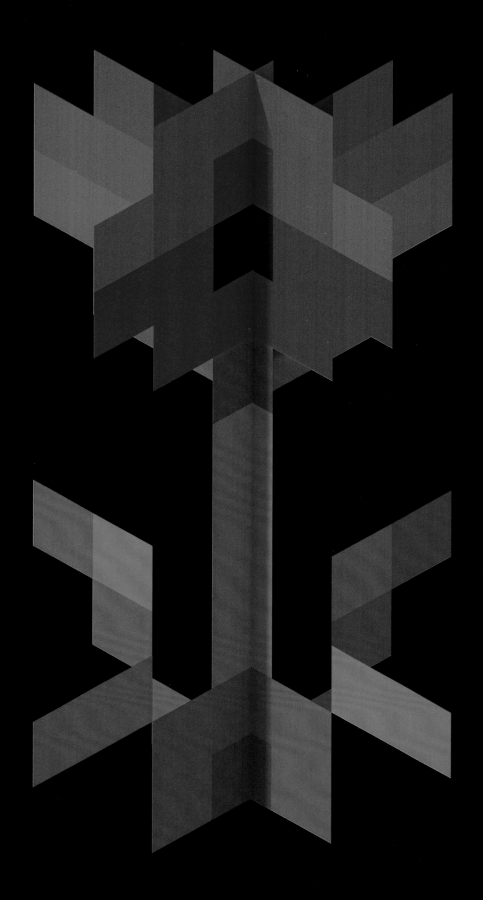

POPPY

SMALL FLOWERS

You'll often see small flowers offering splashes of color in many biomes, particularly in flower forests. Each species will spawn in a different combination of biomes, with some seen in just a single type of biome, like the blue orchid, which appears only in swamps.

STATS

TRANSPARENCY	LIGHT EMISSION
	0

RENEWABLE	BLAST RESISTANCE	HARDNESS
	0	0

FLAMMABLE	SILK TOUCH

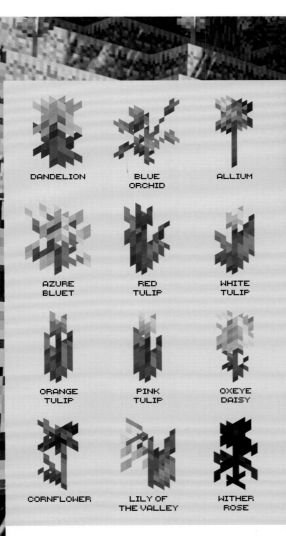

DANDELION   BLUE ORCHID   ALLIUM

AZURE BLUET   RED TULIP   WHITE TULIP

ORANGE TULIP   PINK TULIP   OXEYE DAISY

CORNFLOWER   LILY OF THE VALLEY   WITHER ROSE

GENERATION
Flowers generate on grass and dirt blocks in their respective biomes. The exception is the Wither rose, which only generates when the Wither boss mob kills a mob or player. A Wither rose will be planted on the block on which the mob died and inflict the Wither effect on anyone who touches it.

COLOR INJECTION
You can harvest flowers with any tool, including your hands, and replant them in flower pots. The Wither rose causes damage to any mob that touches it unless it's in a pot. The main use of the flower item is to create dyes to change the color of wool, beds and other customizable blocks.

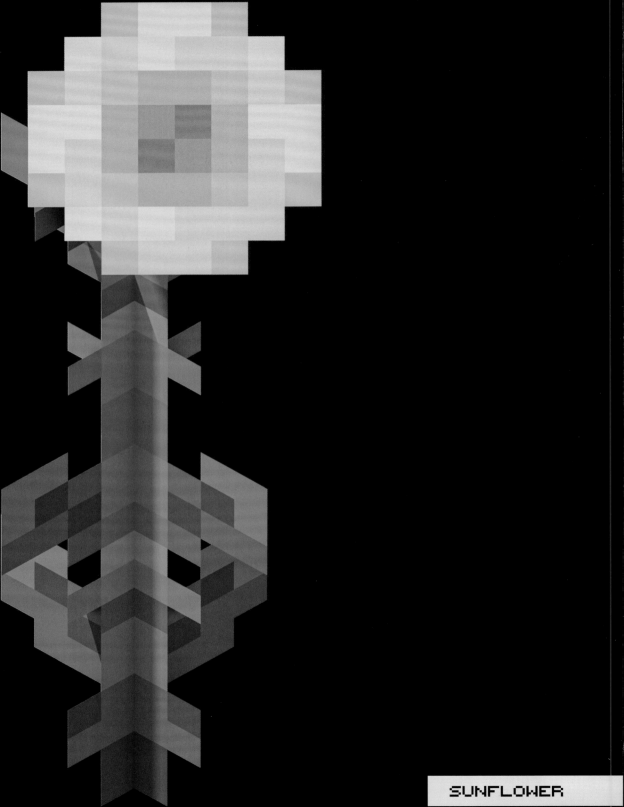

SUNFLOWER

TALL FLOWERS

FOUND:
Sunflower plains or forest biomes

Some flowers can grow to be two blocks high, but they are much rarer than their smaller floral friends. You can make twice as much dye with tall flowers as you can with their smaller counterparts. Fire can spread through tall flowers, so take care to protect your flower beds!

STATS

TRANSPARENCY	LIGHT EMISSION	
	0	
RENEWABLE	BLAST RESISTANCE	HARDNESS
	0	0
FLAMMABLE	SILK TOUCH	

LILAC   ROSEBUSH   PEONY

GENERATION
Large flowers can only spawn on world generation, which means they won't spawn while you're traveling around the world. All tall flowers will spawn in forest biomes and its variants as well as flower forests, except the sunflower, which only spawns in sunflower plains.

BEE HAVEN
Bees will take pollen from flowers big and small, which increases the honey level in beehives and bee nests. Bees also follow players holding flowers, and will enter love mode and breed if given one. Sunflowers always face east toward the rising sun, which makes them useful navigation tools.

 152   270

AZALEA

Deep underground in the lush caves, you'll see the bright leaves of the azalea, a plant block that can cover many ground blocks like dirt and podzol and moss blocks. The flowering variant is adorned with purple petals, too. They have a small chance to drop themselves when mined.

FOUND:
Underground,
in lush caves

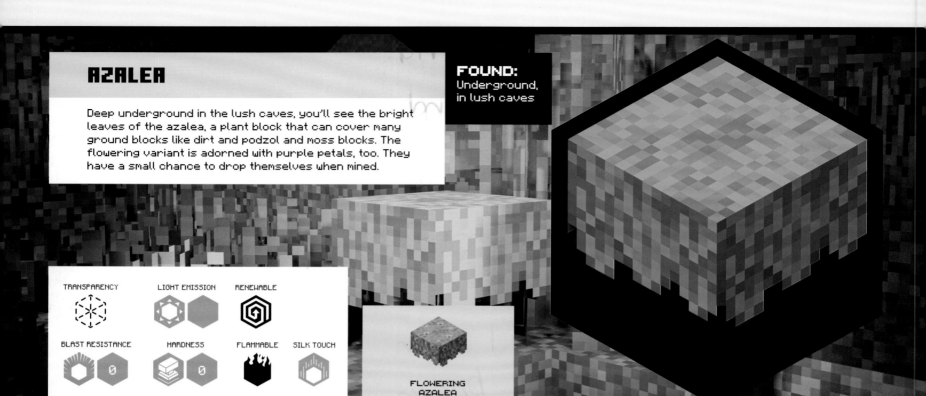

FLOWERING
AZALEA

TRANSPARENCY   LIGHT EMISSION   RENEWABLE

BLAST RESISTANCE   HARDNESS   FLAMMABLE   SILK TOUCH

0   0

FLOWERING AZALEA LEAVES

Like more common leaves on trees, azalea leaves appear as foliage on azalea trees that sprout above lush caves. There are two different types, which match the plant varieties – one is solely formed of leaves while the flowering version has the same pattern of purple petals.

FOUND:
In and above
lush caves

AZALEA
LEAVES

TRANSPARENCY   LIGHT EMISSION   RENEWABLE

BLAST RESISTANCE   HARDNESS   FLAMMABLE   SILK TOUCH

0.2   0.2

HANGING ROOTS

FOUND:
Underground,
in lush caves

Appearing beneath azaleas, hanging roots are an unusual block that attach to whichever block the azalea is topping. They can be detached using shears, then reattached to the underside of other blocks for decoration, or thrown into a composter to increase the compost level.

TRANSPARENCY	LIGHT EMISSION	RENEWABLE
	0	
BLAST RESISTANCE	HARDNESS	FLAMMABLE	SILK TOUCH
0	0		

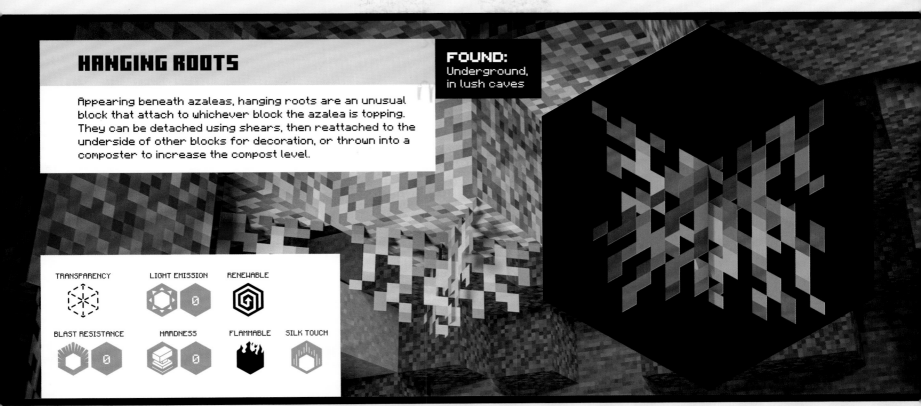

ROOTED DIRT

FOUND:
Underground,
in lush caves

Rooted dirt is an azalea-infused ground block that runs thick with roots. Grass and mycelium can't spread to this block, and you can't plant flowers on it. It's found between azalea trees on the surface and lush caves below. You can collect it without a tool, or use a hoe to turn it into dirt.

TRANSPARENCY	LIGHT EMISSION	RENEWABLE
	0	
BLAST RESISTANCE	HARDNESS	FLAMMABLE	SILK TOUCH
0.5	0.5		

 22 82 86 88

MOSS BLOCK

A block that calls the lush caves home, the moss block is a haven for underground plant life. It's possible to place most plants, except sugar cane and bamboo, on moss blocks, and any saplings planted on moss blocks will remain a sapling instead of growing into a tree.

STATS

TRANSPARENCY		LIGHT EMISSION 0
RENEWABLE	BLAST RESISTANCE 0.1	HARDNESS 0.1
FLAMMABLE		SILK TOUCH

GREEN AND PLEASANT
Using bone meal on a moss block gives the moss a chance to spread to stone blocks – such as stone, deepslate and gravel – up to 7 blocks away! The bone meal can also cause azaleas, grass and moss carpet to grow on top of it. Moss blocks are most easily collected with an axe.

 25   30   81

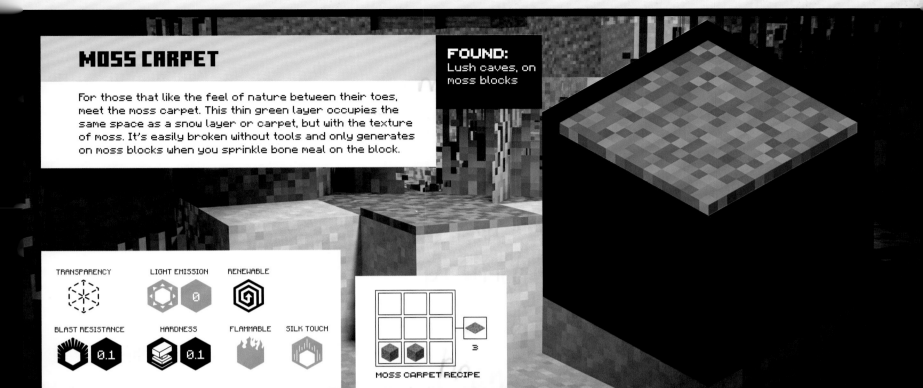

MOSS CARPET

For those that like the feel of nature between their toes, meet the moss carpet. This thin green layer occupies the same space as a snow layer or carpet, but with the texture of moss. It's easily broken without tools and only generates on moss blocks when you sprinkle bone meal on the block.

FOUND:
Lush caves, on moss blocks

TRANSPARENCY	LIGHT EMISSION	RENEWABLE
	0	

BLAST RESISTANCE	HARDNESS	FLAMMABLE	SILK TOUCH
0.1	0.1		

MOSS CARPET RECIPE — 3

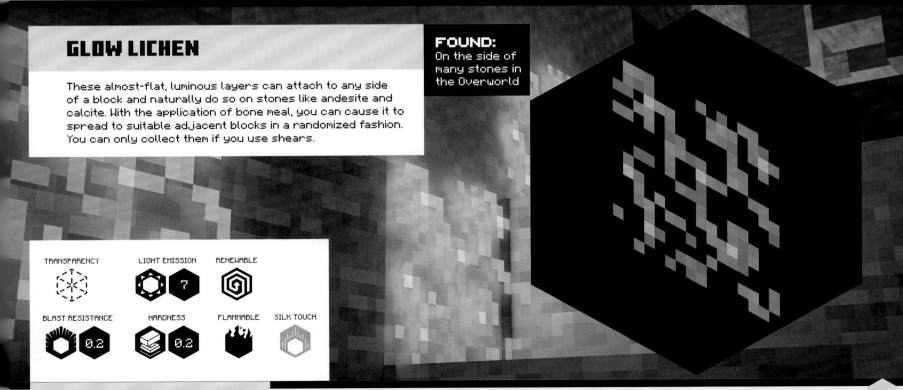

GLOW LICHEN

These almost-flat, luminous layers can attach to any side of a block and naturally do so on stones like andesite and calcite. With the application of bone meal, you can cause it to spread to suitable adjacent blocks in a randomized fashion. You can only collect them if you use shears.

FOUND:
On the side of many stones in the Overworld

TRANSPARENCY	LIGHT EMISSION	RENEWABLE
	7	

BLAST RESISTANCE	HARDNESS	FLAMMABLE	SILK TOUCH
0.2	0.2		

 56 73 312

SPORE BLOSSOM

STATS

TRANSPARENCY	LIGHT EMISSION
	0

RENEWABLE	BLAST RESISTANCE	HARDNESS
	0	0

FLAMMABLE	SILK TOUCH

Like azaleas, spore blossoms add a much-needed splash of color to the cave system, generating in the lush cave areas underground. They can be mined with relative ease and always drop themselves, which makes them a very popular flower to reuse in builds.

ANY MORE FOR ANY SPORE?
Spore blossoms can only be placed on the underside of a block, which means they're most often found on ceilings, where other plants are unable to reach. They release a steady stream of green particles underneath themselves, though the effect is purely aesthetic.

 86 88 90

CACTUS

You'll see this spiky block planted in the sands of deserts and badlands. Cactus doesn't need light to grow and can reach heights of four blocks. It causes a single point of damage to any mob or player that comes into contact with it and is invulnerable to fire.

STATS

TRANSPARENCY	LIGHT EMISSION
	0

RENEWABLE	BLAST RESISTANCE	HARDNESS
	04	04

FLAMMABLE	SILK TOUCH

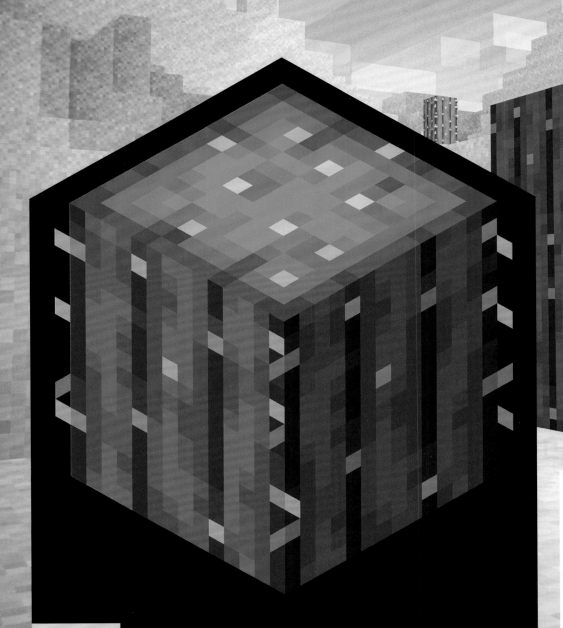

PRICKLY CUSTOMER

Pistons will break a cactus if the arm pushes it, and placing a sign on a cactus will also cause it to break. It will also break any items that it comes into contact with. Unlike most plants, using bone meal on a cactus has no effect on the speed of its growth – it will only try to grow every 16 game ticks. You can destroy a cactus with your hands without taking damage and smelt the block into green dye. Mobs won't try to avoid cacti and will often walk straight into them.

316

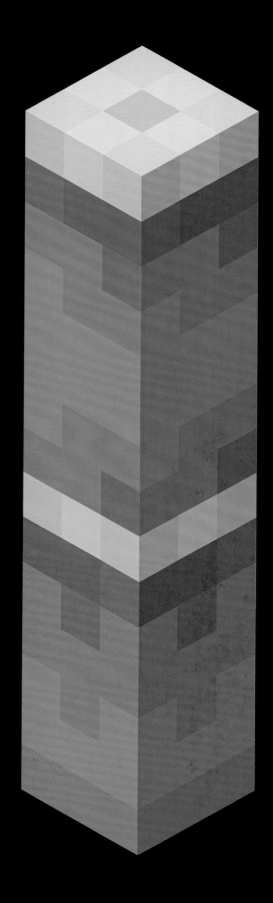

BAMBOO

The fastest-growing plant in Minecraft, bamboo is a valuable resource for crafting and breeding pandas. Bamboo generates from shoots only in jungle biomes, but are easy to harvest in large quantities. You don't need to use a tool to destroy bamboo, but a sword will break it most quickly.

STATS

TRANSPARENCY	LIGHT EMISSION
	0

RENEWABLE	BLAST RESISTANCE	HARDNESS
	1	1

FLAMMABLE	SILK TOUCH

BAMBOO SHOOT

GENERATION

Although it's native to jungles, bamboo can be planted on a variety of ground blocks, including coarse dirt, podzol and mycelium and regular dirt and grass, as long as there's a level 9 light. It can grow up to 16 blocks high and its already fast growth can be sped up with bone meal.

BEHAVIOR

When first planted, bamboo shoots can be displaced by water. Once bamboo grows beyond a single block high, it is able to resist water flow. Mature bamboo becomes flammable and has a different appearance. It can be used as a fuel in furnaces, but will only smelt a quarter of an item.

PANDA PLAYGROUND

Pandas love bamboo, and they will eat the bamboo item if they find it. You can also mate pandas with a bamboo item if they're in close proximity to growing bamboo. Bamboo can be used to create sticks, or more impressively, scaffolding, which also requires string.

DRIPLEAVES

STATS

TRANSPARENCY

LIGHT EMISSION 0

RENEWABLE

BLAST RESISTANCE 0.1

HARDNESS 0.1

FLAMMABLE

SILK TOUCH

Dripleaves are a free-runner's dream. The big ones are natural blocks that grow to different heights and have a large, strong leaf that can support a player ... for a while at least. The small dripleaf can't support weight, but can grow into a big dripleaf with the help of bone meal.

BIG DRIPLEAF

SMALL DRIPLEAF

BIG DRIPLEAF STEM

PLANT PLATFORMING
After a player jumps onto a big dripleaf, they'll have one second to jump off again, or the leaf will tilt and drop the player. The big dripleaf generates naturally in lush caves but can be made taller by applying more bone meal to it, which will increase its height by one block.

DEAD BUSH

The dead bush is a less impressive example of flora – a leafless husk
of a once verdant growth that can't be brought back to life. They're
found in warm biomes like deserts and taigas and are mostly used for
aesthetic purposes to signify barren or desolate parts of a build.

STATS

TRANSPARENCY		LIGHT EMISSION
		0

RENEWABLE	BLAST RESISTANCE	HARDNESS
	0	0

FLAMMABLE	SILK TOUCH

FORGOTTEN FLORA
You can place dead bushes on sand, terracotta,
podzol and dirt blocks, or in flower pots. Being
dead plants, they won't grow or spread to other
blocks. They drop themselves if you break them
with shears; otherwise they drop up to 2 sticks.
You can also fuel furnaces with dead bushes.

99

SUGAR CANE

Originally added to Minecraft as "reeds," sugar cane is a versatile crop that is used in crafting. It grows in plentiful quantities whenever there is water around and shares many qualities and physical features with bamboo, which also grows vertically in stacks.

STATS

TRANSPARENCY

LIGHT EMISSION

0

RENEWABLE

BLAST RESISTANCE
0

HARDNESS
0

FLAMMABLE

SILK TOUCH

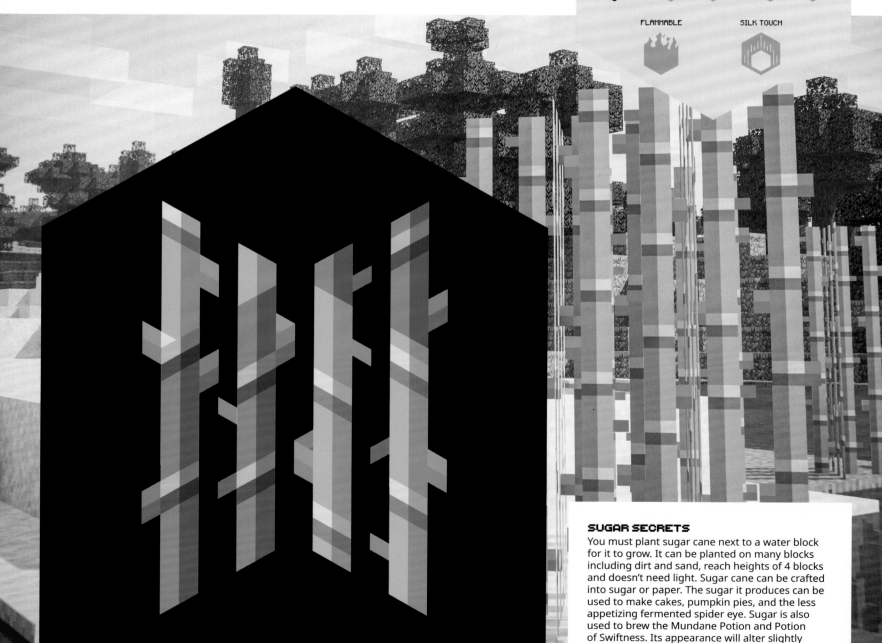

SUGAR SECRETS
You must plant sugar cane next to a water block for it to grow. It can be planted on many blocks including dirt and sand, reach heights of 4 blocks and doesn't need light. Sugar cane can be crafted into sugar or paper. The sugar it produces can be used to make cakes, pumpkin pies, and the less appetizing fermented spider eye. Sugar is also used to brew the Mundane Potion and Potion of Swiftness. Its appearance will alter slightly depending on the biome that it's planted in.

23   96

MUSHROOMS

You will find these tiny fungi in dark, dank biomes, like mushroom fields, swamps, dark oak forests and giant tree taigas, as well as in the Nether. They can easily be collected by hand and are used to make various stews. The brown mushroom also gives off a faint glow.

STATS

TRANSPARENCY	LIGHT EMISSION
	0/1

RENEWABLE	BLAST RESISTANCE	HARDNESS
	0	0

FLAMMABLE	SILK TOUCH

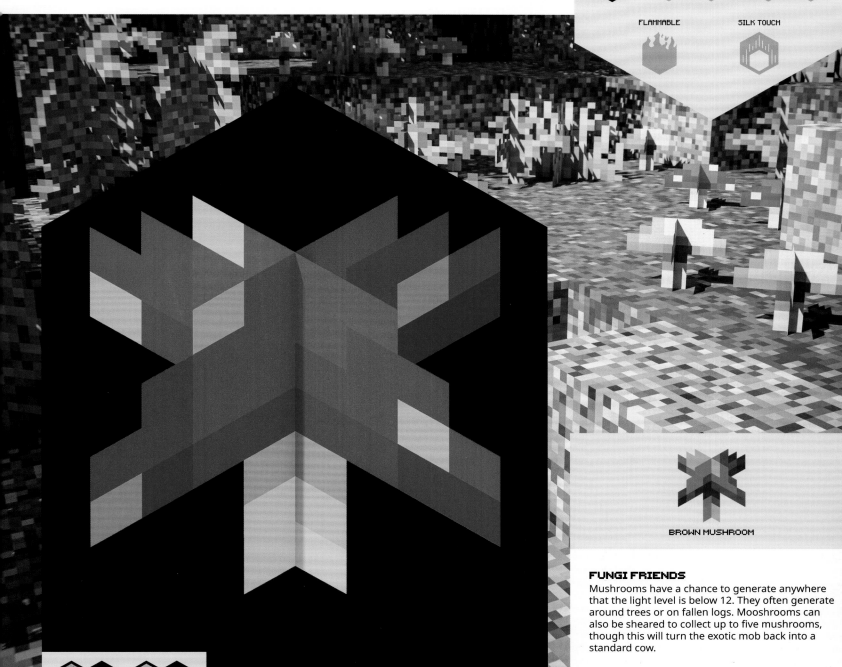

BROWN MUSHROOM

FUNGI FRIENDS

Mushrooms have a chance to generate anywhere that the light level is below 12. They often generate around trees or on fallen logs. Mooshrooms can also be sheared to collect up to five mushrooms, though this will turn the exotic mob back into a standard cow.

20   102

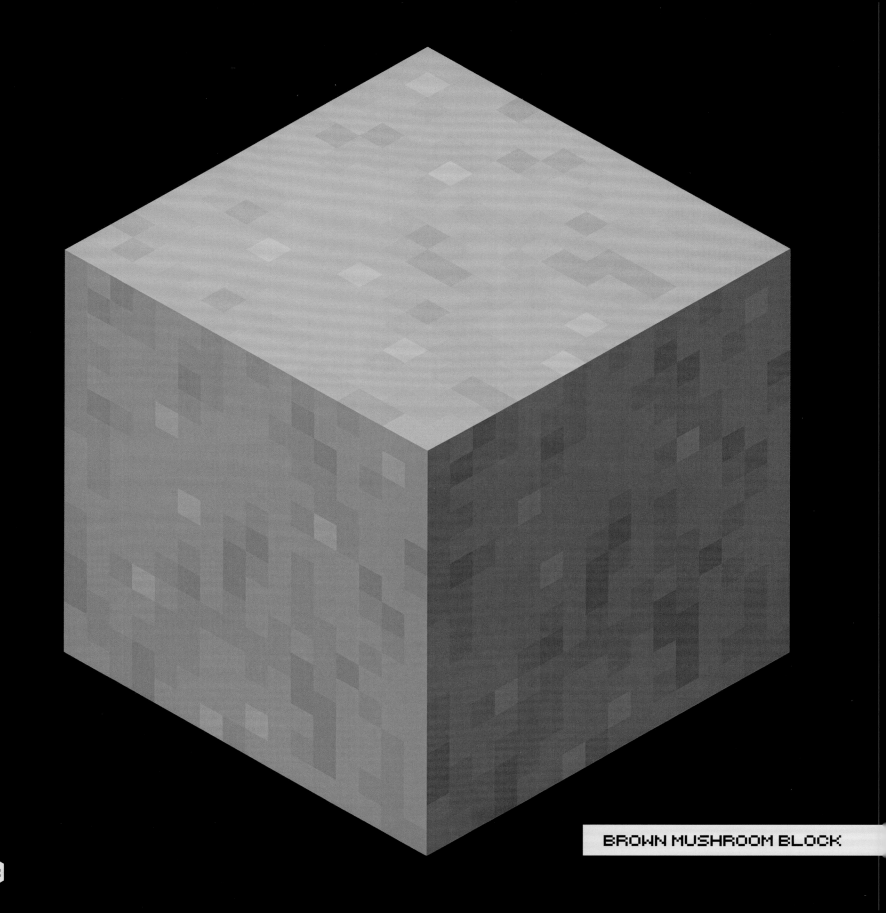

BROWN MUSHROOM BLOCK

MUSHROOM BLOCKS

In swamps, dark forest and mushroom fields, you might come across huge treelike mushrooms, which are composed of mushroom blocks. There are three different types of mushroom block – brown, red and the stem block – all of which will drop small mushrooms when they're broken.

STATS

TRANSPARENCY	LIGHT EMISSION
	0

RENEWABLE	BLAST RESISTANCE	HARDNESS
	0.2	0.2

FLAMMABLE	SILK TOUCH

MUSHROOM STEM RED MUSHROOM BLOCK

GENERATION
As well as their natural biomes of generation, huge mushrooms can be grown from small red and brown mushrooms by applying bone meal to them. The mushroom needs to be planted on podzol or mycelium at any light level, or dirt or grass at a light level below 12. There should to be at least 7 blocks free above the mushroom for it to turn into a huge mushroom.

BEHAVIOR
The red and brown mushroom blocks can be collected as an item with a Silk Touch–enchanted tool, but will drop their small counterparts when destroyed with an unenchanted tool. The stem block can also yield mushrooms, or variant mushroom blocks that have the mushroom texture on all faces.

BIOFUELS
The stem block acts as logs do for trees and travels from the ground to the canopy of red or brown mushroom blocks. Mushroom blocks, like most vegetation, can be used as fuel and also in composters. They have an 85% chance to create a new layer of compost in the composter.

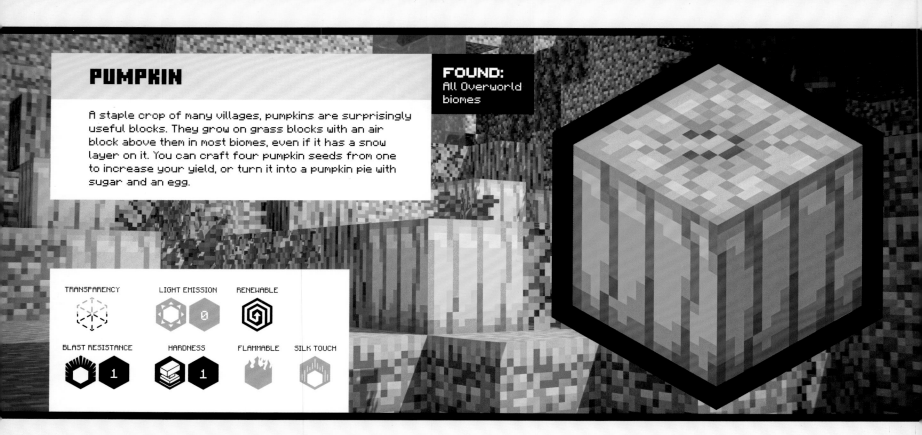

PUMPKIN

A staple crop of many villages, pumpkins are surprisingly useful blocks. They grow on grass blocks with an air block above them in most biomes, even if it has a snow layer on it. You can craft four pumpkin seeds from one to increase your yield, or turn it into a pumpkin pie with sugar and an egg.

TRANSPARENCY	LIGHT EMISSION	RENEWABLE
	0	

BLAST RESISTANCE	HARDNESS	FLAMMABLE	SILK TOUCH
1	1		

PUMPKIN STEM

FOUND:
All Overworld biomes

A pumpkin stem is the block that grows above ground from planted pumpkin seeds before the pumpkin appears. It has eight stages of growth and will transform into an "attached" version once the pumpkin has fully grown. They will only grow from seeds placed on farmland.

TRANSPARENCY	LIGHT EMISSION	RENEWABLE
	0	

BLAST RESISTANCE	HARDNESS	FLAMMABLE	SILK TOUCH
0	0		

GROWTH STAGES
OF PUMPKIN STEM

CARVED PUMPKIN

If you take a pair of shears to a pumpkin, you'll be able to make a spooky-faced gourd known as the carved pumpkin, as well as receive some pumpkin seeds. It can then be worn as a helmet, so you don't anger Endermen, or placed on snow or blocks of iron configurations to summon golems to aid you.

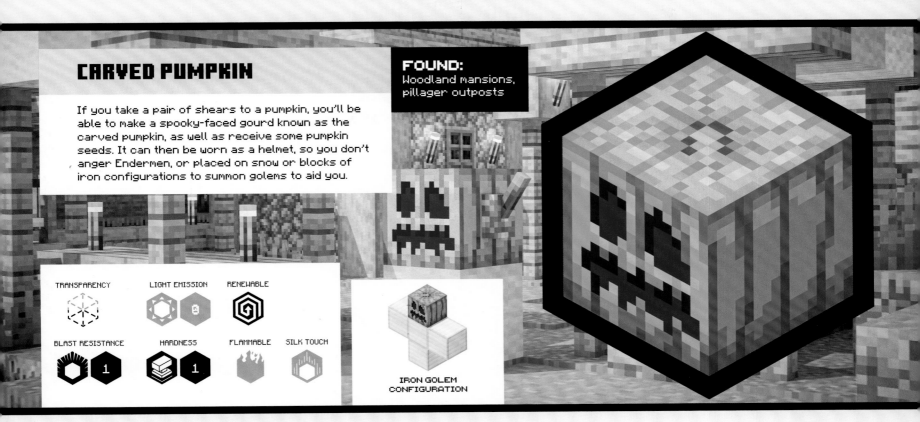

TRANSPARENCY	LIGHT EMISSION	RENEWABLE
	0	

BLAST RESISTANCE	HARDNESS	FLAMMABLE	SILK TOUCH
1	1		

IRON GOLEM
CONFIGURATION

JACK-O'-LANTERN

Like carved pumpkins, these luminous variants can be worn or used to summon snow and iron golems. They're crafted with a torch and a carved pumpkin and produce the brightest possible light. They also generate in taiga and snowy taiga villages.

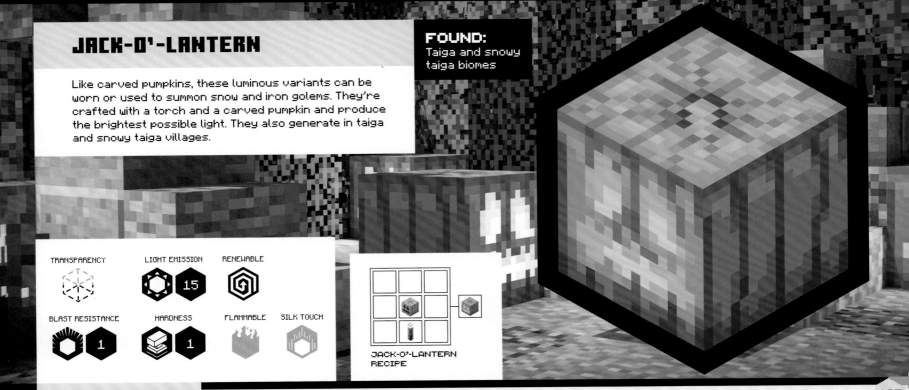

TRANSPARENCY	LIGHT EMISSION	RENEWABLE
	15	

BLAST RESISTANCE	HARDNESS	FLAMMABLE	SILK TOUCH
1	1		

JACK-O'-LANTERN
RECIPE

 55 214

MELON

Generating in jungle biomes, savanna villages and inside some woodland mansions, melons are a juicy source of food. They are a product of melon seeds, and grow in much the same way as a pumpkin does, appearing above ground once the seed growth has reached its final stage.

STATS

TRANSPARENCY	LIGHT EMISSION
	0

RENEWABLE	BLAST RESISTANCE	HARDNESS
	1	1

FLAMMABLE	SILK TOUCH

SLICES ALL AROUND

Melons need a level 9 light to grow. The stem will not produce another melon until the first is harvested. When broken by anything but a Silk Touch-enchanted tool, the melon will drop up to 7 melon slices, though you need 9 to craft a full melon again. You can also craft the slices with gold nuggets to create a glistering melon slice.

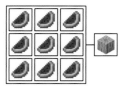

MELON RECIPE

MELON STEM

Melon seeds germinate and grow into melon stems, which go through an eight-stage cycle before producing a single melon. Like pumpkins, the stem will attach to the melon once it is produced in an adjacent block and will stay attached until the melon is harvested.

STATS

TRANSPARENCY

LIGHT EMISSION 0

RENEWABLE

BLAST RESISTANCE 0

HARDNESS 0

FLAMMABLE

SILK TOUCH

SNEAKY CROP

Despite the fact that melons naturally grow in jungles, you will only be able to find melon stems naturally in the patches of savanna and desert villages, or in some woodland mansions if they have a stem room. The best way to generate a melon stem is from melon seeds, which can be crafted from a melon slice.

GROWTH STAGES OF MELON STEM

WHEAT

FOUND:
Village farms in
the Overworld

Loved by farm animals and players alike, wheat is a common crop that you can craft into treats galore. It's a common sight in villages, where you'll often see farmer villagers reaping and planting their crops. Wheat can be used to lead, tame and breed animals, too.

STATS

TRANSPARENCY

LIGHT EMISSION 0

RENEWABLE

BLAST RESISTANCE 0

HARDNESS 0

FLAMMABLE

SILK TOUCH

BEHAVIOR

When harvested in a fully mature state, wheat will drop itself as an item as well as dropping seeds, but if harvested in an earlier state only the seeds drop. Wheat is used to craft foodstuffs – cake, bread and cookies – as well as hay bales. When wheat is held, cows, sheep, goats and mooshrooms will follow players, and it can also be used to breed these mobs.

ANIMAL APPLICATIONS

Wheat seeds are often also dropped when breaking grass or ferns. The seeds can also be used to tame parrots and breed chickens. Bees can also pollinate wheat – as they do other crops – which speeds up their growth, similarly to the way that bone meal advances them.

GROWTH STAGES OF WHEAT

GENERATION

Wheat seeds must be planted on farmland in order to grow. Wheat goes through 7 stages of growth before it's considered fully mature, and bone meal can be used to speed up the process. Well-hydrated farmland also helps to speed up maturity. Wheat crops are often found on village farms.

 23 209 318

CARROT

A common garden vegetable, carrots are grown in villages across the land. They each replenish 3 hunger points, but you can double their effectiveness by crafting them with gold nuggets to create golden carrots. You can also plant harvested carrots to grow new crops.

STATS

TRANSPARENCY	LIGHT EMISSION
	0

RENEWABLE	BLAST RESISTANCE	HARDNESS
	0	0

FLAMMABLE	SILK TOUCH

BEHAVIOR

Bone meal can be used on planted carrots to speed up their growth. Harvesting carrot crops will yield up to five carrots. Rabbits are attracted to carrot crops and will eat them, decreasing their growth by a single stage. The smart farmer would do well to fence off their carrots to prevent them being eaten.

FOODSTUFFS

Harvested carrots can be used to breed rabbits and pigs. Farmer villagers will also tend to carrot crops, harvesting them when they're fully grown. The same villagers also often have carrots to trade. Carrots can also be used in food recipes and to make a carrot on a stick, which can be used to guide saddled pigs.

GENERATION

Like wheat, melon and pumpkin, carrots also have eight growth stages, including the ripened state, however, carrots only have four textures to represent this. When fully ripe, you'll be able to see the orange carrot top poking out of the ground. They also need farmland to grow and spawn in village vegetable plots.

GROWTH STAGES OF CARROT

 23

BEETROOT

Often overlooked in favor of more common vegetables, beetroots are packed with color and uses, as well as being one of the fastest growers. They can restore a hunger point when they're harvested, or you can craft them into delicious beetroot soup instead.

STATS

TRANSPARENCY

LIGHT EMISSION 0

RENEWABLE

BLAST RESISTANCE 0

HARDNESS 0

FLAMMABLE

SILK TOUCH

VEGETABLE TREASURE

Beetroot is rarely grown on village farms, but can drop up to 3 beetroot seeds when harvested, as well as the beetroot item itself. The seeds can be used for breeding chickens, while the beetroot, as with many foodstuffs, can breed villagers and pigs. The vegetable can also be turned into a red dye. They're often found in loot chests in structures like dungeons and mine shafts.

GROWTH STAGES OF BEETROOT

POTATO

The staple food of the Minecraft world, potatoes are found on village farms. They're also a common loot item in generated structures, and can be found in villages, pillager outposts and shipwreck chests. They drop up to five potatoes when the fully ripe crop is harvested.

STATS

TRANSPARENCY	LIGHT EMISSION	
		0
RENEWABLE	BLAST RESISTANCE	HARDNESS
	0	0
FLAMMABLE	SILK TOUCH	

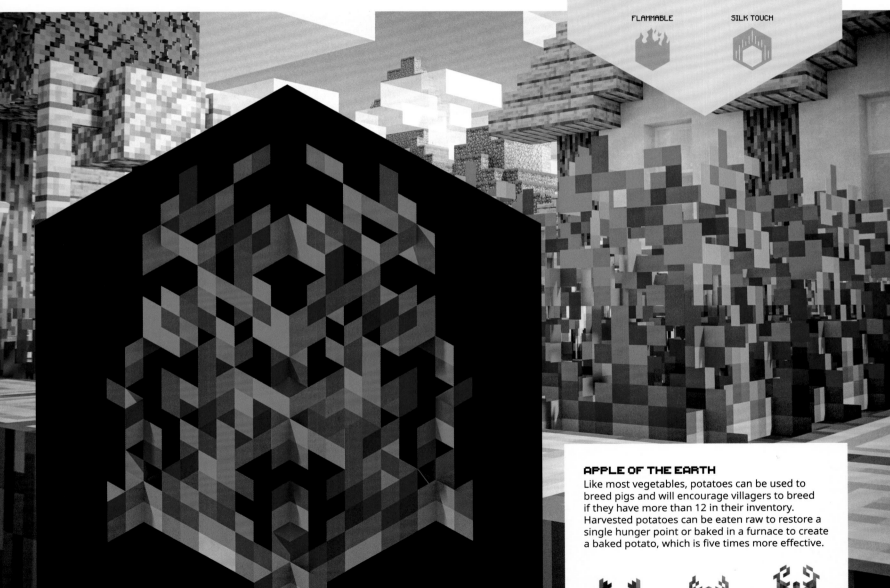

APPLE OF THE EARTH
Like most vegetables, potatoes can be used to breed pigs and will encourage villagers to breed if they have more than 12 in their inventory. Harvested potatoes can be eaten raw to restore a single hunger point or baked in a furnace to create a baked potato, which is five times more effective.

GROWTH STAGES OF POTATO

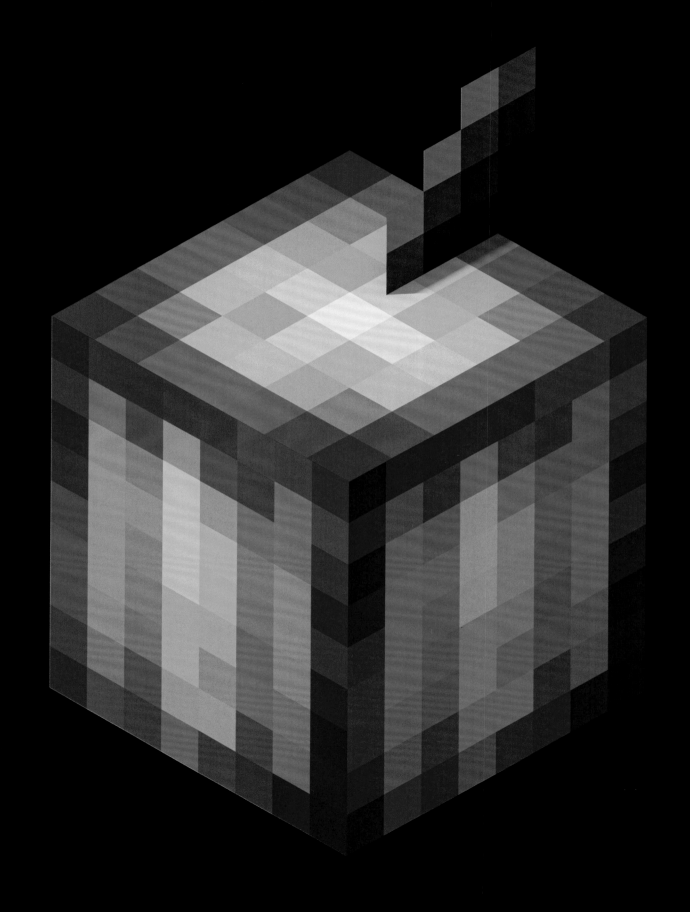

COCOA

Native to the jungle biomes, cocoa is a dye and an ingredient in tasty foods, which you can find on the trunks of jungle trees. Cocoa pods can't be collected as an item, but will instead drop cocoa beans when you destroy them, which you can easily do with any tool, though axes are quickest.

STATS

TRANSPARENCY	LIGHT EMISSION
	0

RENEWABLE	BLAST RESISTANCE	HARDNESS
	3	0.2

FLAMMABLE	SILK TOUCH

BEHAVIOR

Bone meal can advance the growth stage when applied to cocoa pods. The cocoa beans the pod drops can be used to craft cookies or turned into a brown dye. Unusually, the beans themselves can be used as a replacement for a dye and used in recipes for crafts like brown beds.

TAKE THE JUNGLE WITH YOU

Although they only naturally generate in jungles, you can plant cocoa beans on any jungle log, which means you can place a jungle log in any biome and start a crop. Cocoa beans will also drop from the pods if the log they're attached to is destroyed by any means, or if the pod is hit by water or a piston head.

GROWTH STAGES OF COCOA

GENERATION

Cocoa goes through three stages of growth. If it is harvested in either of the first two stages, it will only drop a single cocoa bean, but if you have patience and wait until the final stage of growth, it will drop a maximum of three cocoa beans.

SWEET BERRY BUSH

Commonly found in the taiga biomes, sweet berry bushes are productive plants that you can repeatedly harvest to collect sweet berries. They're more versatile than vegetables in terms of where they can be planted, though they don't have as many uses as other crops.

STATS

TRANSPARENCY	LIGHT EMISSION
	0

RENEWABLE	BLAST RESISTANCE	HARDNESS
	 0	0

FLAMMABLE	SILK TOUCH

BUSH BLOCKER

Sweet berry bushes can grow on farmland, dirt, coarse dirt, podzol and grass blocks. The berries they produce are used as seeds to plant more bushes. Only two of its four growth stages can be harvested for fruit – you can reap two berries in the third stage, and three berries in the fourth. When harvested, the bush will reset to stage 1 and begin to grow again. Fully grown sweet berry bushes will slow down and damage players and mobs that pass through them, except foxes, which can also be bred with sweet berries.

GROWTH STAGES OF SWEET BERRY BUSH

 18 19 22 23

CAVE VINES

Is glowing food safe? Only one way to find out ... Cave vines radiate light at all times, but shine brighter with every glow berry that emerges. Each glow berry you eat will replenish two hunger points. You'll find them in lush caves, and like much of the flora there, they only dangle from the bottom of blocks.

STATS

TRANSPARENCY	LIGHT EMISSION
	10-14

RENEWABLE	BLAST RESISTANCE	HARDNESS
	0	0

FLAMMABLE	SILK TOUCH

CAVE VINE BODY

BERRY NICE INDEED
The fruit of cave vines is the glow berry, which can be collected by interacting with the vine. The glow berries are also the seed that you can plant on the bottom of blocks to make new plants. They can reach up to 26 blocks long, and each cave vine block has the chance to bear fruit!

CAVE VINE HEAD

83	131

KELP

A type of aquatic flora, kelp is a tall underwater plant that appears in ocean biomes, except frozen and warm variants. It doesn't require light and can reach a massive 26 blocks tall. When you destroy it, it drops itself as an item, and any kelp above the broken one will also break.

STATS

TRANSPARENCY	LIGHT EMISSION
	0

RENEWABLE	BLAST RESISTANCE	HARDNESS
	0	0

FLAMMABLE	SILK TOUCH

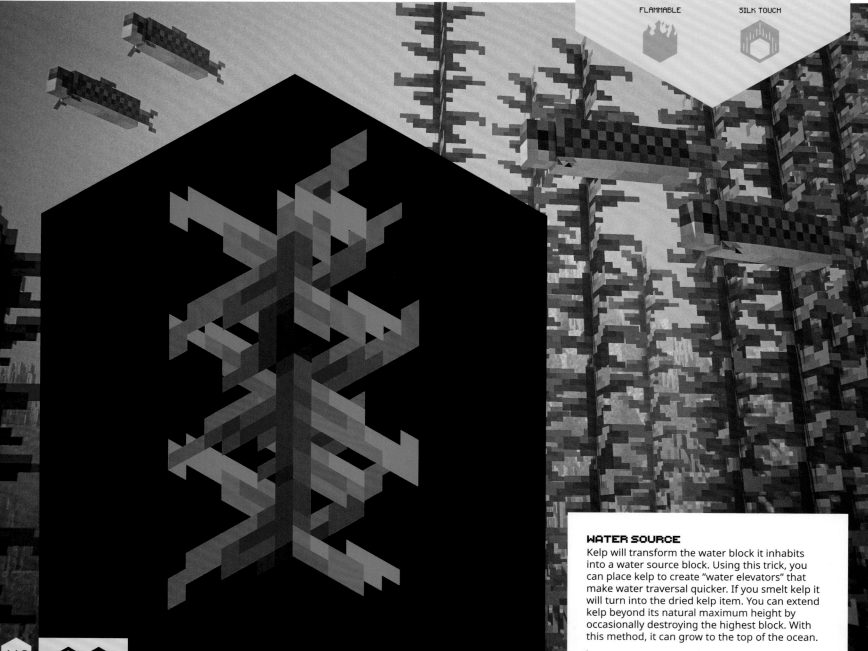

WATER SOURCE

Kelp will transform the water block it inhabits into a water source block. Using this trick, you can place kelp to create "water elevators" that make water traversal quicker. If you smelt kelp it will turn into the dried kelp item. You can extend kelp beyond its natural maximum height by occasionally destroying the highest block. With this method, it can grow to the top of the ocean.

DRIED KELP BLOCK

FOUND:
By crafting only

Unusually for an item that originates in water, dried kelp blocks make excellent fuel items, more powerful even than coal. A single dried kelp block can smelt 20 items! They're crafted with nine blocks of dried kelp, which is a food item that you can eat very quickly!

STATS

TRANSPARENCY

LIGHT EMISSION
0

RENEWABLE

BLAST RESISTANCE
2.5

HARDNESS
0.5

FLAMMABLE

SILK TOUCH

BUTCHER'S BLOCK
For some reason, butcher villagers offer you an emerald in exchange for 10 dried kelp blocks. When placed, they're mineable using any tool, though hoes are the most efficient. Their ribbon-wrap texture also makes them a common block used in decorative building.

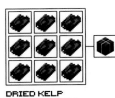

DRIED KELP
BLOCK RECIPE

CORAL

You'll find coral generating as part of reef structures on the seabed of warm oceans. There are five different types of coral, each with its own color and foliage pattern. These delicate lifeforms can't be obtained without the aid of Silk Touch, but are easily destroyed, even without a tool.

STATS

TRANSPARENCY	LIGHT EMISSION
	0

RENEWABLE	BLAST RESISTANCE	HARDNESS
	0	0

FLAMMABLE	SILK TOUCH

BUBBLE CORAL

120

 BRAIN CORAL

 TUBE CORAL

 FIRE CORAL

 HORN CORAL

 DEAD BUBBLE CORAL

DEAD BRAIN CORAL

 DEAD TUBE CORAL

 DEAD FIRE CORAL

 DEAD HORN CORAL

UNDERWATER LIFE
Coral are excellent for decoration, but can be difficult to feature in builds as they require an adjacent block of water to stay alive; otherwise they will turn into their dead variants. If you use bone meal on an underwater ground block in a warm ocean, there's a chance that coral will form.

CORAL FANS

Coral fans share many properties with their non-fan variants – they're transparent, can only be harvested with Silk Touch–enchanted tools and generate in warm ocean biomes. Their foliage is arranged in a fan shape, and you can place them on all faces of a block except the top.

STATS

TRANSPARENCY	LIGHT EMISSION
	0

RENEWABLE	BLAST RESISTANCE	HARDNESS
	0	0

FLAMMABLE	SILK TOUCH

BUBBLE CORAL FAN

 16   122

BRAIN CORAL FAN	TUBE CORAL FAN	FIRE CORAL FAN
HORN CORAL FAN	DEAD BUBBLE CORAL FAN	DEAD BRAIN CORAL FAN
DEAD TUBE CORAL FAN	DEAD FIRE CORAL FAN	DEAD HORN CORAL FAN

FLANKING FANS

Coral fans can be placed on the sides of blocks so that they can theoretically cover all visible sides of a placed block. They are available in five different styles and will turn into dead variants if not adjacent to a water block. Once coral is dead, it can't be brought back to life.

CORAL BLOCKS

The core of reef structures is made up of solid coral blocks, on which coral and coral fans appear. They are available in the same styles as coral and fans, and also die if not exposed to water. Unlike those blocks, they also have some hardness, meaning that you need a pickaxe to mine them.

STATS

TRANSPARENCY	LIGHT EMISSION
	0

RENEWABLE	BLAST RESISTANCE	HARDNESS
	6	1.5

FLAMMABLE	SILK TOUCH

TUBE CORAL BLOCK

BRAIN
CORAL BLOCK

BUBBLE
CORAL BLOCK

FIRE
CORAL BLOCK

HORN
CORAL BLOCK

DEAD TUBE
CORAL BLOCK

DEAD BRAIN
CORAL BLOCK

DEAD BUBBLE
CORAL BLOCK

DEAD FIRE
CORAL BLOCK

DEAD HORN
CORAL BLOCK

BASE REEF

When mined, coral blocks will drop the dead variant of itself unless a Silk Touch–enchanted tool is used, in which case it will drop itself as an item. Wandering traders have obviously spent some time on coral reefs, as they often have coral blocks available for you to buy.

SEA PICKLE

FOUND:
Warm ocean biomes

Spawning in colonies, sea pickles are light-emitting underwater plants. Their luminosity increases with quantity, beginning at 6 for one, up to 15 for a full four – but only if they're in water. You can mine them without a tool to make all the sea pickles drop, before turning them into lime dye.

STATS

TRANSPARENCY

  6-15
LIGHT EMISSION

RENEWABLE

BLAST RESISTANCE 0

HARDNESS 0

FLAMMABLE

SILK TOUCH

PICKLE MULTIPLICATION

Sea pickles can generate in the same conditions as coral – in warm water oceans – but also on top of coral, too. Bone meal placed on a sea pickle that lives on top of coral will increase the number in the colony, and also has the chance to spread pickles to other adjacent coral blocks.

DIFFERENT CONFIGURATIONS OF SEA PICKLES

SEAGRASS

Seagrass is a common underwater plant in oceans and other waters. It generates in single block form, as well as a 2-block-high tall seagrass variant. You can collect seagrass with shears – the tall variant will drop two pieces – which can be used to breed turtles.

STATS

TRANSPARENCY	LIGHT EMISSION
	0

RENEWABLE	BLAST RESISTANCE	HARDNESS
	0	0

FLAMMABLE	SILK TOUCH

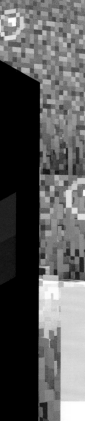

TALL SEAGRASS

GROWING UNDER THE SEA

Bone meal can be used on solid blocks to grow seagrass – though there's a chance it could grow coral instead. If you use bone meal on seagrass, it will turn it into tall seagrass. Lava that flows over water containing seagrass will be resisted, allowing the water to remain unaltered.

LILY PAD

FOUND:
Swamp biomes

On some bodies of water, you might see smatterings of lily pads — flat, floating leaves. Though they're not a full block, players and mobs can still jump on them to avoid getting their feet wet. They're easily broken — even when a boat runs over them — and drop themselves as an item.

STATS

TRANSPARENCY	LIGHT EMISSION
	0

RENEWABLE	BLAST RESISTANCE	HARDNESS
	0	0

FLAMMABLE	SILK TOUCH

CURIOUS PLACEMENT

You can't place blocks on a lily pad, but you can place them underneath. Placement will destroy the lily pad but the block will stay in place, which makes it useful when building structures on the surface of water. As well as water, they can also be placed on top of ice and frosted ice.

 16 51 54

NETHER WART

Stroll through a Nether fortress or bastion remnant structure and you'll likely see patches of Nether wart. Its primary use when you've harvested it is to brew Awkward Potions – which you can use as a basis for almost any other potion – by combining it with a bottle of water on a brewing stand.

STATS

TRANSPARENCY	LIGHT EMISSION 0	
RENEWABLE	BLAST RESISTANCE 0	HARDNESS 0
FLAMMABLE	SILK TOUCH	

NETHER WART GROWTH STAGES

SOMETHING'S BREWING

As well as being a useful brewing ingredient, you can also use it in recipes for the Nether wart block and red Nether bricks. It goes through four stages of growth and it will drop four Nether warts if you harvest it at the final stage, or just one at any of the previous stages.

NETHER SPROUTS

Found only in the warped forest biome of the Nether, Nether sprouts are similar in appearance to Overworld grass and have some similar properties. You can cause the sprouts to spread to other blocks by using bone meal on them.

STATS

TRANSPARENCY	LIGHT EMISSION
	0

RENEWABLE	BLAST RESISTANCE	HARDNESS
	0	0

FLAMMABLE	SILK TOUCH

KEEP OFF THE SPROUTS
Nether sprouts can be harvested with any item and can flourish on a range of blocks, including nylium, podzol and dirt, which means you can take them back to the Overworld to plant. They're decent as a composting material, with a 50% chance of increasing the level of a composter.

22   61   84

127

STEMS

As wood logs are to Overworld trees, stems are to the Nether's huge fungus. Unlike their wooden counterparts, they are not flammable, either by fire or lava, though they are slightly easier to destroy. Crimson stems only generate in crimson forest biomes naturally.

STATS

TRANSPARENCY	LIGHT EMISSION
	0

RENEWABLE	BLAST RESISTANCE	HARDNESS
	2	2

FLAMMABLE	SILK TOUCH

CRIMSON STEM

WARPED STEM

RESISTANT FOREST
Stems are resistant to fire and lava, which makes them more durable than Overworld trees. The trunks that they form can reach heights of up to 26 blocks tall. They can be grown by players manually, by using bone meal on warped or crimson fungi, as long as they're on their respective nyliums. Either stem can replace logs in most recipes.

 62 80

FUNGUS

These little Nether-flavored mushrooms can be found in the crimson and warped forest biomes, growing on crimson and warped nylium respectively. They can be generated on nylium by using bone meal on the block, which you can also use to further transform the fungi into the huge treelike variants.

STATS

TRANSPARENCY	LIGHT EMISSION
	0

RENEWABLE	BLAST RESISTANCE	HARDNESS
	0	0

FLAMMABLE	SILK TOUCH

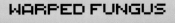
WARPED FUNGUS

101

CRIMSON FUNGUS

WHERE HOGLINS FEAR TO TREAD

The warped version can be used to craft a warped fungus on a stick. You can use this treat to direct striders, which is very useful as they can walk on lava! Hoglins have an aversion to warped fungus and will run away from any that are planted in the ground or a flower pot. Both fungi are used for breeding – the warped version breeds striders, while crimson fungus works on hoglins.

ROOTS

You can find exotic roots in the warped and crimson forest biomes of the Nether. They can grow on their corresponding nylium or on soul sand. You can sprinkle bone meal on nylium to generate more roots. You don't need a tool to harvest roots, and they'll always drop themselves.

STATS

TRANSPARENCY	LIGHT EMISSION
	0

RENEWABLE	BLAST RESISTANCE	HARDNESS
	0	0

FLAMMABLE	SILK TOUCH

WARPED ROOTS

CRIMSON ROOTS

CUBE ROOTS

Roots are generally thought of as a decorative block, as you might use them as ethereal alternatives to traditional flowers. You can even plant them in flower pots, where they will take on a slightly different look from their natural form.

WEEPING VINES

One of two types of vines that can be found in the Nether, weeping vines are the more common variety. Like vines, they can be climbed, and they also have the advantage of not being flammable. They can be broken instantly and drop themselves as an item, which can be replanted.

TRANSPARENCY

LIGHT EMISSION   0

RENEWABLE

BLAST RESISTANCE 0

HARDNESS   0

FLAMMABLE

SILK TOUCH

WEEPING VINES PLANT

TWISTING VINES

While in a warped forest biome, you might see these twisting vines shooting out of the ground. They have almost identical properties to the weeping vines, but are styled to fit the dark foreboding greens of the warped forest.

TRANSPARENCY

LIGHT EMISSION   0

RENEWABLE

BLAST RESISTANCE 0

HARDNESS   0

FLAMMABLE

SILK TOUCH

TWISTING VINES PLANT

CHORUS PLANT

If you manage to reach the End islands, you might see the End's only native flora – the chorus plant. This block can be broken most easily with an axe but won't drop itself as an item, even with Silk Touch. The plants can turn into tall trees that reach up to 22 blocks high.

STATS

TRANSPARENCY	LIGHT EMISSION
	0

RENEWABLE	BLAST RESISTANCE	HARDNESS
	04	04

FLAMMABLE	SILK TOUCH

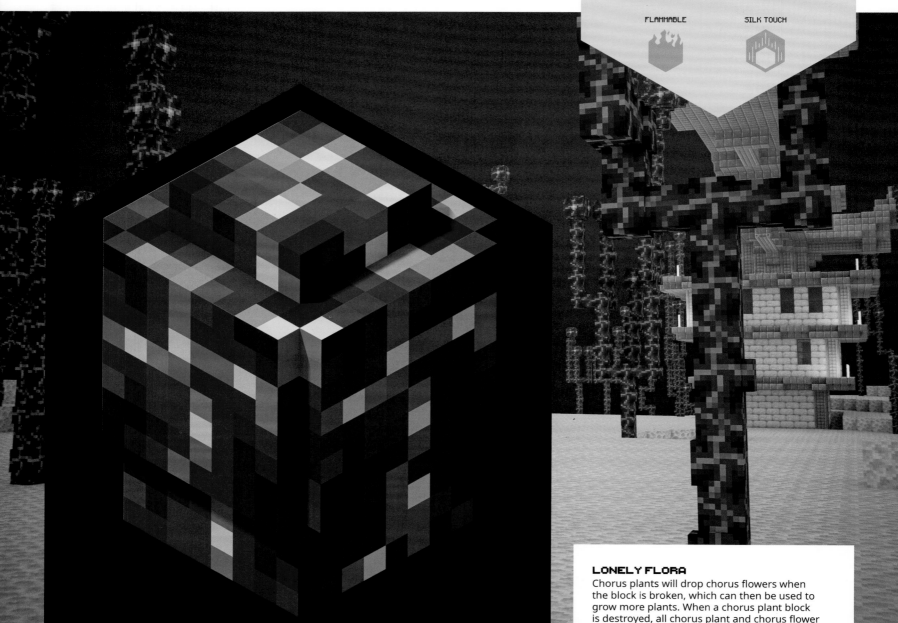

LONELY FLORA

Chorus plants will drop chorus flowers when the block is broken, which can then be used to grow more plants. When a chorus plant block is destroyed, all chorus plant and chorus flower blocks above will be destroyed, too. You can only obtain chorus plants in the Creative inventory.

CHORUS FLOWER

The blooms of the chorus plant are chorus flowers, which, unlike most flowers, are block-shaped. Before they fully mature, they appear primarily white, but switch to a mostly purple pattern when of age. You can harvest chorus flowers with any tool in order to collect them.

STATS

TRANSPARENCY	LIGHT EMISSION 0
RENEWABLE	BLAST RESISTANCE 0.4
	HARDNESS 0.4
FLAMMABLE	SILK TOUCH

CHORUS PLANTS AT VARIOUS AGES

SEEDS OF THE END
Chorus flowers generate on fully grown chorus plants. They have six stages of growth and will turn horizontally or grow more flowers on the same plant at each stage. Harvested chorus flowers can be planted in End stone at any light level to spawn more chorus plants.

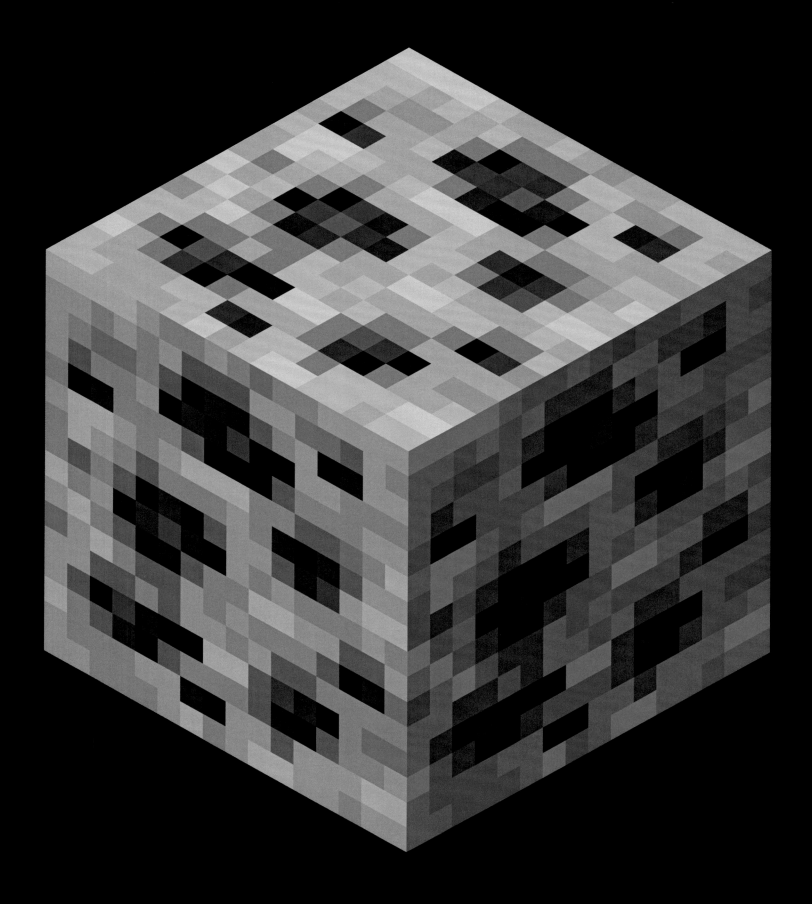

COAL ORE

The most common ore block is the one you're most likely to stumble across first – coal ore. It's prevalent in all biomes and you'll often see it dotting the hallways of mine shafts and caverns. Along with iron ore, it was the first ore to be added to Minecraft.

STATS

TRANSPARENCY	LIGHT EMISSION
	0

RENEWABLE	BLAST RESISTANCE	HARDNESS
	3	3

FLAMMABLE	SILK TOUCH

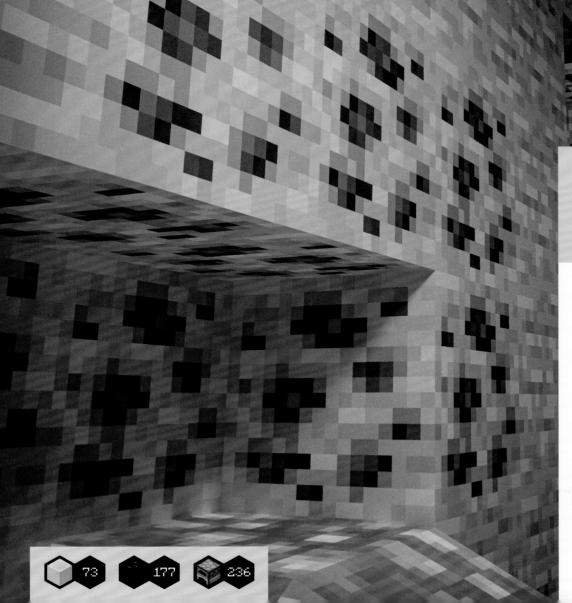

DEEPSLATE COAL ORE

BEHAVIOR
When mined, coal ore will drop a single piece of coal, which is useful for powering furnaces or crafting torches that can illuminate further mining expeditions. It requires only a wooden pickaxe to be mined, or will drop itself as an item if the pickaxe is enchanted with Silk Touch. Coal ore can also be smelted down into coal using a furnace.

GENERATION
Coal ore commonly generates underground in mineral veins, and is a frequent sight for any miner. The deepslate variant generates in place of deepslate and tuff, but is only visually different.

BLACK GOLD
The amount of coal gained from mining coal ore can be increased by enchanting a pickaxe with Fortune – at the highest level of enchantment, it can drop 4 pieces of coal. When fossils generate underground, there's a chance that some of the bone blocks will be replaced by a coal ore block.

73	177	236

IRON ORE

Iron is one of Minecraft's oldest ores and, next to coal, is one of the most common. By using a stone pickaxe or better, you can collect raw iron, which you can smelt into iron ingots. Dozens of important recipes use these ingots – from iron swords and tools to rails and pressure plates.

STATS

TRANSPARENCY	LIGHT EMISSION
	0

RENEWABLE	BLAST RESISTANCE	HARDNESS
	3	3

FLAMMABLE	SILK TOUCH

DEEPSLATE IRON ORE

SHALLOW MINING
Iron ore is found in every biome of the Overworld. It generates in large veins, within a wide range of elevations. If iron ore attempts to generate within layers of deepslate and tuff, it turns into the slightly more hardy deepslate iron ore variant.

LAPIS LAZULI ORE

The ore of lapis lazuli is rarer than coal or iron ores, though it can still generate in all biomes. It's the only source of lapis lazuli, a vital resource for enchanting, which unlocks up to three possible enchantment options on an item. It can also be crafted into blue dye.

STATS

TRANSPARENCY	LIGHT EMISSION
	0

RENEWABLE	BLAST RESISTANCE	HARDNESS
	3	3

FLAMMABLE	SILK TOUCH

DEEPSLATE LAPIS ORE

LUCKY FIND
Though rare, each lapis lazuli ore will drop up to 9 pieces of lapis lazuli, which can be increased to 36 if the pickaxe is enchanted with Fortune. If it generates deep enough in the world, there's a chance that it will appear as its deepslate variant.

GOLD ORE

FOUND:
Underground in
the Overworld

All that glitters is indeed gold. Gold ore, that is. It's a rare find, though it can be found within a wide span of levels. You need an iron pickaxe to mine it, and it drops raw gold, which will smelt into gold ingots that, in turn, you can craft into gold armor, weapons and tools.

STATS

TRANSPARENCY	LIGHT EMISSION
	0

RENEWABLE	BLAST RESISTANCE	HARDNESS
	3	3

FLAMMABLE   SILK TOUCH

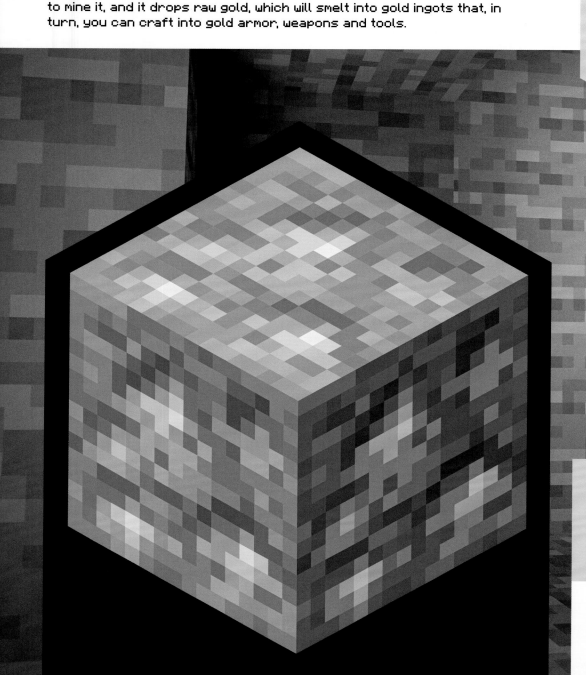

DEEPSLATE
GOLD ORE

HEAVY METAL

If you travel to the badlands biome, gold becomes a lot more common. You can use Silk Touch to make the block drop itself, which you can then smelt into gold ingots. If you descend to the deepest underground levels, you may find deepslate gold ore.

 149   180

REDSTONE ORE

Now we're playing with power! Redstone ore is the source of redstone dust, the conduit for all mechanical items and contraptions in Minecraft. When mined with a stone pickaxe or better, you'll be able to collect up to five pieces of redstone dust, or the block itself if you use Silk Touch.

STATS

TRANSPARENCY	LIGHT EMISSION
	9

RENEWABLE	BLAST RESISTANCE	HARDNESS
	3	3

FLAMMABLE	SILK TOUCH

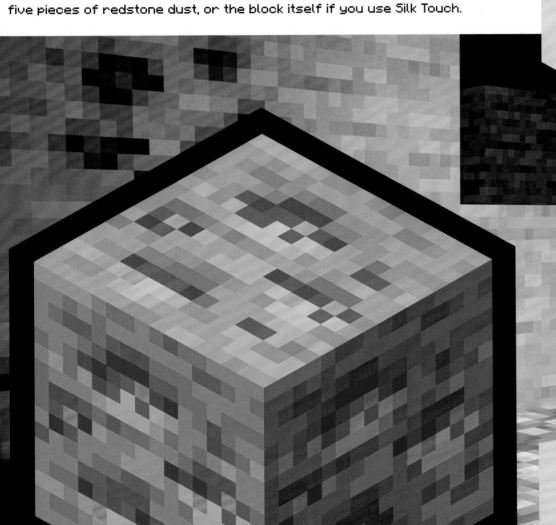

**DEEPSLATE
REDSTONE ORE**

POWER SOURCE

If redstone ore generates toward the lowest depths of the world, there's a chance it will replace deepslate or tuff and become deepslate redstone ore. It will become a level 9 light source when touched by a mob or player – unless sneaking – or when a player interacts with the block.

DIAMOND ORE

Found in the deepest layers of the world, diamond ore generates in big veins, which you'll need an iron pickaxe to mine. Diamonds are used to craft armor and tools, like the diamond pickaxe, which is essential to mine the strongest blocks in the game, such as obsidian.

STATS

TRANSPARENCY	LIGHT EMISSION
	0

RENEWABLE	BLAST RESISTANCE	HARDNESS
	3	3

FLAMMABLE	SILK TOUCH

DEEPSLATE DIAMOND ORE

A MINER'S BEST FRIEND

Fortune can increase the number of diamonds that diamond ore will drop, though it can only drop up to 4 diamonds. Like other ores, there's a finite amount of diamond ore in each world. You can get the block to drop itself with a Silk Touch tool, and there's also a deepslate variant that occurs when it generates in deepslate or tuff.

EMERALD ORE

rarest Overworld ore is the emerald ore, mostly because each ore
ck will only ever drop a single emerald without enchantments. Emeralds
a valuable currency, used to trade with villagers around the world. An
pickaxe or better is required to mine it.

STATS

TRANSPARENCY	LIGHT EMISSION
	0

RENEWABLE	BLAST RESISTANCE		HARDNESS
		3	3

FLAMMABLE	SILK TOUCH

**DEEPSLATE
EMERALD ORE**

SCARY SCARCITY

As with other ores, Silk Touch will allow you
to mine the block as an item, and the Fortune
enchantment can increase the drop rate fourfold.
Emerald ore has a deepslate variant like other
ores, but it doesn't generate naturally, so you can
only find it in Creative mode.

PPER ORE

changeable copper ore block drops raw copper that you can fashion
copper ingots. Like other ores, it generates in veins underground, at
und the same rate as iron ore. You may notice a bit of discoloration on
re, which hints at its variable nature ...

STATS

TRANSPARENCY

LIGHT EMISSION
0

RENEWABLE

BLAST RESISTANCE
3

HARDNESS
3

FLAMMABLE

SILK TOUCH

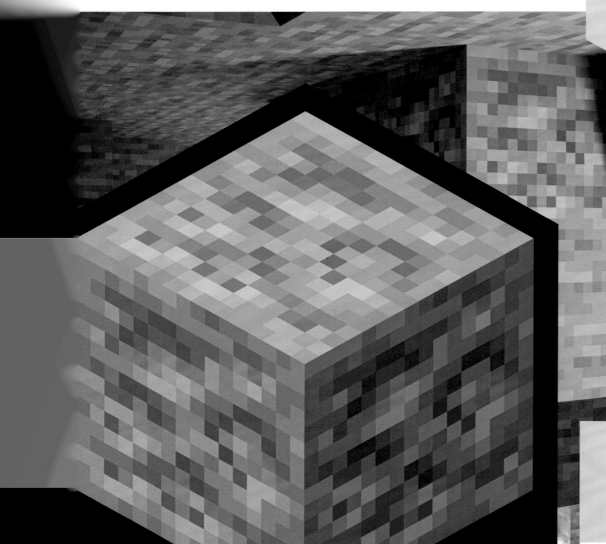

DEEPSLATE
COPPER ORE

WHATEVER THE WEATHER

You can smelt copper ingots from copper ore to
craft lightning rods, spyglasses and copper blocks,
which will weather and change appearance with
time. Copper and raw copper blocks can also be
crafted back into ingots or raw copper. You need
at least a stone pickaxe to mine copper ore.

 136   184   186   187

AMETHYST CLUSTER

This delicate gem emerges from budding amethysts in one of four growth stages. Only the fully grown amethyst cluster will drop amethyst shards, unless you mine earlier stages with a Silk Touch-enchanted tool. These shards can be used to craft spyglasses and tinted glass.

STATS

TRANSPARENCY	LIGHT EMISSION
	1-5

RENEWABLE	BLAST RESISTANCE	HARDNESS
	1.5	1.5

FLAMMABLE	SILK TOUCH

SMALL BUD   MEDIUM BUD   LARGE BUD

FINE CRYSTALS
The first three stages of amethyst growths are called "buds." Every few ticks, there's a chance that the budding amethyst will grow a bud, or increase an existing bud by one stage, on any of its faces. All sizes of bud will also give off a small amount of light, more so with each growth stage, up to a maximum of 5 for a cluster.

CRYING OBSIDIAN

A glowing version of obsidian, crying obsidian shares many similarities with its darker cousin. It has identical blast resistance and hardness, and you can only mine it with a diamond or netherite pickaxe. It's also resistant to fire and lava, as well as the push and pull of pistons.

STATS

TRANSPARENCY	LIGHT EMISSION
	10

RENEWABLE	BLAST RESISTANCE	HARDNESS
	1200	50

FLAMMABLE	SILK TOUCH

BEHAVIOR
The main difference that crying obsidian has from the normal variant is the fact that it has dripping purple particles, and emits a light level of 10. When you eventually mine the block, you'll be able to use it to craft a respawn anchor, which allows you to set a spawn point in the Nether.

GENERATION
You'll only find crying obsidian naturally in ruined portals of the Nether and Overworld, where it has a small chance to replace the obsidian blocks of the portal. However, this is a bit of a red herring as you can't use it in place of obsidian to create the frames for Nether portals.

WEEPING TREASURE
Though it's rare as a naturally generated block, if you're lucky you'll find crying obsidian in the chests of bastion remnant structures, or by trading with piglins. Jeb added the texture for crying obsidian to the beta of Minecraft, but it wasn't used for an actual block until nine years later!

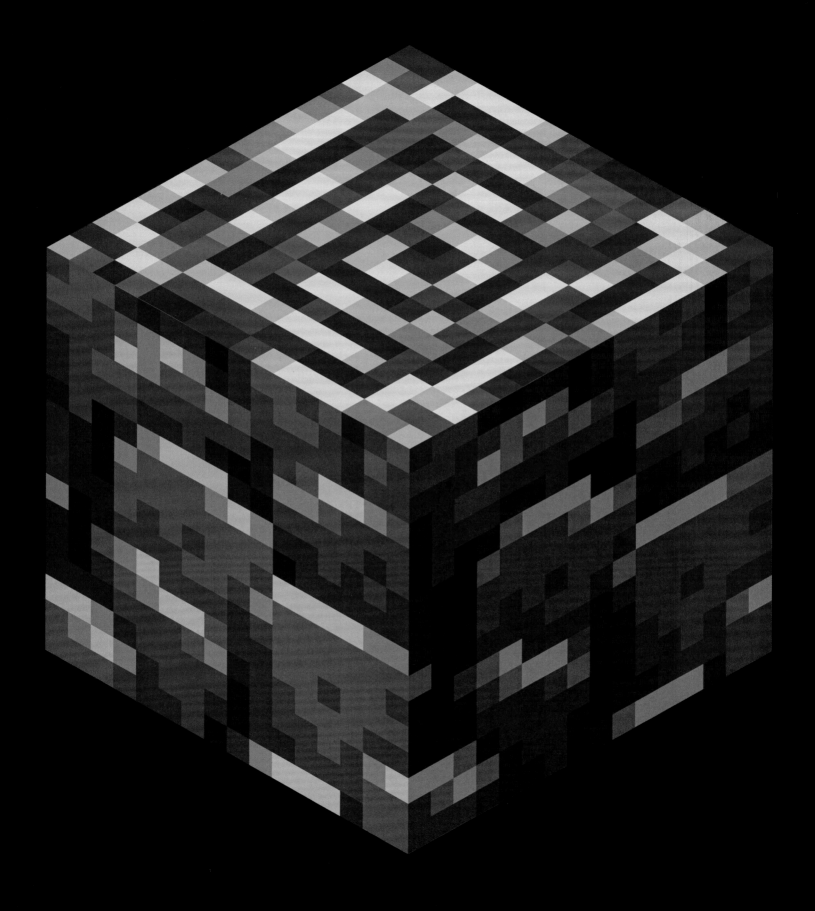

ANCIENT DEBRIS

A resilient ore block, as tough as crying obsidian in terms of its blast resistance, ancient debris is the sole source of netherite scrap. You can only mine it with a diamond pickaxe or better, just like obsidian, and it drops itself as an item without the need for Silk Touch enchantments.

STATS

TRANSPARENCY	LIGHT EMISSION
	0

RENEWABLE	BLAST RESISTANCE	HARDNESS
	1200	30

FLAMMABLE	SILK TOUCH

BEHAVIOR
Ancient debris is highly resistant to fire and lava, and will resist burning and even float on lava when it's in item form. Fittingly, you can smelt it into netherite scrap, which is used to create some of the most powerful tools in Minecraft, and which is also fire resistant and buoyant in lava.

GENERATION
Ancient debris spawns the same way that Overworld ores do, in mineral veins of up to 3 blocks. It can replace netherrack, basalt or blackstone when it generates. Like crying obsidian, it is most often found in the loot chests of bastion remnants.

ALLOY INGREDIENT
You can't use netherite scrap alone to craft any items. Instead, it must be combined with gold ingots to make netherite ingots, which can then be crafted together with diamond tools and armor to make netherite equivalents.

46   48   201

NETHER QUARTZ ORE

FOUND:
In the Nether

Found in clusters within the netherrack that forms the majority of the Nether, Nether quartz ore is the source of Nether quartz, which is used to craft several decorative quartz blocks and is used in recipes for redstone items like observers. You can also smelt the ore into Nether quartz using a furnace.

STATS

TRANSPARENCY	LIGHT EMISSION
	0

RENEWABLE	BLAST RESISTANCE	HARDNESS
	3	3

FLAMMABLE	SILK TOUCH

FIERY ORE

Nether quartz is a much more common ore in the Nether than ancient debris and will generate in veins of up to 14 blocks. It can be found between levels 10 and 117 in any biome of the dimension. It's slightly rarer in basalt deltas as there is less netherrack for it to try to replace.

 62
 204

NETHER GOLD ORE

Gold isn't only found in the Overworld – you can find Nether gold ore in the fiery dimension, too. It generates between the same levels and in similar quantities as Nether quartz ore. Be careful if you choose to mine it – any nearby piglins will become enraged and attack!

STATS

TRANSPARENCY	LIGHT EMISSION
	0

RENEWABLE	BLAST RESISTANCE	HARDNESS
	3	3

FLAMMABLE	SILK TOUCH

NUGGET HACK
Nether gold drops up to 6 gold nuggets when you break it with any pickaxe, However, you need 9 gold nuggets to make a gold ingot, so it's more efficient to mine the block with Silk Touch to make the Nether gold ore drop itself, before smelting that block down into a single gold ingot.

 138   180

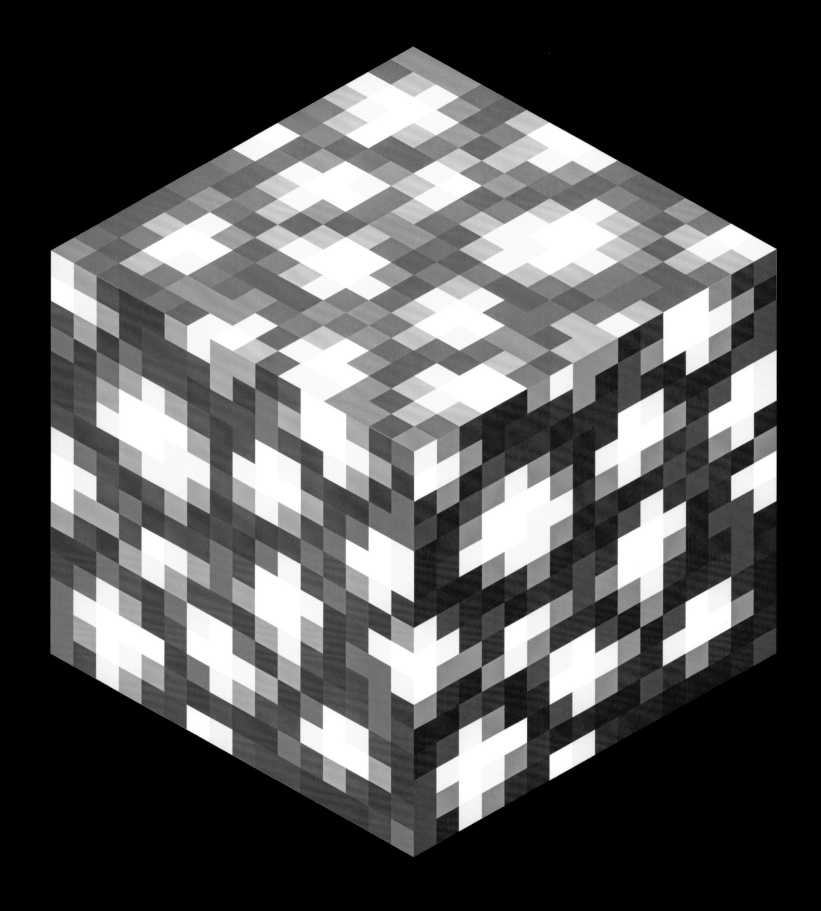

GLOWSTONE

Glowstone is one of few light sources you'll see illuminating the Nether. Unlike other lights, it's considered a transparent block. You can mine it with a pickaxe to produce glowstone dust, or use Silk Touch to make it drop itself. Both block and dust have many uses in crafts and potions.

STATS

TRANSPARENCY	LIGHT EMISSION
	15

RENEWABLE	BLAST RESISTANCE	HARDNESS
	0.3	0.3

FLAMMABLE	SILK TOUCH

BEHAVIOR
The block produces the brightest possible light to penetrate the Nether's dim gloom. It is a vital ingredient in crafting – you can use it to create redstone lamps and respawn anchors. The glowstone dust it produces is also used in brewing to increase the strength of the potion's effect.

GENERATION
Glowstone generates in hanging configurations from ceilings, or within naturally generated bastion remnant structures. As well as generating naturally, you can craft glowstone using 4 pieces of glowstone dust.

A LIGHT IN THE DARK
You can increase the amount of glowstone dust you receive by using the Fortune enchantment, though 4 pieces is the maximum. Redstone dust placed atop glowstone will carry a signal upward, but not downward, which makes it a useful block to have to hand when building redstone circuits.

 63   307

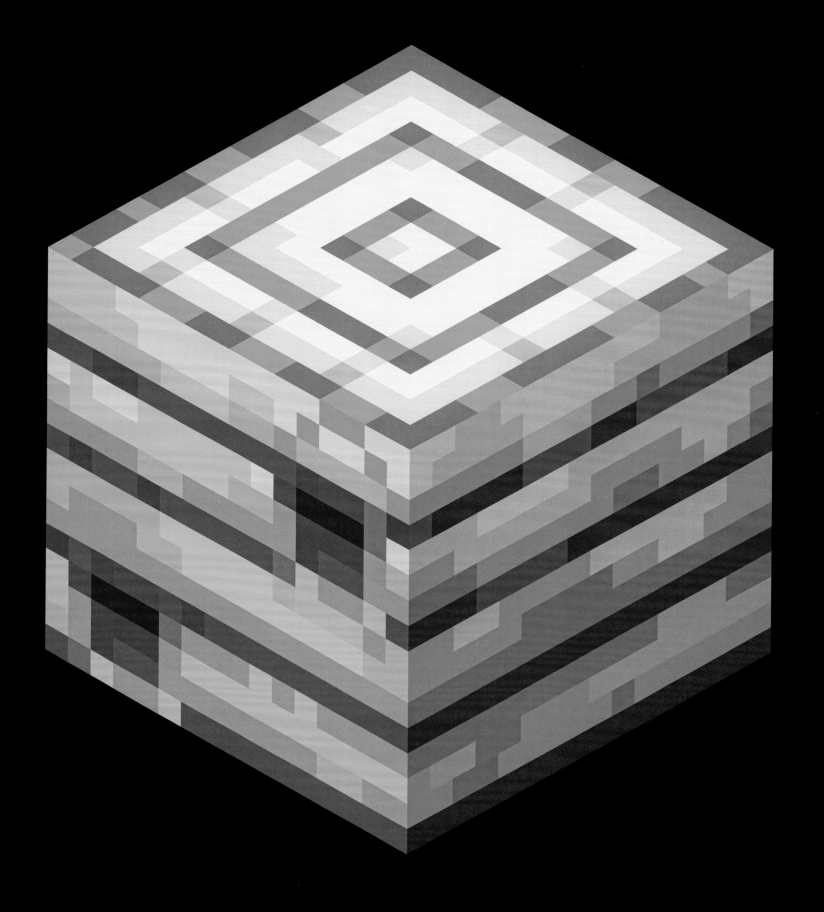

BEE NEST

The natural home to bees of the Overworld, bee nests are important in maintaining the flora of the dimension. They can hold a maximum of three bees per nest who will collect pollen from nearby plants to produce delicious honey and honeycomb.

STATS

TRANSPARENCY

LIGHT EMISSION
0

RENEWABLE

BLAST RESISTANCE
0.3

HARDNESS
0.3

FLAMMABLE

SILK TOUCH

BEHAVIOR
Bees will fly to flowers, collect pollen and work away in the bee nest to increase the honey by a single level. Once the nest is full of honey, you can use a glass bottle on it to transform it into a bottle of honey, which is great for battling hunger as well as removing any Poison effect!

GENERATION
Bee nests generate in plains and forest biomes, where flowers and trees are most abundant. You can destroy them with any tool, but they'll break and make the bees angry. If you use the Silk Touch enchantment, the bees will remain calm and in the nest. You can't craft bee nests, so if you want to replace one, you'll need to craft a beehive, which has the same functions.

BUZZ OFF
You can also shear bee nests to harvest the block for honeycomb, though this will also anger the bees. You can avoid infuriating them by lighting a campfire within five blocks of the bee nest or setting a fire directly underneath it.

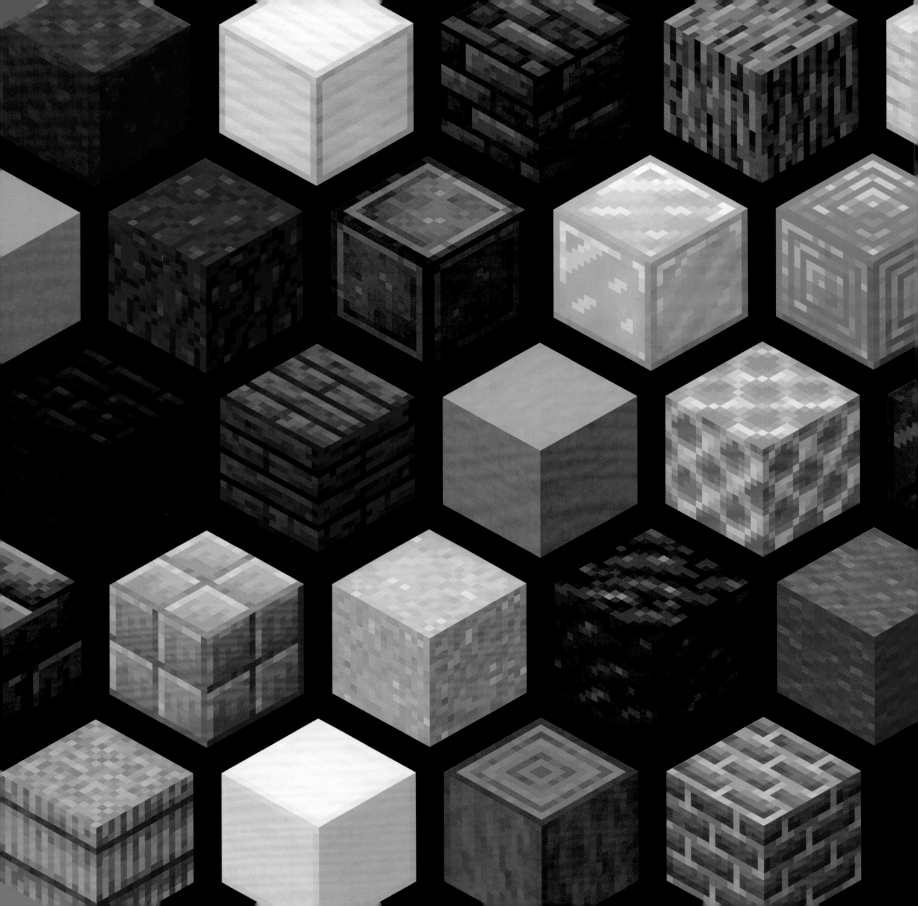

REFINED BLOCKS

WOOD

Wood and hyphae are crafted from the logs of trees and stems of huge fungi. These blocks have bark textures on all sides, and you can use them in a similar number of crafting recipes as their unrefined counterparts, such as those for planks, campfires and smokers.

STATS

TRANSPARENCY

LIGHT EMISSION
0

RENEWABLE

BLAST RESISTANCE
2

HARDNESS
2

FLAMMABLE

SILK TOUCH

OAK WOOD

ACACIA WOOD · BIRCH WOOD · DARK OAK WOOD · JUNGLE WOOD

SPRUCE WOOD · CRIMSON HYPHAE · WARPED HYPHAE

DIMENSION DIFFERENCES

Wood is available in all the same types as logs, while hyphae is available in crimson and warped varieties. Wood made from Overworld logs burns in fire and lava, while the Nether hyphae do not. You can also smelt wood, logs and their stripped variants into charcoal, which is a fuel that can be used to power more smelting.

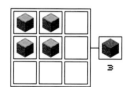
WOOD RECIPE

 80 128 159

STRIPPED WOOD

If you interact with a placed piece of wood or hyphae – rather than mining it – with an axe in hand, you'll create a stripped variant of the block. You can then collect it by harvesting it with an axe as usual. It has identical properties to the unstripped version of woods and hyphaes.

STATS

TRANSPARENCY	LIGHT EMISSION 0
RENEWABLE	BLAST RESISTANCE 2	HARDNESS 2
FLAMMABLE	SILK TOUCH

STRIPPED JUNGLE WOOD

STRIPPED BIRCH WOOD | STRIPPED DARK OAK WOOD | STRIPPED JUNGLE WOOD | STRIPPED OAK WOOD

STRIPPED SPRUCE WOOD | STRIPPED CRIMSON HYPHAE | STRIPPED WARPED HYPHAE

WOOD WORLDWIDE

You can find stripped oak, spruce and acacia wood in plains, snowy tundra and savanna villages respectively. You can use stripped woods in any recipe that features normal unstripped wood. Its texture resembles the inside of logs rather than the bark, which gives it a unique look that you can use as an interesting decoration.

STRIPPED LOGS

You can create stripped logs using the same method as stripped wood –
by using an axe on a placed block, but this time the placed block is a log.
The stripped stems aren't flammable like the Overworld logs, though they
are slightly easier to harvest; otherwise their properties are identical.

STATS

TRANSPARENCY	LIGHT EMISSION
	0

RENEWABLE	BLAST RESISTANCE	HARDNESS
	2	2

FLAMMABLE	SILK TOUCH

STRIPPED SPRUCE LOG

STRIPPED
ACACIA
LOG

STRIPPED
BIRCH
LOG

STRIPPED
DARK OAK
LOG

STRIPPED
JUNGLE
LOG

STRIPPED
OAK
LOG

STRIPPED
CRIMSON
STEM

STRIPPED
WARPED
STEM

ALL BITE NO BARK
Stripped logs and stems maintain the concentric
top and bottom faces of normal logs, but have a
different texture on the sides. The direction the log
faces depends on where you place it – if placed on
the ceiling or floor, the rings will face up and down;
place them on a wall and they'll face sideways.

PLANKS

FOUND:
Many Overworld structures

STATS

TRANSPARENCY	LIGHT EMISSION
	0

RENEWABLE	BLAST RESISTANCE	HARDNESS
	3	2

FLAMMABLE	SILK TOUCH

The most productive wooden block is planks, which you can craft from any log, wood or stripped variant of either. You will also see them naturally generate in many structures, from shipwrecks to witch huts. Like their source blocks, only the Overworld planks are flammable.

ACACIA PLANKS **BIRCH PLANKS** **DARK OAK PLANKS** **JUNGLE PLANKS**

OAK PLANKS **SPRUCE PLANKS** **WARPED PLANKS**

MULTI-PURPOSE PRODUCT

You can use wood planks in a multitude of recipes, from boats and beehives to wooden tools and many others. Nether wood planks can be used interchangeably in any recipe except for the creation of boats, though they don't directly pass on their fire-resistant properties to any product.

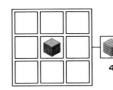

PLANKS RECIPE

CRIMSON PLANKS

 156

 159

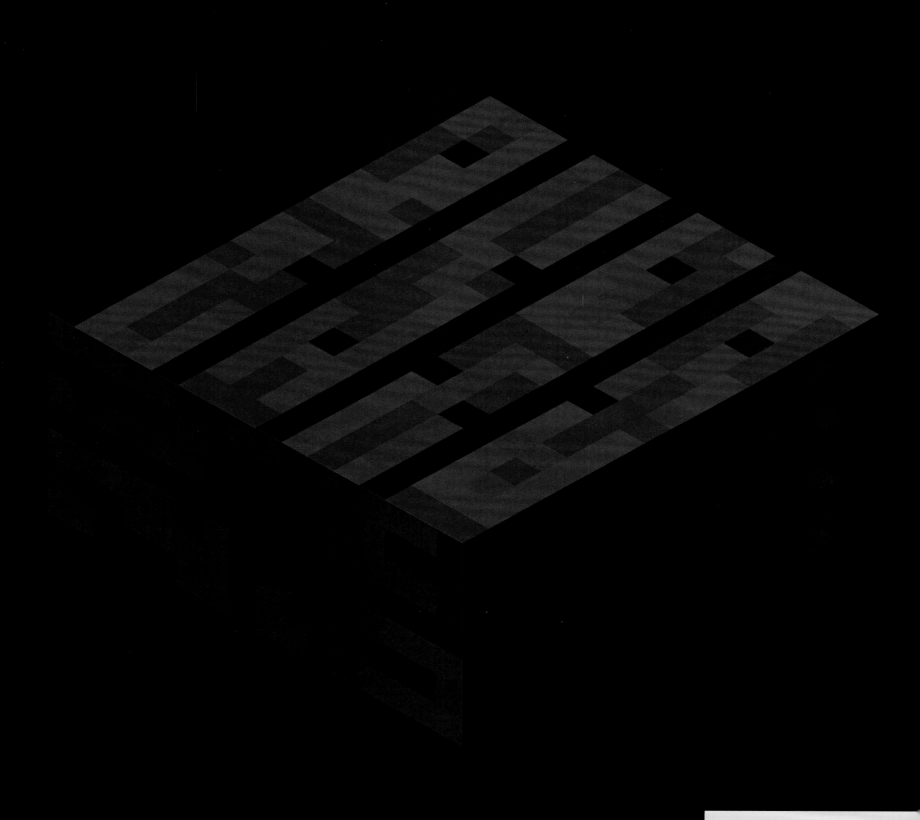

DARK OAK SLAB

WOOD SLABS

Slabs are half-height blocks that are available in all varieties of Overworld wood and Nether hyphae. You can craft six of them with three plank blocks, and they're easily collected with an axe once placed. You can position them in the top or bottom part of any block space if there's a block adjacent.

STATS

TRANSPARENCY	LIGHT EMISSION
	0

RENEWABLE	BLAST RESISTANCE	HARDNESS
	3	2

FLAMMABLE	SILK TOUCH

ACACIA SLAB   BIRCH SLAB   JUNGLE SLAB

OAK SLAB   SPRUCE SLAB   CRIMSON SLAB

WARPED SLAB

GENERATION
Though they're largely crafted blocks, you can find slabs in buildings across the world. You'll see oak, acacia and spruce slabs in villages of the savanna, plains and snowy taiga biomes. Others still can be found in woodland mansions, igloos, pillager outposts and shipwrecks.

BEHAVIOR
If you place a slab on top of a block, or the bottom half of the side of a block, the slab will occupy the bottom part of the block space. If you place it on the underside of a block or the top half of a block's side then it will occupy the top part of the space. You can place two slabs of the same type in a block space to create a double slab.

SLAB CRAFTS
You can use wooden slabs in recipes for barrels, composters, lecterns and more. Slabs occupying the top of a block space can be used in redstone builds to transmit a signal upward and horizontally, without passing it down. Like other wood products, slabs can also be used as a fuel.

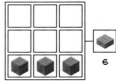

WOODEN SLAB RECIPE

 162   168

WOOD DOUBLE SLABS

FOUND:
Only when placing slabs together

Though these might look very similar to wooden planks, double slabs are a distinct block in their own right. You can only create them by placing a wooden slab on top of or underneath an identical wooden slab within a single block space.

STATS

TRANSPARENCY

LIGHT EMISSION — 0

RENEWABLE

BLAST RESISTANCE — 3

HARDNESS — 2

FLAMMABLE

SILK TOUCH

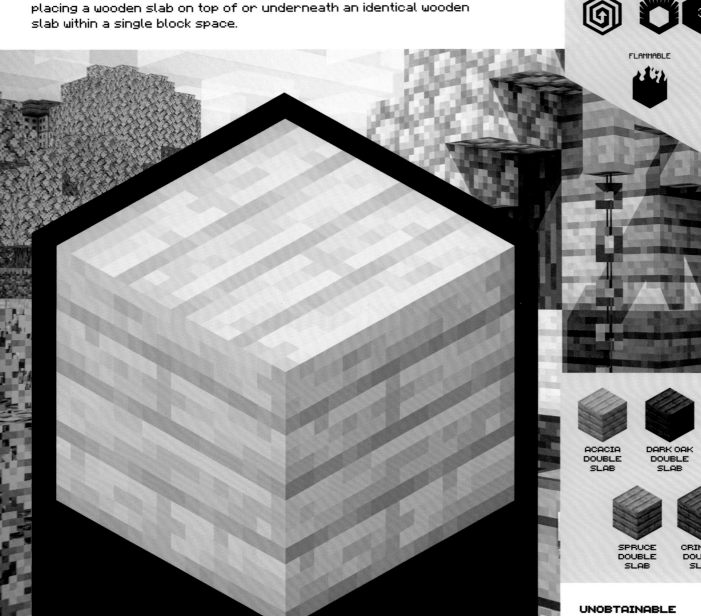

BIRCH DOUBLE SLAB

ACACIA DOUBLE SLAB	DARK OAK DOUBLE SLAB	JUNGLE DOUBLE SLAB	OAK DOUBLE SLAB

SPRUCE DOUBLE SLAB	CRIMSON DOUBLE SLAB	WARPED DOUBLE SLAB

UNOBTAINABLE

When you destroy a double slab, it will drop two slab blocks instead of itself. In fact, it's impossible to obtain the double slabs in your inventory, even in Creative mode. They have similar qualities to slabs, except the obvious size difference and the fact they're not transparent.

WOOD STAIRS

Wooden stairs appear in villages and other structures around the Overworld. You can get your hands on them by crafting six planks together, and they'll make it much easier to get around buildings. Unlike other stairs, you don't need a pickaxe to break these – any tool will make them drop.

STATS

TRANSPARENCY	LIGHT EMISSION
	0

RENEWABLE	BLAST RESISTANCE	HARDNESS
	3	2

FLAMMABLE	SILK TOUCH

JUNGLE STAIRS

ACACIA STAIRS

BIRCH STAIRS

DARK OAK STAIRS

OAK STAIRS

SPRUCE STAIRS

CRIMSON STAIRS

WARPED STAIRS

STEPPING UP
The benefit of stairs is that they allow you to easily travel between different block heights without jumping. They will create continuous staircases if placed horizontally adjacent and will also curve inward or outward when placed to connect two stair blocks that are a diagonal space apart.

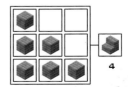

WOODEN STAIR RECIPE

 159   172   174

BRICKS

A common decorative block, bricks are often used to create modern exteriors, and you can sometimes see them in the houses of plains villages. Brick will drop itself as an item if you mine it with a pickaxe and you can use it to craft similarly styled walls, slabs and stairs, or make banner patterns.

STATS

TRANSPARENCY	LIGHT EMISSION
	0

RENEWABLE	BLAST RESISTANCE	HARDNESS
	6	2

FLAMMABLE	SILK TOUCH

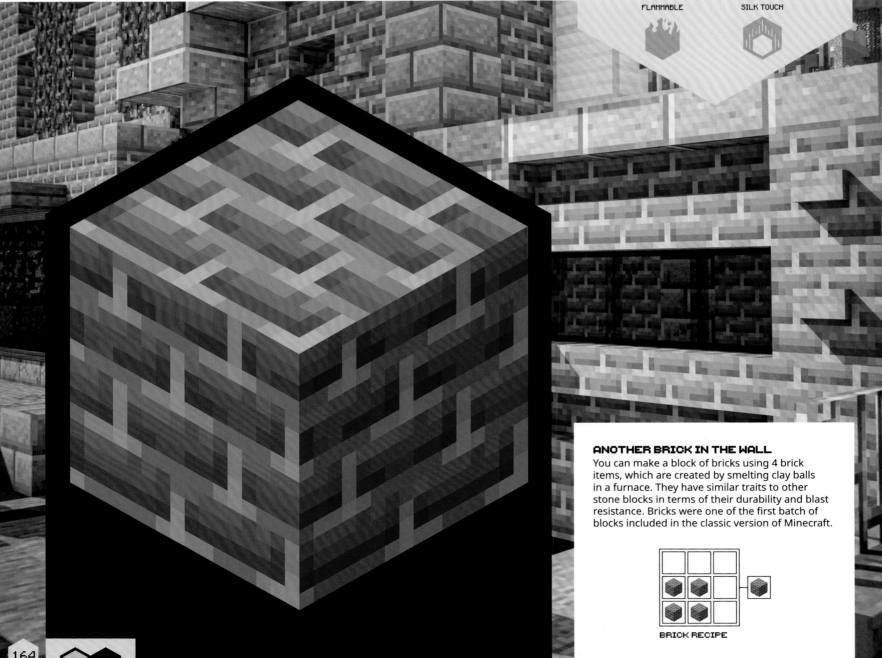

ANOTHER BRICK IN THE WALL
You can make a block of bricks using 4 brick items, which are created by smelting clay balls in a furnace. They have similar traits to other stone blocks in terms of their durability and blast resistance. Bricks were one of the first batch of blocks included in the classic version of Minecraft.

BRICK RECIPE

DEEPSLATE BRICKS

FOUND:
By crafting only

With a pattern more reminiscent of stone bricks than the finer texture of polished deepslate, deepslate bricks are dark, bold and primarily used for aesthetics. You can make four of them with as many blocks of polished deepslate, though they're only half as strong as their source block.

CRACKED DEEPSLATE BRICKS

DARK MATERIALS

Putting deepslate bricks through a furnace will give you the cracked variant, which is used for a slightly more distressed look. You can also craft slabs, stairs and wall variants with deepslate bricks. The block's final trick is that you can use it to craft deepslate tiles, which have a more varied brick texture than deepslate bricks themselves.

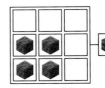

DEEPSLATE BRICKS RECIPE

 35   166

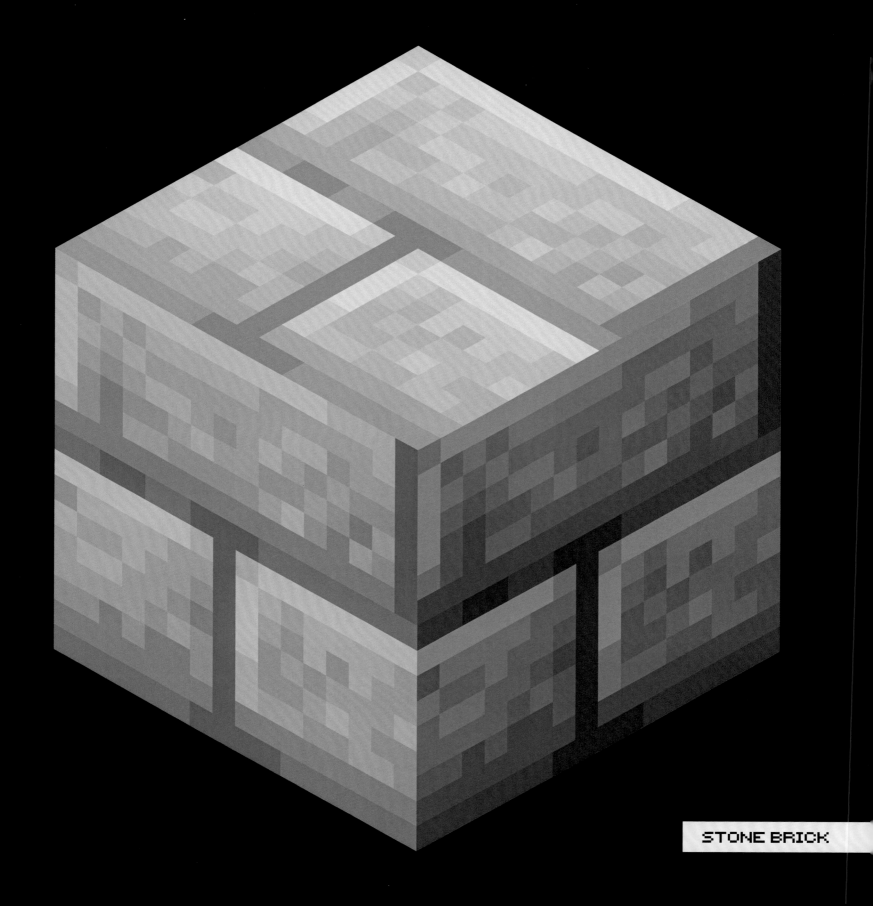

STONE BRICK

STONE BRICKS

Not content with one type of bricks? There are four versions based on stone! They're common blocks in villages but you can also spot them in rare igloo basements and strongholds. You can use them to craft decorative blocks, and the chiseled stone brick is also used to make a lodestone.

STATS

TRANSPARENCY	LIGHT EMISSION
	0

RENEWABLE	BLAST RESISTANCE	HARDNESS
	6	1.5

FLAMMABLE	SILK TOUCH

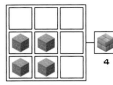

CRACKED STONE BRICKS	MOSSY STONE BRICKS	CHISELED STONE BRICKS

A CUT ABOVE
You can craft stone bricks with 4 stone blocks or by putting a single block through a stonecutter. Chiseled stone bricks are also made with the stonecutter, while you can combine stone bricks and a vine to make mossy stone bricks. Cracked stone bricks can only be found in strongholds.

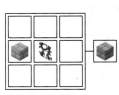

STONE BRICKS RECIPE

MOSSY STONE BRICKS RECIPE

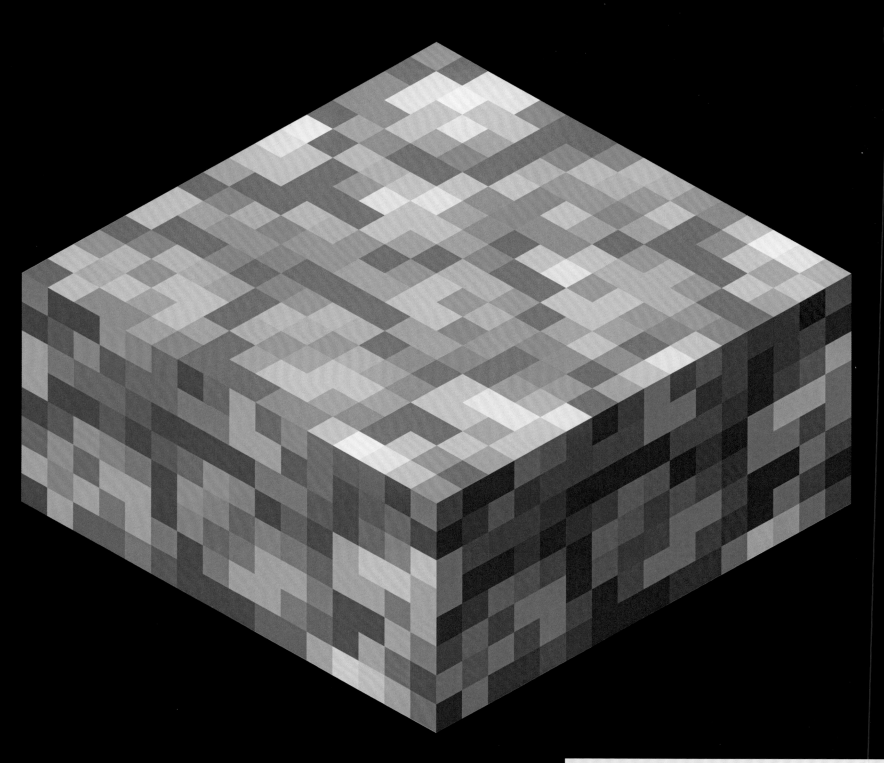

MOSSY COBBLESTONE SLAB

STONE SLABS

Stone slabs share the block placement mechanics of wooden slabs, but offer an immunity to fire and lava, as well as a better blast resistance. They're best mined with pickaxes, and you'll find a few of the stone slabs – the sandstone and quartz ones – are easier to mine than wood.

STATS

TRANSPARENCY	LIGHT EMISSION
	0

RENEWABLE	BLAST RESISTANCE	HARDNESS
	6	1.5

FLAMMABLE	SILK TOUCH

GRANITE SLAB | POLISHED GRANITE SLAB | STONE SLAB | SMOOTH STONE SLAB | COBBLESTONE SLAB

STONE BRICK SLAB | MOSSY STONE BRICK SLAB | ANDESITE SLAB | POLISHED ANDESITE SLAB | DIORITE SLAB

POLISHED DIORITE SLAB | SANDSTONE SLAB | CUT SANDSTONE SLAB | SMOOTH SANDSTONE SLAB | RED SANDSTONE SLAB

CUT RED SANDSTONE SLAB | SMOOTH RED SANDSTONE SLAB | BRICK SLAB | PRISMARINE SLAB | PRISMARINE BRICK SLAB

DARK PRISMARINE SLAB | NETHER BRICK SLAB | RED NETHER BRICK SLAB | QUARTZ SLAB | SMOOTH QUARTZ SLAB

PURPUR SLAB | BLACKSTONE SLAB | POLISHED BLACKSTONE SLAB | POLISHED BLACKSTONE BRICK SLAB | DEEPSLATE SLAB

POLISHED DEEPSLATE SLAB | COBBLED DEEPSLATE SLAB | DEEPSLATE BRICK SLAB

GENERATION

Stone slabs are ubiquitous in structures throughout the world. You can discover cobblestone slabs in woodland mansions, blackstone slabs in bastion remnants of the Nether and stone brick slabs in the ruined portals found in the Overworld.

MYRIAD SLABS

You can craft stone slabs on a stonecutter, which will result in 2 slabs from each source block. On a crafting table, 3 source blocks produce 6 slabs, so it's as efficient as the stonecutter, unlike crafting stair blocks. They also have the same redstone-transmitting properties as the wooden versions.

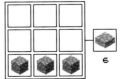

MOSSY COBBLESTONE SLAB RECIPE

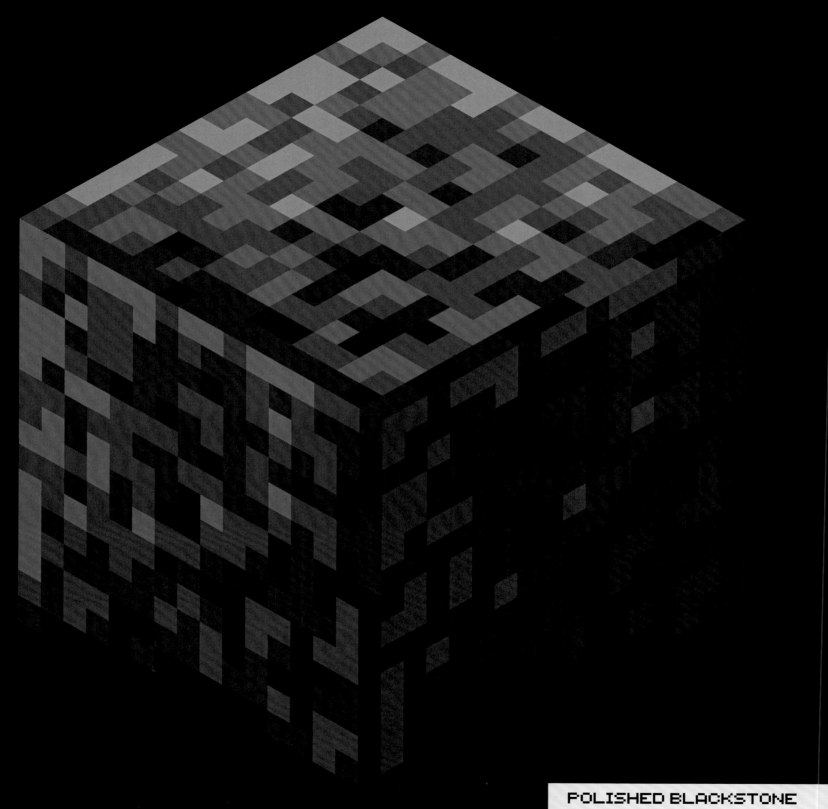

POLISHED BLACKSTONE
DOUBLE SLAB

STONE DOUBLE SLABS

If you combine two identical stone slabs in the same block space, it will turn into a stone double slab! Like wooden double slabs, the stone version can't be added to inventories. If you destroy a double slab, it drops two slabs, and using a pickaxe is the fastest method of destruction.

STATS

TRANSPARENCY	LIGHT EMISSION
	0

RENEWABLE	BLAST RESISTANCE	HARDNESS
	6	1.5

FLAMMABLE	SILK TOUCH

GRANITE DOUBLE SLAB · **POLISHED GRANITE DOUBLE SLAB** · **STONE DOUBLE SLAB** · **SMOOTH STONE DOUBLE SLAB** · **COBBLESTONE DOUBLE SLAB**

MOSSY COBBLESTONE DOUBLE SLAB · **STONE BRICK DOUBLE SLAB** · **MOSSY STONE BRICK DOUBLE SLAB** · **ANDESITE DOUBLE SLAB** · **POLISHED ANDESITE DOUBLE SLAB**

DIORITE DOUBLE SLAB · **POLISHED DIORITE DOUBLE SLAB** · **SANDSTONE DOUBLE SLAB** · **CUT SANDSTONE DOUBLE SLAB** · **SMOOTH SANDSTONE DOUBLE SLAB**

RED SANDSTONE DOUBLE SLAB · **CUT RED SANDSTONE DOUBLE SLAB** · **SMOOTH RED SANDSTONE DOUBLE SLAB** · **BRICK DOUBLE SLAB** · **PRISMARINE DOUBLE SLAB**

PRISMARINE BRICK DOUBLE SLAB · **DARK PRISMARINE DOUBLE SLAB** · **NETHER BRICK DOUBLE SLAB** · **RED NETHER BRICK DOUBLE SLAB** · **QUARTZ DOUBLE SLAB**

SMOOTH QUARTZ DOUBLE SLAB · **PURPUR DOUBLE SLAB** · **BLACKSTONE DOUBLE SLAB** · **POLISHED BLACKSTONE BRICK DOUBLE SLAB** · **DEEPSLATE DOUBLE SLAB**

DEEPSLATE BRICK DOUBLE SLAB · **POLISHED DEEPSLATE DOUBLE SLAB** · **COBBLED DEEPSLATE DOUBLE SLAB**

INHERITED STATS

The properties of double slabs depend on the source blocks that comprise them. They all have the differing resilience of their composite slabs, yet share the same blast resistance among all variants. They're solid and opaque, unlike slabs, so they carry redstone transmissions as any normal block does.

 162   168

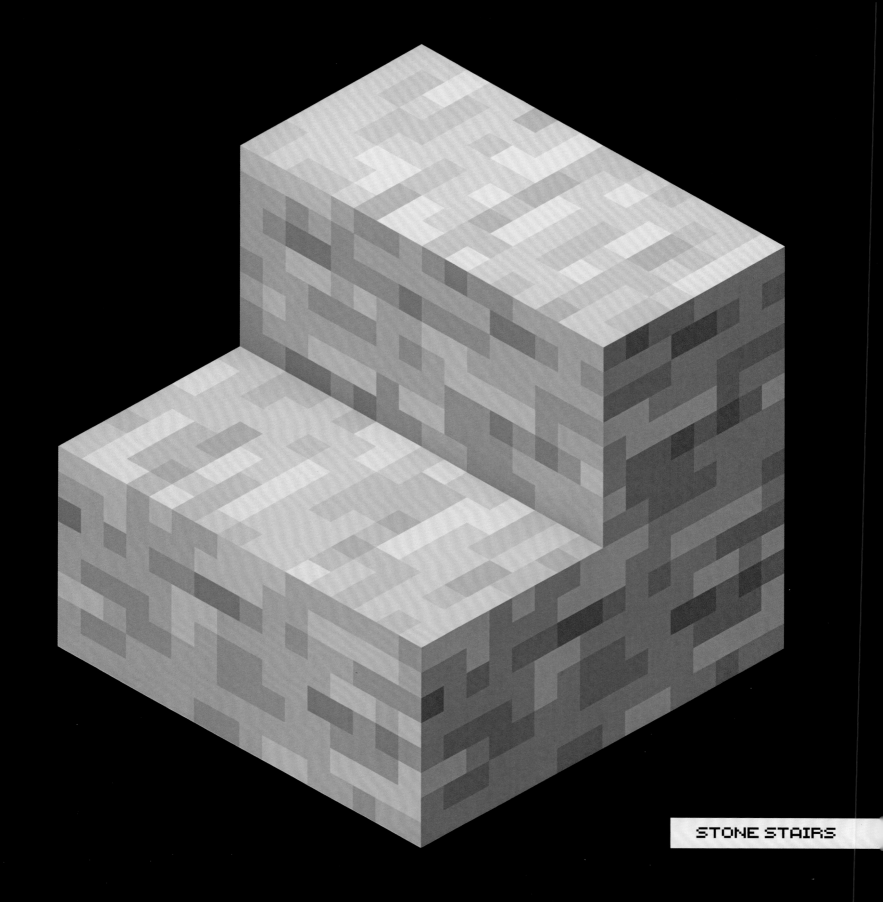

STONE STAIRS

STONE STAIRS

A sturdier foothold for 'crafters can be found in the stone stairs selection. They're mostly stronger than wooden stairs and are less affected by explosions, as well as being fireproof. You can use them to traverse levels with ease and to create decorative roofs and overhangs.

STATS

TRANSPARENCY

LIGHT EMISSION
0

RENEWABLE

BLAST RESISTANCE
6

HARDNESS
1.5

FLAMMABLE

SILK TOUCH

STONE BRICK STAIRS

MOSSY STONE BRICK STAIRS

COBBLESTONE STAIRS

MOSSY COBBLESTONE STAIRS

BRICK STAIRS

ANDESITE STAIRS

POLISHED ANDESITE STAIRS

DIORITE STAIRS

POLISHED DIORITE STAIRS

GRANITE STAIRS

POLISHED GRANITE STAIRS

PRISMARINE STAIRS

PRISMARINE BRICK STAIRS

DARK PRISMARINE STAIRS

PURPUR STAIRS

NETHER BRICK STAIRS

RED NETHER BRICK STAIRS

BLACKSTONE STAIRS

POLISHED BLACKSTONE STAIRS

POLISHED BLACKSTONE BRICK STAIRS

COBBLED DEEPSLATE STAIRS

DEEPSLATE BRICK STAIRS

DEEPSLATE TILE STAIRS

POLISHED DEEPSLATE STAIRS

GENERATION

You can craft stone stairs in a similar way to wooden ones, but using stone blocks instead of planks. However, you can also create them more efficiently by using the source block on a stonecutter. You can find them in structures across all three dimensions, from the Overworld's ocean ruins, throughout the End city and in ruined portals of the Nether and Overworld.

ANOTHER LEVEL

The hardness of stone stairs differs, with some, such as granite and polished blackstone stairs, easier to mine than wooden versions, and others, like deepslate, which are much harder than stone stairs. Unlike wooden stairs, the most efficient tool for mining stone stairs is a pickaxe, which is also the only way you will get them to drop themselves.

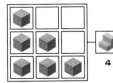
4

STONE STAIRS RECIPE

SOFT STONE STAIRS

This set of stairs is quicker to mine than any variant and has the lowest blast resistance among its peers. Soft stone stairs are crafted like any stair block, with six source blocks or by using the stonecutter. Sandstone stairs generate in ocean ruins and desert structures.

STATS

TRANSPARENCY	LIGHT EMISSION
	0

RENEWABLE	BLAST RESISTANCE	HARDNESS
	0.8	0.8

FLAMMABLE	SILK TOUCH

SANDSTONE
STAIRS

RED SANDSTONE
STAIRS

QUARTZ
STAIRS

STEP ON IT
The sandstone stairs that generate in ocean ruins only do so when the ruins are in a warm ocean, so keep an eye out for coral. As you only craft 4 stairs from 6 source blocks, it's cheaper to use a stonecutter, which uses one block for each set of stairs.

SMOOTH SOFT STONE STAIRS

FOUND: Desert villages

Unlike normal sandstone and quartz, the smooth stairs variants have a resilience equivalent to wood and some other stone stairs, like those made of cobblestone. However, the blast resistance is equally low. Smooth sandstone stairs can be found in desert village structures.

STATS

TRANSPARENCY

LIGHT EMISSION   0

RENEWABLE

BLAST RESISTANCE 2

HARDNESS 2

FLAMMABLE

SILK TOUCH

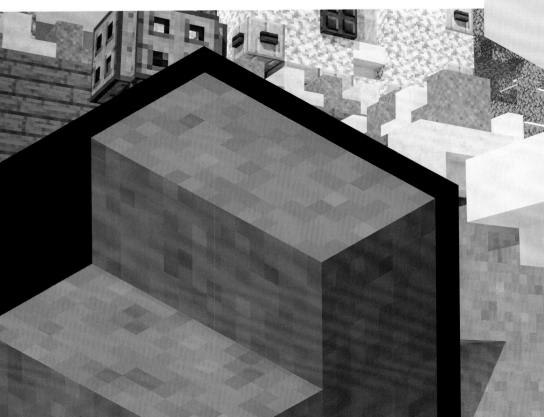

SMOOTH RED SANDSTONE STAIRS

 163   172

SMOOTH SANDSTONE STAIRS

SMOOTH QUARTZ STAIRS

SURPRISING STRENGTH

Smooth soft stone stairs have a greater hardness than a lot of stone stairs, such as blackstone and purpur stairs, which means they take longer to mine. You must use a pickaxe to collect them.

DEEPSLATE TILES

Like many of the deepslate variants, deepslate tiles have several useful purposes. Their varied brick texture makes them great for decoration, but they also have their own set of shaped blocks – you can use deepslate tiles to make stairs, slabs and even walls.

STATS

TRANSPARENCY

  0
LIGHT EMISSION

RENEWABLE

 6
BLAST RESISTANCE

 3.5
HARDNESS

FLAMMABLE

SILK TOUCH

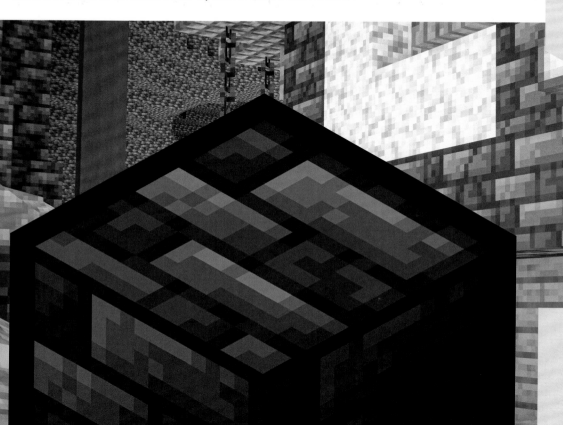

CRACKED DEEPSLATE TILES

ON THE TILES
The shaped blocks can be made either on a crafting table or by using a stonecutter. They also have a cracked variant that can be created by smelting. Deepslate tiles must be mined with a pickaxe; otherwise it won't drop itself as a block. Unusually, a gold pickaxe will mine deepslate tiles the fastest.

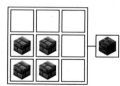
DEEPSLATE TILES RECIPE

BLOCK OF COAL

The block of coal is a mineral block that you can craft with nine pieces of coal. You can use blocks of coal to power furnaces, where they'll smelt 80 items per block. Coal can only smelt eight items apiece, so the block of coal is a more efficient energy source. It drops itself when mined with any pickaxe.

STATS

TRANSPARENCY	LIGHT EMISSION
	0

RENEWABLE	BLAST RESISTANCE	HARDNESS
	6	5

FLAMMABLE	SILK TOUCH

FIREPOWER

Crafting works both ways with a block of coal, so you can turn a block of coal back into coal items, which is useful for storing excess fuels, especially as the blocks of coal stack. Unlike other mineral blocks, a block of coal is flammable if you place it in the world.

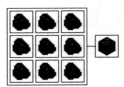

BLOCK OF COAL RECIPE

BLOCK OF IRON

FOUND:
In loot chests
or by crafting

If you find yourself with an abundance of iron ingots or raw iron in your inventory, you can combine nine pieces to create a block of iron or block of raw iron to help store them. You can reverse the process to turn them back into ingots or raw iron, or use the blocks to create an anvil.

STATS

TRANSPARENCY	LIGHT EMISSION
	0

RENEWABLE	BLAST RESISTANCE	HARDNESS
	6	5

FLAMMABLE	SILK TOUCH

**BLOCK OF
RAW IRON**

SOLID AS A BLOCK

A block of iron is common as a decorative block, but you can also use it in a few handy builds. Combining 4 blocks of iron and a pumpkin will summon an iron golem, and you can create pyramids that can house a beacon with them as well, though other minerals can be used for this.

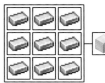

BLOCK OF IRON RECIPE

BLOCK OF LAPIS LAZULI

You can craft the rare gem lapis lazuli into this solid mineral block, which is often used as a very expensive decoration due to its deep blue color. A lapis lazuli block features as part of illager statues within woodland mansions, but you'll need a stone pickaxe to collect it.

STATS

TRANSPARENCY	LIGHT EMISSION
	0

RENEWABLE	BLAST RESISTANCE	HARDNESS
	3	3

FLAMMABLE	SILK TOUCH

STORAGE STONE
As lapis lazuli is an important component in enchanting, you might find it useful to craft them into a lapis lazuli block and vice versa, so you always have enough materials to forge ahead. It has a lower blast resistance than any other mineral block, and is slightly weaker than all but the block of gold, too.

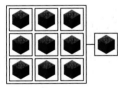

LAPIS LAZULI
BLOCK RECIPE

BLOCK OF GOLD

FOUND:
Ocean monuments, ruined portals and bastion remnants

Be careful when you mine the block of gold, as you could infuriate any piglins that spot you. It's a mineral block that you can craft with nine gold ingots and back again, which makes it great for storing the precious yellow metal. You can also craft a block of raw gold by replacing the ingots with raw gold.

STATS

TRANSPARENCY	LIGHT EMISSION
	0

RENEWABLE	BLAST RESISTANCE	HARDNESS
	6	3

FLAMMABLE	SILK TOUCH

**BLOCK OF
RAW GOLD**

PRECIOUS TREASURE
Blocks of gold spawn naturally in a couple of structures, such as bastion remnants and ruined portals. Explorers can also find 8 of them encased in dark prismarine at the heart of ocean monuments. Like blocks of iron, they can be used to create the platforms that power a beacon, too.

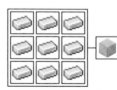

BLOCK OF GOLD RECIPE

 138

 149

BLOCK OF REDSTONE

FOUND:
By crafting only

A power source commonly used in mechanisms, the block of redstone is a mineral block crafted from nine redstone dust. Engineers can reverse the craft to ensure they always have redstone dust on hand. You can mine it with any pickaxe to easily move it between circuits.

STATS

TRANSPARENCY	LIGHT EMISSION
	0

RENEWABLE	BLAST RESISTANCE	HARDNESS
	6	5

FLAMMABLE	SILK TOUCH

PLAYING WITH POWER

The block of redstone has an innate function beyond storage of redstone dust – it is a power source for redstone circuits. Unlike some power sources, the block of redstone is always "on" and will constantly send a redstone signal to any connected component. It's often combined with sticky pistons to make a toggleable power source.

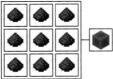

BLOCK OF
REDSTONE RECIPE

 139 282

BLOCK OF DIAMOND

The bright blue block of diamond is as desirable for decor as it is for storage. Diamonds are always handy for crafting strong weapons and armor, so craft a block of diamond with nine diamonds, then back into diamonds as you need them. You need at least an iron pickaxe to mine the block.

STATS

TRANSPARENCY	LIGHT EMISSION
	0

RENEWABLE	BLAST RESISTANCE	HARDNESS
	6	5

FLAMMABLE	SILK TOUCH

DIAMOND ECONOMY

It's possible to find a block of diamond in a few different rooms of a woodland mansion. It can also be used in the beacon pyramid configurations, though it is an expensive choice considering the alternatives. In the early days of Minecraft, a block of diamond only required 4 diamonds to craft.

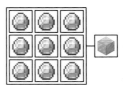

BLOCK OF DIAMOND RECIPE

BLOCK OF EMERALD

Guess what a block of emerald is made from? Kelp! Oh, wait, it's emeralds. Mine it with an iron pickaxe or better, then use a crafting table to break the block into nine emeralds – perfect for transporting currency. It can only be mined with an iron pickaxe or stronger, or it will drop nothing.

STATS

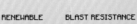

TRANSPARENCY	LIGHT
RENEWABLE	BLAST RESISTANCE

BLAST RESISTANCE: 6

5

FLAMMABLE

SILK TOUCH

GREEN WITH ENVY
Blocks of emerald can't be found anywhere in a naturally generated world, meaning they can only be obtained by crafting. Its bright jade color makes it useful in the construction of eye-catching builds, while you can also use it to power up beacons by featuring it in the platform or pyramid configurations.

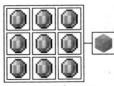

**BLOCK OF EMERALD
RECIPE**

BLOCK OF COPPER

FOUND:
By crafting only

The block of copper is a mineral crafted with copper ingots. Its appearance transforms over time through four stages, from orange to turquoise. You can craft a block of raw copper in a similar way, using raw copper instead of ingots, and both blocks can be changed back to their source items.

EXPOSED   WEATHERED   OXIDIZED   RAW COPPER

TRANSPARENCY	LIGHT EMISSION	RENEWABLE

BLAST RESISTANCE	HARDNESS	FLAMMABLE	SILK TOUCH
6	3		

BLOCK OF COPPER RECIPE

CUT COPPER

FOUND:
By crafting only

Combine four blocks of copper, or run one block through a stonecutter, and you'll end up with the patterned cut copper. They experience the same oxidization as their source block, but the level can be reduced by lightning strikes or by hitting it with an axe, as with other copper blocks.

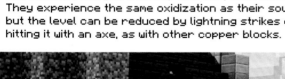

EXPOSED   WEATHERED   OXIDIZED

TRANSPARENCY	LIGHT EMISSION	RENEWABLE
	0	

BLAST RESISTANCE	HARDNESS	FLAMMABLE	SILK TOUCH
6	3		

4

CUT COPPER RECIPE

184

WAXED BLOCK OF COPPER

FOUND:
By crafting
only

Apply honeycomb to a block of copper to turn it into this waxed variant, which looks identical, but won't oxidize any further, allowing you to preserve blocks at your favorite level of copper. The copper block can be crafted with honeycomb at any stage to make waxed variants.

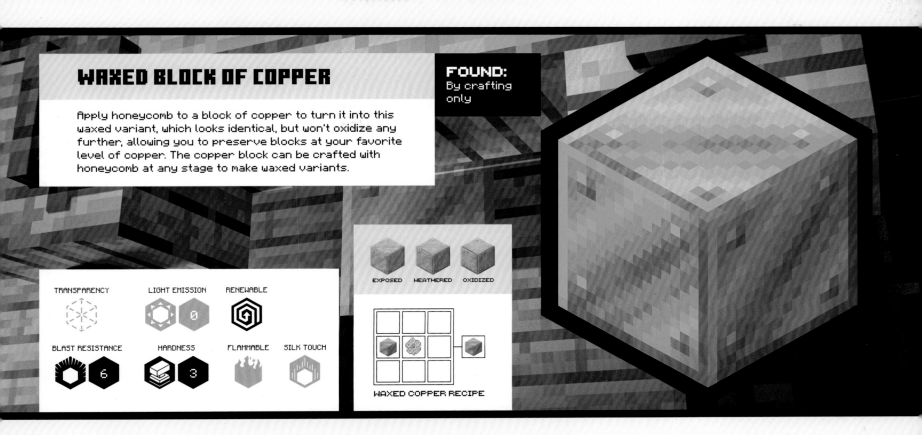

EXPOSED   WEATHERED   OXIDIZED

WAXED COPPER RECIPE

TRANSPARENCY	LIGHT EMISSION	RENEWABLE
	0	

BLAST RESISTANCE	HARDNESS	FLAMMABLE	SILK TOUCH
6	3		

WAXED CUT COPPER

FOUND:
By crafting
only

Like normal cut copper, waxed cut copper is primarily used to craft other forms like slabs and stairs. It's created by using waxed blocks of copper instead of the unwaxed ones, and will again resist the ravages of time and remain in the state that it was in when the waxing process occurred.

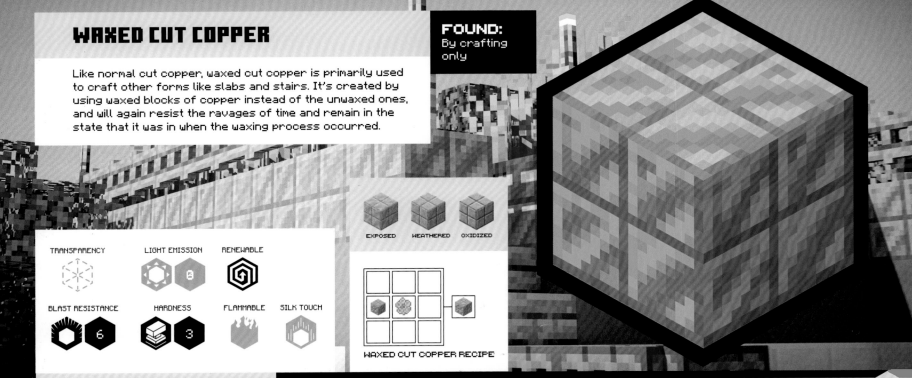

EXPOSED   WEATHERED   OXIDIZED

WAXED CUT COPPER RECIPE

TRANSPARENCY	LIGHT EMISSION	RENEWABLE
	0	

BLAST RESISTANCE	HARDNESS	FLAMMABLE	SILK TOUCH
6	3		

COPPER SLABS

STATS

FOUND:
By crafting only

By crafting cut copper or waxed cut copper, you can create these strong half-height variants. The cut copper slabs will still experience the oxidization process like cut copper, though the waxed variants are resistant. Both versions can also be made on a stonecutter.

TRANSPARENCY   LIGHT EMISSION

0

RENEWABLE   BLAST RESISTANCE   HARDNESS

6   3

FLAMMABLE   SILK TOUCH

WEATHERED
COPPER SLAB

EXPOSED
COPPER SLAB

OXIDIZED
COPPER SLAB

WAXED CUT
COPPER SLAB

WAXED EXPOSED
CUT COPPER SLAB

WAXED
WEATHERED CUT
COPPER SLAB

WAXED OXIDIZED
CUT COPPER SLAB

COPPER BOTTOM

The group of copper slabs are among the strongest in the game, with a hardness and blast resistance greater than all but End stone slabs. The waxed cut copper slabs can also be created by crafting the cut copper slab with honeycomb, much like you can do with the full blocks.

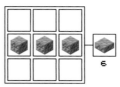

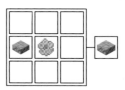

CUT COPPER
SLAB RECIPE

WAXED CUT COPPER
SLAB RECIPE

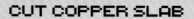

CUT COPPER SLAB

 70   160   168

COPPER STAIRS

Take your copper game to another level by crafting your cut copper into stair blocks. As with other copper blocks, the waxed ones will not experience oxidization, but unwaxed ones will. The waxed versions can also be crafted using cut copper stairs and a piece of honeycomb.

STATS

TRANSPARENCY

LIGHT EMISSION 0

RENEWABLE

BLAST RESISTANCE 6

HARDNESS 3

FLAMMABLE

SILK TOUCH

WEATHERED CUT COPPER STAIRS

EXPOSED CUT COPPER STAIRS

OXIDIZED COPPER STAIRS

WAXED CUT COPPER STAIRS

WAXED EXPOSED CUT COPPER STAIRS

WAXED WEATHERED CUT COPPER STAIRS

WAXED OXIDIZED CUT COPPER STAIRS

ELEVATED STRENGTH

Like cut copper slabs, cut copper stairs are among the strongest stairs available. You need a wooden pickaxe at least to mine cut copper stairs and have them drop themselves. They can also be made on stonecutters. They can be broken with lesser tools, but won't drop a thing.

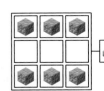

CUT COPPER STAIRS RECIPE

4

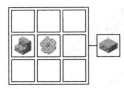

WAXED CUT COPPER STAIRS RECIPE

CUT COPPER STAIRS

70   163   172

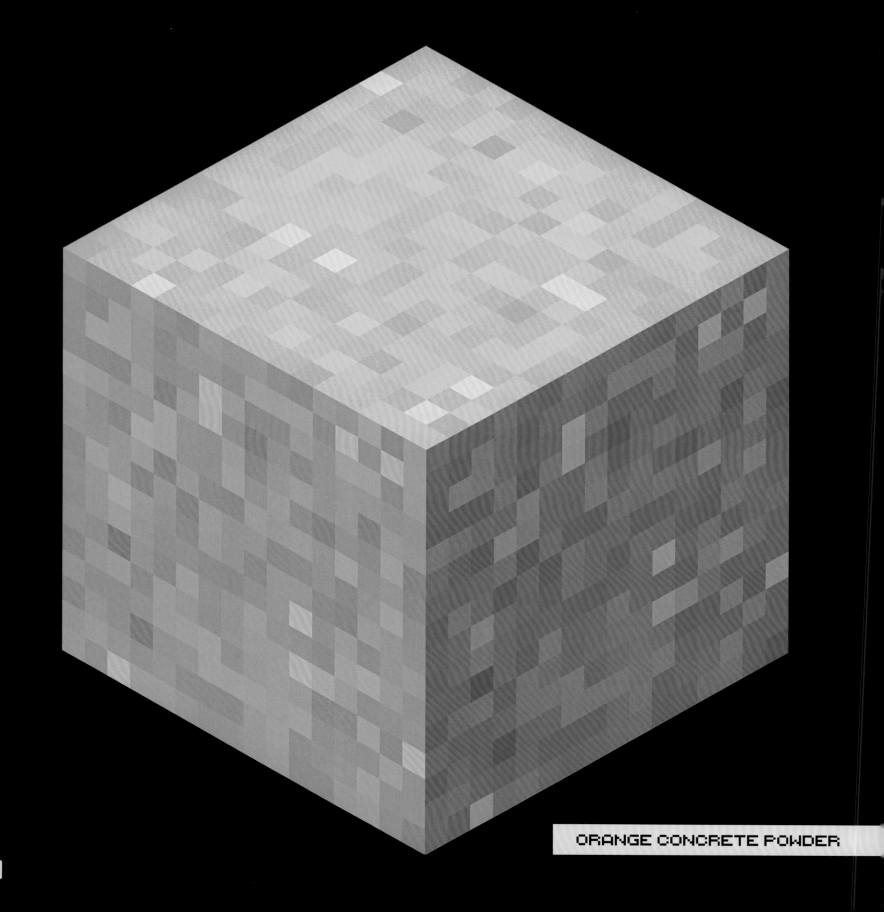

ORANGE CONCRETE POWDER

CONCRETE POWDER

One of few gravity-abiding blocks in Minecraft, concrete powder will turn into concrete when exposed to water. It's available in the usual kaleidoscope of colors, so it's perfect for creating eye-catching builds. It's very weak and prone to blasts, which is to be expected of a powder.

STATS

TRANSPARENCY	LIGHT EMISSION
	0

RENEWABLE	BLAST RESISTANCE	HARDNESS
	0.5	0.5

FLAMMABLE	SILK TOUCH

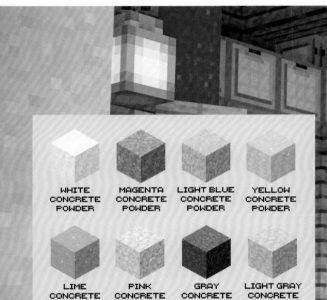

WHITE CONCRETE POWDER | MAGENTA CONCRETE POWDER | LIGHT BLUE CONCRETE POWDER | YELLOW CONCRETE POWDER

LIME CONCRETE POWDER | PINK CONCRETE POWDER | GRAY CONCRETE POWDER | LIGHT GRAY CONCRETE POWDER

CYAN CONCRETE POWDER | PURPLE CONCRETE POWDER | BLUE CONCRETE POWDER | BROWN CONCRETE POWDER

GREEN CONCRETE POWDER | RED CONCRETE POWDER | BLACK CONCRETE POWDER

GENERATION

Concrete powder doesn't generate naturally, so you'll need to craft it using 4 pieces each of sand and gravel, as well as one of the 16 available dye ingredients. Items that can be used in place of dyes, such as cocoa beans, can be substituted into the recipe, too.

 25
 26
 190

BEHAVIOR

Like the sand and gravel used to craft concrete powder, concrete powder will fall whenever there is no solid block underneath it. When it comes into contact with flowing water or a water source, it will solidify and turn into a concrete block. If it falls on a player or mob's head, it will suffocate them until they move or it's destroyed.

PROTOTYPE BUILDS

Some Minecrafters prefer to build with concrete powder. They will form the shape of the build, easily destroying and replacing blocks as they go, then apply a bucket of water to turn the finished product into concrete. Placing concrete powder beside lava has a similar hardening effect as water.

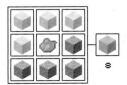

8

CONCRETE POWDER RECIPE

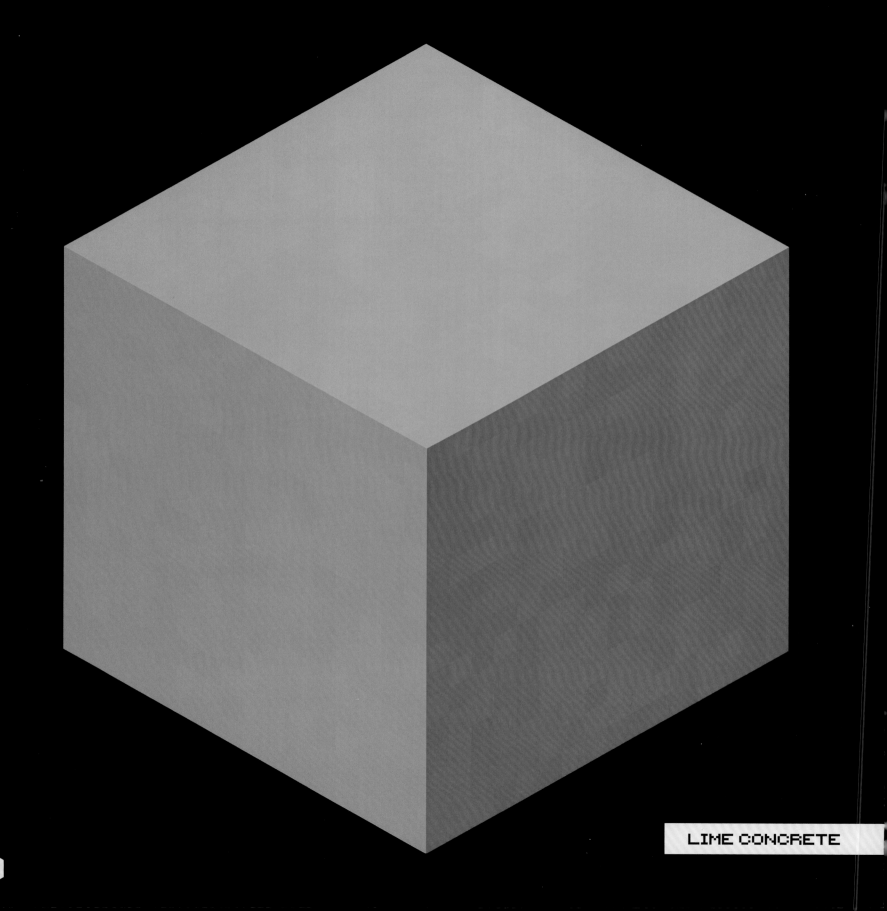

LIME CONCRETE

CONCRETE

Produced when concrete powder comes into contact with water, concrete is a colorful building block that is harder even than most stone blocks, though it is weaker against explosions in comparison. Unlike the powder that forms it, you should mine concrete with a pickaxe for maximum efficiency.

STATS

TRANSPARENCY	LIGHT EMISSION	
		0

RENEWABLE	BLAST RESISTANCE		HARDNESS	
		1.8		1.8

FLAMMABLE	SILK TOUCH

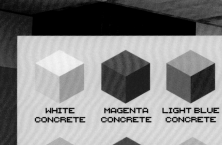

WHITE CONCRETE — **MAGENTA CONCRETE** — **LIGHT BLUE CONCRETE** — **YELLOW CONCRETE**

PINK CONCRETE — **GRAY CONCRETE** — **LIGHT GRAY CONCRETE** — **CYAN CONCRETE**

PURPLE CONCRETE — **BLUE CONCRETE** — **BROWN CONCRETE** — **GREEN CONCRETE**

RED CONCRETE — **BLACK CONCRETE** — **ORANGE CONCRETE**

GENERATION

Concrete can only be created by players when you expose concrete powder to water. The color of concrete that's formed can only be altered by using different colors of concrete powder, as you can't apply dye directly to concrete. It's also available in the Creative inventory.

BEHAVIOR

You need a pickaxe to collect concrete; otherwise it won't drop anything. Though concrete is most commonly used as a decorative building block, you can also make note blocks play a bass drum sound if it is directly underneath the note block.

JUST ADD WATER

Concrete can't be created using water in bottles or cauldrons, nor rainfall, only by exposure to flowing water, water sources or a bucket of water. Its colors are similar to wool blocks, and more vivid than stained terracotta. Unlike wool, however, it's resistant to fire.

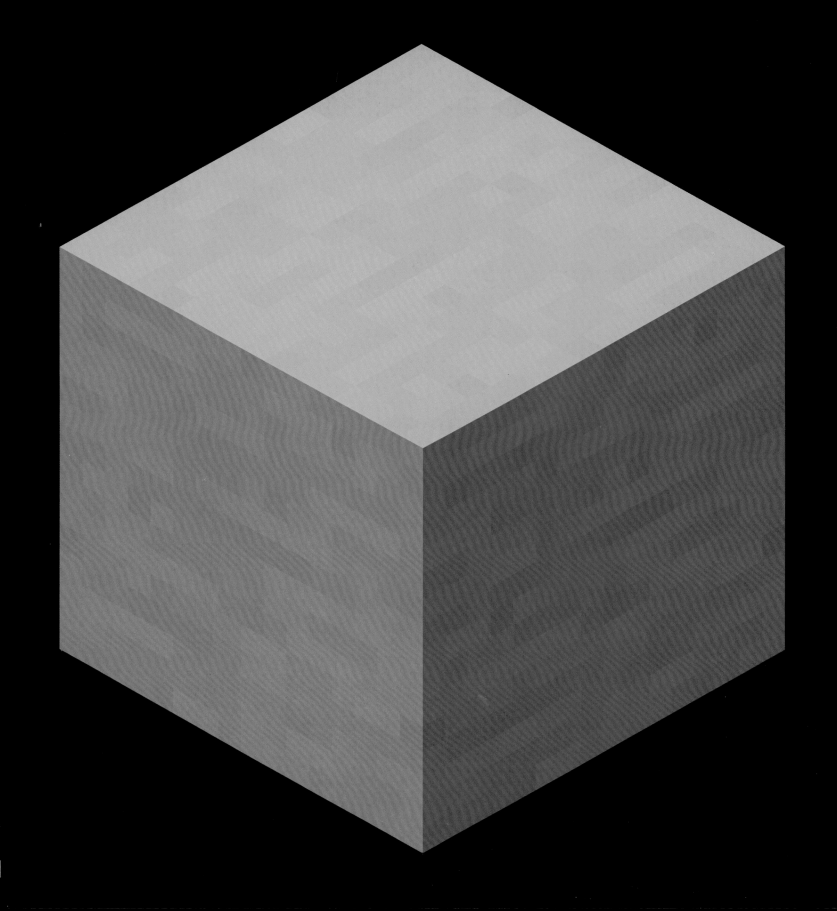

TERRACOTTA

STATS

TRANSPARENCY

LIGHT EMISSION

0

RENEWABLE

BLAST RESISTANCE

4.2

HARDNESS

1.25

FLAMMABLE

SILK TOUCH

A craftable block that's also found all around the Overworld, terracotta is highly desired for decorative purposes and can be collected with any pickaxe. Raw terracotta blocks can be colored with any of the myriad dyes, though the resulting blocks have more muted tones than their concrete equivalents.

WHITE TERRACOTTA · MAGENTA TERRACOTTA · LIGHT BLUE TERRACOTTA · YELLOW TERRACOTTA

LIME TERRACOTTA · PINK TERRACOTTA · GRAY TERRACOTTA · LIGHT GRAY TERRACOTTA

CYAN TERRACOTTA · PURPLE TERRACOTTA · BLUE TERRACOTTA · BROWN TERRACOTTA

GREEN TERRACOTTA · RED TERRACOTTA · BLACK TERRACOTTA · ORANGE TERRACOTTA

GENERATION

The best place to find terracotta is a badlands biome, where undyed and 6 different colors of terracotta can be found. Undyed terracotta can also be created by smelting a block of clay in a furnace, while 8 blocks of terracotta and a suitable dye can be used to form the colored versions.

BEHAVIOR

Dyed terracotta can be placed in a furnace again to smelt glazed terracotta. The dying process is irreversible, and it's also impossible to apply another dye to change the color of dyed terracotta. The blast resistance of terracotta is more similar to stone than the clay that was used to create it.

WORLDWIDE RESOURCE

Different terracottas can also be found in villages of the plains, savanna and desert biomes, as well as pyramids and ocean ruins structures. Terracotta is often carried by mason villagers who will trade you their wares for an emerald.

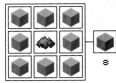

BLUE TERRACOTTA RECIPE

27   194

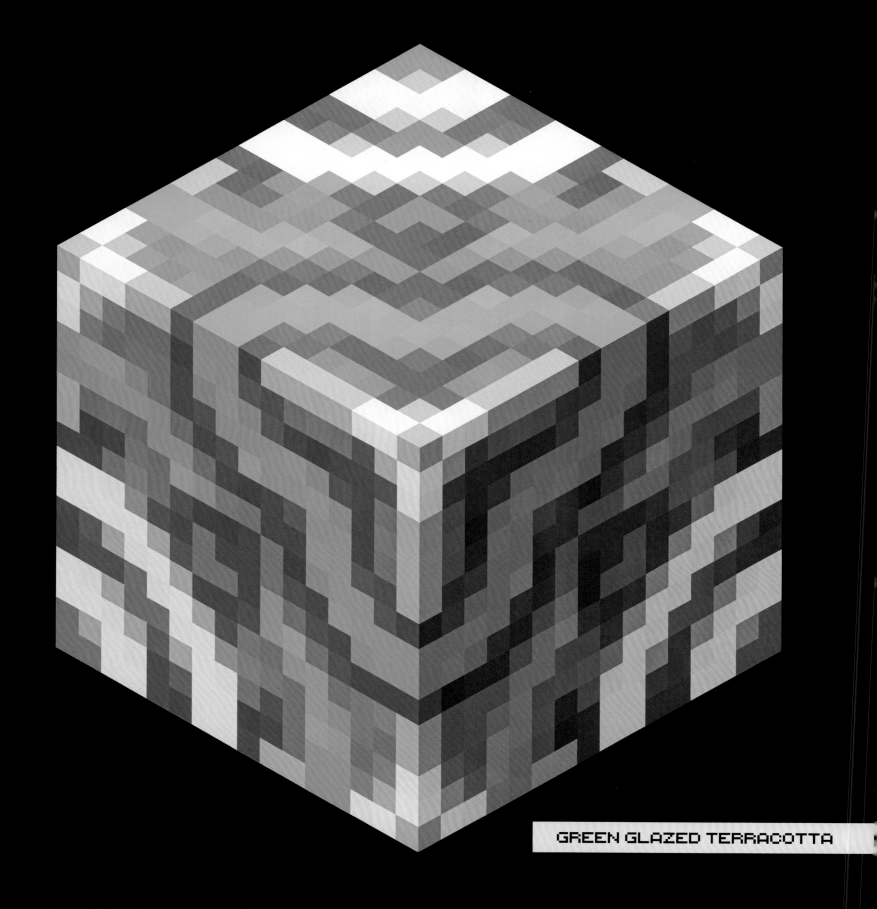

GREEN GLAZED TERRACOTTA

GLAZED TERRACOTTA

FOUND:
Some villages, underwater ruins, or by smelting colored terracotta

While dyes tend to produce simple colored blocks, glazed terracotta blocks all have dramatically different textures that really catch the eye. The smelting process reduces glazed terracotta's blast resistance in comparison to its terracotta source, but the aesthetic more than makes up for it.

STATS

TRANSPARENCY	LIGHT EMISSION
	0

RENEWABLE	BLAST RESISTANCE	HARDNESS
	1.4	1.4

FLAMMABLE	SILK TOUCH

WHITE GLAZED TERRACOTTA	MAGENTA GLAZED TERRACOTTA	LIGHT BLUE GLAZED TERRACOTTA	YELLOW GLAZED TERRACOTTA

LIME GLAZED TERRACOTTA	PINK GLAZED TERRACOTTA	GRAY GLAZED TERRACOTTA	LIGHT GRAY GLAZED TERRACOTTA

CYAN GLAZED TERRACOTTA	PURPLE GLAZED TERRACOTTA	BLUE GLAZED TERRACOTTA	BROWN GLAZED TERRACOTTA

RED GLAZED TERRACOTTA	BLACK GLAZED TERRACOTTA	ORANGE GLAZED TERRACOTTA

GENERATION

Glazed terracotta is made by smelting any dyed terracotta in a furnace. When it is placed, you'll need to use a pickaxe to mine it again. You can also find various glazed terracotta blocks in the wild – most are found in some villages, but the purple variant is found in some ocean ruins, and you can see the lime one in desert village temples.

PERPLEXING PATTERNS

The intricate patterns of glazed terracotta can be combined and extended to create even larger patterns; 2x2 placements of identical glazed terracotta, each of them rotated 90 degrees to the last, will create a secret pattern. Rotate all the blocks again to reveal yet more patterns!

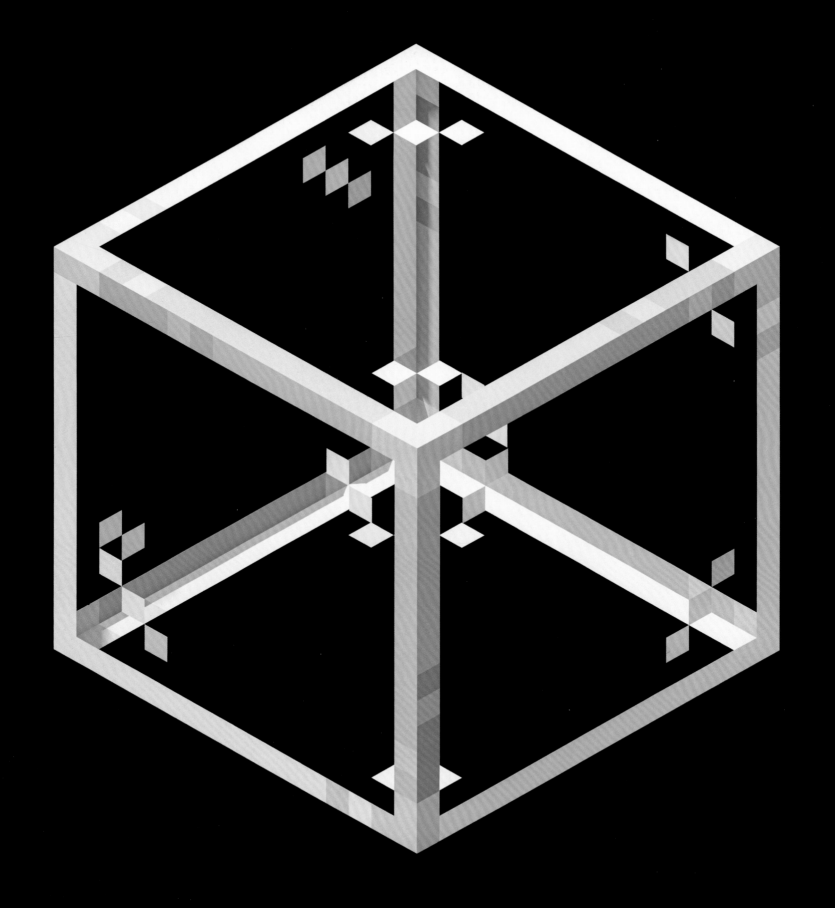

GLASS

Glass is a full-size block that allows you to see outside from the safety of your base, which makes it an obvious choice in builds. It's a versatile crafting ingredient that can be used for beacons, End crystals and glass bottles, as well as variants like the glass panes.

STATS

TRANSPARENCY	LIGHT EMISSION
	0

RENEWABLE	BLAST RESISTANCE	HARDNESS
	0.3	0.3

FLAMMABLE	SILK TOUCH

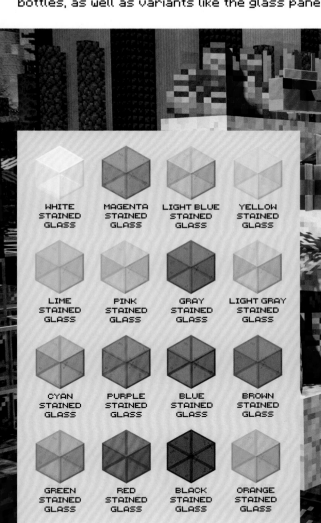

WHITE STAINED GLASS · MAGENTA STAINED GLASS · LIGHT BLUE STAINED GLASS · YELLOW STAINED GLASS

LIME STAINED GLASS · PINK STAINED GLASS · GRAY STAINED GLASS · LIGHT GRAY STAINED GLASS

CYAN STAINED GLASS · PURPLE STAINED GLASS · BLUE STAINED GLASS · BROWN STAINED GLASS

GREEN STAINED GLASS · RED STAINED GLASS · BLACK STAINED GLASS · ORANGE STAINED GLASS

GENERATION

Glass isn't as common as glass panes. You can only find it in secret rooms of woodland mansions, or End cities, where you can see the magenta variant. In an earlier version of Minecraft, you could also find glass pillars atop strongholds. You can create plain glass by smelting sand or red sand, and combine dye with 8 glass blocks to make stained variants.

BEHAVIOR

The most obvious use for the completely transparent glass block is as a window, allowing players to see out of structures and to let natural light in. It offers little protection from explosions, which isn't surprising, nor is it particularly hard to break, though you can only collect it as an item if you use a Silk Touch–enchanted tool.

CLEARLY VISIBLE

Librarians in villages often stock glass among their available trades. Glass is resistant to fire and lava, and because it is a solid block you can use it to make attractive features like fish tanks or lava columns.

GLASS RECIPE

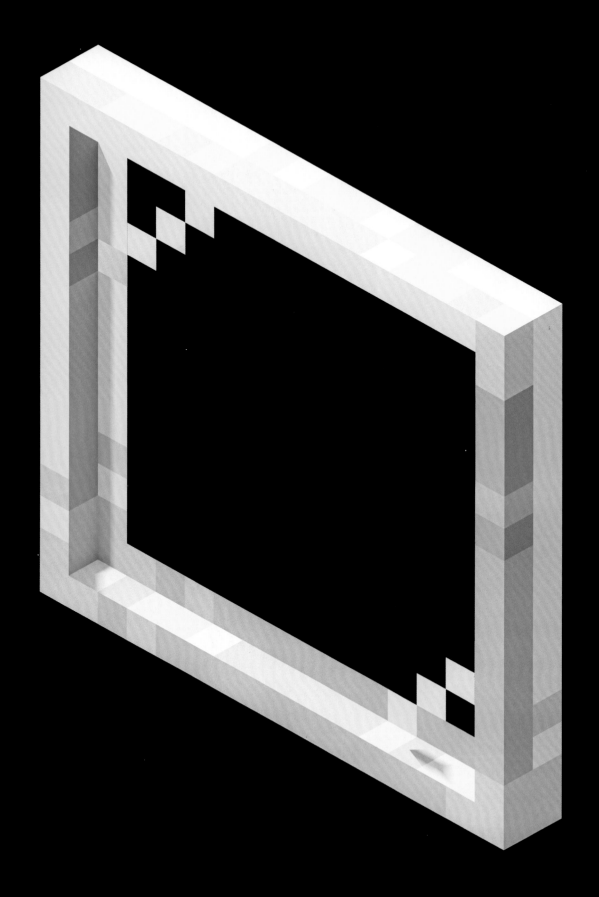

GLASS PANE

Glass panes are a thinner, more versatile version of glass that can be used to cover a wider area with fewer resources. They have similar properties to their source block and you can only obtain them with a Silk Touch-enchanted tool. They're available in all 16 colors as well as an undyed version.

STATS

TRANSPARENCY

LIGHT EMISSION

0

RENEWABLE

BLAST RESISTANCE

0.3

HARDNESS

0.3

FLAMMABLE

SILK TOUCH

WHITE STAINED GLASS PANE

MAGENTA STAINED GLASS PANE

LIGHT BLUE STAINED GLASS PANE

YELLOW STAINED GLASS PANE

LIME STAINED GLASS PANE

PINK STAINED GLASS PANE

GRAY STAINED GLASS PANE

LIGHT GRAY STAINED GLASS PANE

CYAN STAINED GLASS PANE

PURPLE STAINED GLASS PANE

BLUE STAINED GLASS PANE

BROWN STAINED GLASS PANE

GREEN STAINED GLASS PANE

RED STAINED GLASS PANE

BLACK STAINED GLASS PANE

ORANGE STAINED GLASS PANE

GENERATION

You can craft 16 panes of glass from 6 glass blocks, which means that you can cover more than twice the area of block spaces with panes as with the full blocks. Stained glass panes can be made in the same way with stained glass blocks, or you can craft 8 glass panes with any dye to produce the same effect.

BEHAVIOR

When placed beside a glass pane that is perpendicular to the current placement, the glass pane will turn into a corner configuration. If a pane is placed in the block behind a row of glass panes, one of the panes will change to a T-configuration. Adding a pane in front of this will create a cross-configuration of glass.

THROUGH THE LOOKING GLASS

You'll often see glass panes as windows in villages and temples in many biomes. You can sell excess glass panes to cartographers in villages, but what on earth do they use them for? Well, if you use a glass pane on a cartography table, it will lock the map and stop it from updating any further, which perhaps explains why they find them useful.

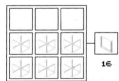

16

GLASS PANE RECIPE

TINTED GLASS

Crafted with four amethyst shards and a block of glass, the tinted window is a glass block that doesn't allow light through, though you can still see through its transparent faces. You can use it to dim light sources completely or direct light in certain directions.

STATS

TRANSPARENCY

LIGHT EMISSION
0

RENEWABLE

BLAST RESISTANCE
0.3

HARDNESS
0.3

FLAMMABLE

SILK TOUCH

REINFORCED GLASS
Tinted glass shares most properties with glass, although it is slightly more practical as you don't need a Silk Touch–enchanted tool to collect it – nor any tool in fact. It has no use in crafts and there isn't a pane version, nor does it have any color variants like other glass blocks do.

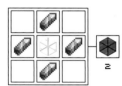

TINTED GLASS RECIPE

 143　 196　 198

BLOCK OF NETHERITE

FOUND:
By crafting only

Crafted from nine netherite ingots, the block of netherite is a strong mineral block that is as durable as obsidian. Unlike similar strong blocks, it can be pushed and pulled by pistons, which makes it very useful in redstone contraptions, even those that use TNT, as it can withstand blasts!

STATS

TRANSPARENCY	LIGHT EMISSION
	0

RENEWABLE	BLAST RESISTANCE	HARDNESS

| | 1200 | 50 |

FLAMMABLE	SILK TOUCH

MAKING MOVES
Due to its significant strength, you can only mine a block of netherite with a diamond or netherite pickaxe. You can use it as efficient storage for netherite ingots by crafting them with 9 such items. The block of netherite can be used as a part of a beacon's platform like other mineral blocks.

BLOCK OF
NETHERITE RECIPE

46   146

NETHER BRICKS

Nether bricks are dark crimson variants of the Overworld's bricks that you'll find in Nether fortresses. You can destroy them with any tool, but they'll only drop themselves if you use a pickaxe. They're not particularly strong but they are resistant to ghast fireballs.

STATS

TRANSPARENCY	LIGHT EMISSION
	0

RENEWABLE	BLAST RESISTANCE	HARDNESS
	6	2

FLAMMABLE	SILK TOUCH

RED NETHER BRICKS

CRACKED NETHER BRICKS

CHISELED NETHER BRICKS

DARK DECORATION

You can craft Nether bricks using 4 Nether brick items, which are made from smelted netherrack. Smelting Nether bricks in a furnace will turn them into their cracked variant, while you can add 2 Nether warts to 2 Nether brick items to create red Nether bricks. Finally, the chiseled version is crafted with 2 Nether brick slabs.

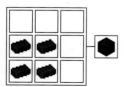

NETHER BRICKS RECIPE

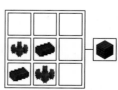

RED NETHER BRICKS RECIPE

PURPUR BLOCK

These lavender-colored blocks are the stuff that End cities and End ships are made from. Their stats are similar to those of stone blocks in the Overworld, and you need to mine them with a pickaxe to collect them. You can also craft decorative stairs and slabs with a purpur block.

STATS

TRANSPARENCY	LIGHT EMISSION	
		0

RENEWABLE	BLAST RESISTANCE		HARDNESS	
		6		1.5

FLAMMABLE	SILK TOUCH

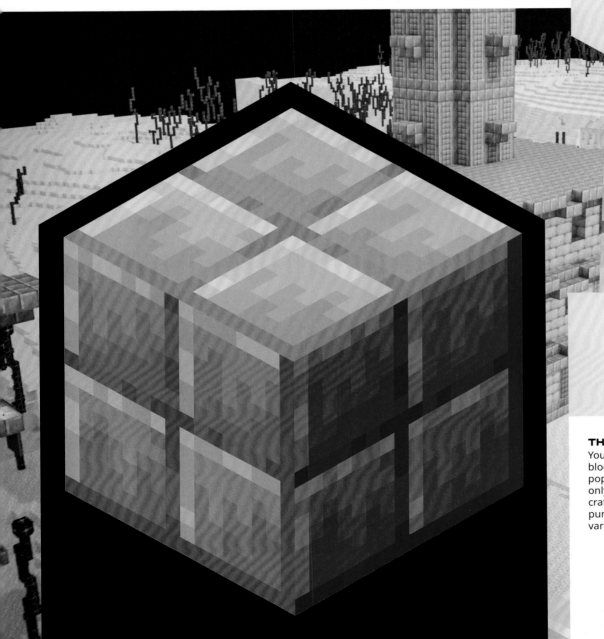

PURPUR
PILLAR

THE FRUIT BLOCK
You can also craft both variants of purpur. The blocks are made when you craft 4 pieces of popped chorus fruit – a refined version of the End's only foodstuff. You can make purpur pillars by crafting 2 purpur slabs, or more simply, by using a purpur block on a stonecutter. The slab and stairs variants can also be made using this tool.

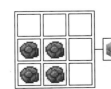

PURPUR BLOCK RECIPE

BLOCK OF QUARTZ

FOUND: Bastion remnants of the Nether

The block of quartz and its variants are among the weakest mineral blocks, though they're highly desired as decoration. You can craft a block of quartz with just four pieces of Nether quartz, but unlike other mineral blocks, you can't craft it back into Nether quartz items.

STATS

TRANSPARENCY	LIGHT EMISSION 0
RENEWABLE	BLAST RESISTANCE 0.8
	HARDNESS 0.8
FLAMMABLE	SILK TOUCH

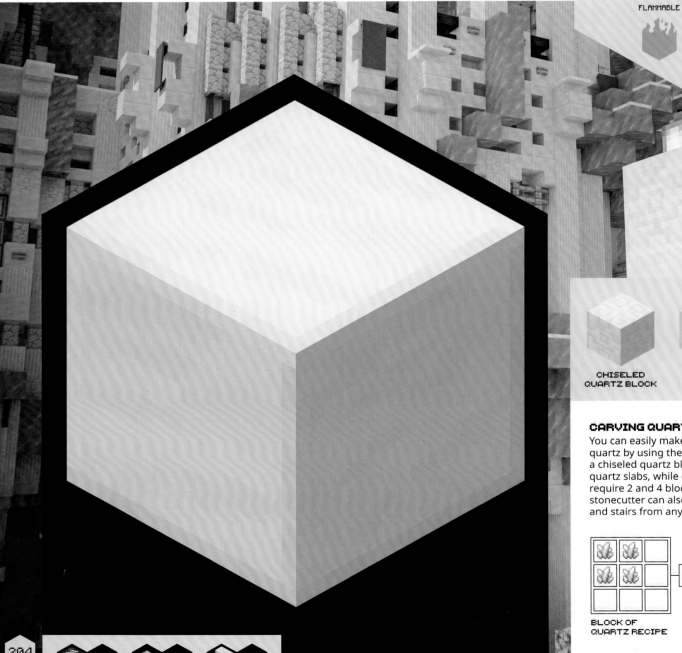

CHISELED QUARTZ BLOCK · QUARTZ PILLAR · QUARTZ BRICKS

CARVING QUARTZ

You can easily make all variants of a block of quartz by using the block on a stonecutter. To craft a chiseled quartz block, you need to combine 2 quartz slabs, while quartz pillars and quartz bricks require 2 and 4 blocks of quartz respectively. A stonecutter can also be used to create quartz slabs and stairs from any quartz variant.

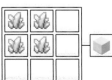

BLOCK OF QUARTZ RECIPE

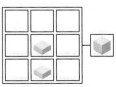

CHISELED QUARTZ BLOCK RECIPE

148 · 168 · 174

SMOOTH QUARTZ BLOCK

FOUND: Bastion remnants of the Nether

Unlike other quartz blocks, a smooth quartz block has hardness and blast resistance comparable to normal stone blocks. You'll be able to find them around bastion remnant structures in the Nether, and you can mine them with any pickaxe, though it will take a little longer than normal quartz.

STATS

TRANSPARENCY

LIGHT EMISSION

RENEWABLE   BLAST RESISTANCE   HARDNESS

6

2

FLAMMABLE   SILK TOUCH

QUARTZ APART

You can smelt a smooth quartz block from a single block of quartz. While you can use the chiseled, pillar or bricks variants of quartz to craft quartz slabs and stairs, smooth quartz can't be used as a substitute for the same purpose. Instead you can craft smooth quartz variants of slabs and stairs, either on crafting tables or on a stonecutter.

SMOOTH QUARTZ
BLOCK RECIPE

NETHER WART BLOCK

The foliage on huge fungi is made up of wart blocks – Nether wart tops crimson fungus and warped wart appears atop warped fungus. You can destroy them with any tool and they'll drop themselves, but a hoe is best. They're good for composting, and have an 85% chance of adding a layer.

STATS

TRANSPARENCY	LIGHT EMISSION
	0

RENEWABLE	BLAST RESISTANCE	HARDNESS
	1	1

FLAMMABLE	SILK TOUCH

WARPED WART
BLOCK

SPORADIC SPORE

Though they're most often seen on huge fungi, you may also spot wart blocks in the ground and ceiling of the Nether. Nether wart blocks can be crafted using 9 Nether warts, though there's no way to craft the warped wart block. As native blocks of the Nether, they're, understandably, resistant to fire and lava.

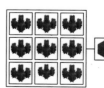

NETHER WART
BLOCK RECIPE

HONEY BLOCK

FOUND:
By crafting only

The product of industrious buzzing bees all across the Minecraft world, honey blocks are sticky blocks that are useful in slowing down movement and as a component in redstone mechanisms. You can destroy them instantly with any tool, and they'll always drop themselves as an item.

STATS

TRANSPARENCY	LIGHT EMISSION
	0

RENEWABLE	BLAST RESISTANCE	HARDNESS
	0	0

FLAMMABLE	SILK TOUCH

STICKY SITUATION

Honey blocks are sticky, and will attempt to move all adjacent blocks when shifted by a piston, including players, mobs or items that are on top of the block. They will slow anything that's moving across, and also beside, the block, so players can travel farther without touching the floor, or slow a fall, if there are adjacent honey blocks they can direct themselves toward. When you craft a honey block from bottles of honey, 4 glass bottles will be left on the crafting table.

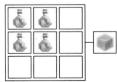

HONEY BLOCK RECIPE

152	208	270	273

HONEYCOMB BLOCK

FOUND:
By crafting only

A uniquely patterned block that you can make with the honeycomb item, honeycomb blocks are purely decorative and have no function, unlike the utilitarian honey block. It's easy to mine and has a low resistance to explosion, but always drops itself as an item when you break one.

STATS

TRANSPARENCY	LIGHT EMISSION
	0

RENEWABLE	BLAST RESISTANCE	HARDNESS
	0.6	0.6

FLAMMABLE	SILK TOUCH

SWEET DECOR
You can combine 4 pieces of honeycomb, collected from bee nests or beehives, to make a honeycomb block. You can't craft it back into honeycomb, so it doesn't work as storage. Unlike honey, it isn't considered transparent, so you can place all the normal blocks on it when building.

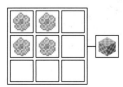

HONEYCOMB
BLOCK RECIPE

 152   207   270

HAY BALE

Often seen in the fields of village farms, hay bales are useful blocks for breeding, decoration and storing wheat. You can mine them easily with any tool, or craft them using wheat. You may spot them in pillager outposts as part of the scarecrows that the illagers use to strike fear into invaders.

STATS

TRANSPARENCY	LIGHT EMISSION 0
RENEWABLE	BLAST RESISTANCE 0.5	HARDNESS 0.5
FLAMMABLE	SILK TOUCH

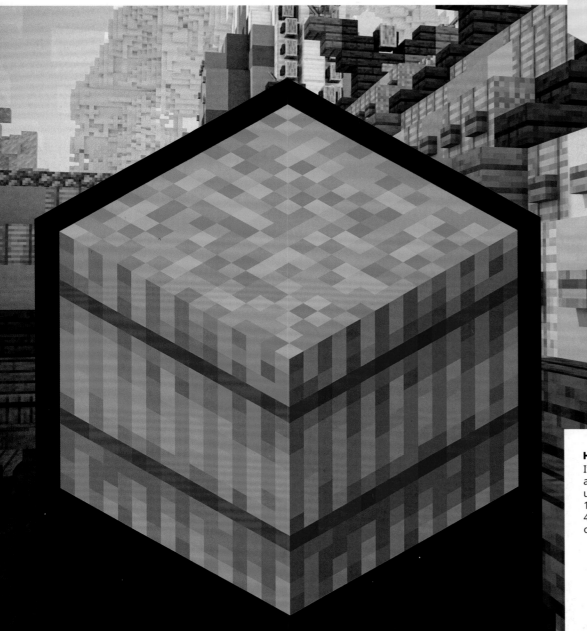

HUMBLE VERSATILITY

If you want to breed horses or llamas, hay bales are the items you need. When you place one under a campfire, the smoke it produces will float 15 blocks higher. If you combine a hay bale with 4 redstone dusts, it'll yield a target block. Falling onto a hay bale will cut the fall damage by 80%.

HAY BALE RECIPE

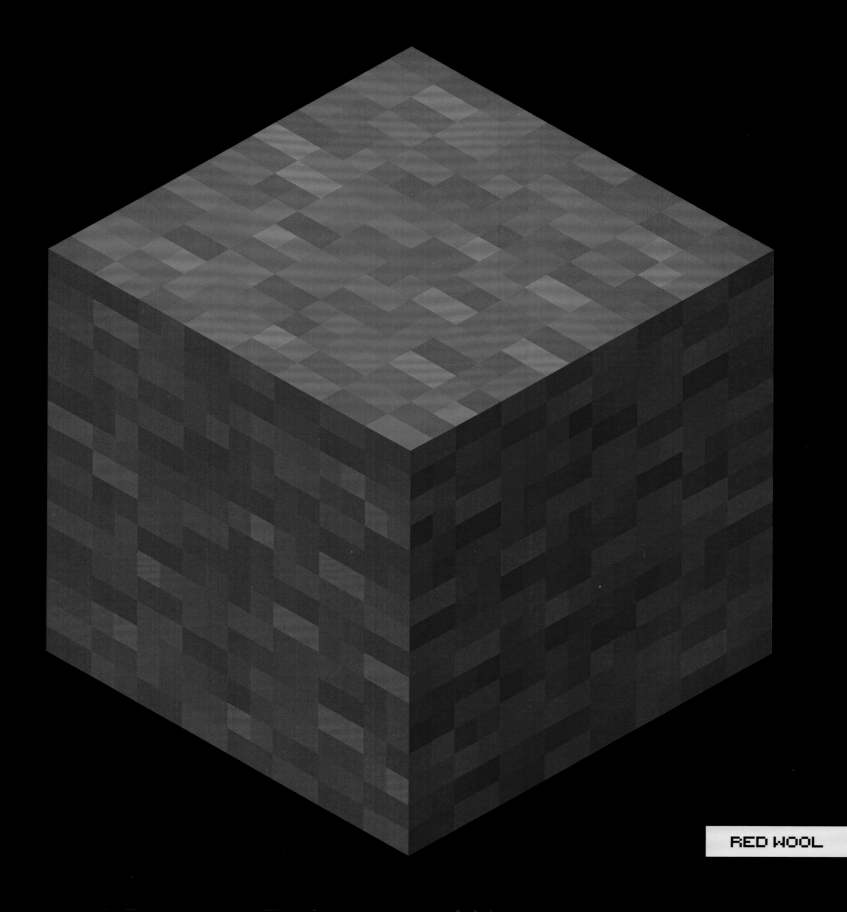

RED WOOL

WOOL

The original dyeable item, wool has been available in Minecraft, in all 16 colors, for over a decade! It's extremely flammable, though its bright hues and mottled texture still make it a popular choice in builds. You can use it for a wide range of decorative crafts, such as beds, carpets and banners.

STATS

TRANSPARENCY	LIGHT EMISSION
	0

RENEWABLE	BLAST RESISTANCE	HARDNESS
	0.8	0.8

FLAMMABLE	SILK TOUCH

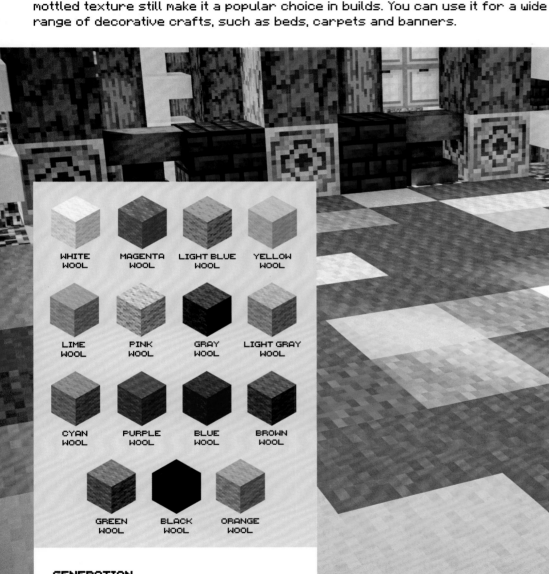

WHITE WOOL · MAGENTA WOOL · LIGHT BLUE WOOL · YELLOW WOOL

LIME WOOL · PINK WOOL · GRAY WOOL · LIGHT GRAY WOOL

CYAN WOOL · PURPLE WOOL · BLUE WOOL · BROWN WOOL

GREEN WOOL · BLACK WOOL · ORANGE WOOL

GENERATION

Wool originates from sheep, and each one will drop up to 3 wools when you shear it, though it does grow back. You can craft wool with a dye to change its color, or you can dye sheep so that they always produce a certain color of wool. You'll also be able to spot wool in woodland mansions, villages and pillager outposts.

BEHAVIOR

The primary use of wool is in crafting, where you can use its many colors to create and customize other items. You can craft carpets with 2 pieces of wool, banners with 6 pieces and a stick, paintings are from a single piece of wool and 8 sticks, and beds, which you craft by combining 3 wools and 3 wood planks.

SHEAR EFFICIENCY

You can collect wool most quickly with shears, and it always drops itself as an item. Sheep also drop wool when they are defeated, though it's a much less efficient method of gaining wool than shears. Wool used in recipes must be matching and will result in a similarly colored product. Shepherds in villages will buy wool in exchange for emeralds, though they must have plenty of wool already ...

 246   312   314

UTILITY BLOCKS

TORCH

You'll often find torches, a common light source, lining the walls of villages and abandoned mine shafts. You can break them by hand to collect them, or craft them with a stick and a piece of coal or charcoal. They give off a bright light that's just short of the maximum.

STATS

TRANSPARENCY	LIGHT EMISSION
	14

RENEWABLE	BLAST RESISTANCE	HARDNESS
	0	0

FLAMMABLE	SILK TOUCH

WALL
TORCH

LIGHTING THE WAY

You can place torches on the side or top of solid blocks, and their appearance will differ slightly depending on which face they're attached to. They're most commonly used in crafting to create other light sources, such as lanterns and jack-o'-lanterns.

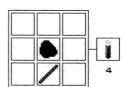

TORCH RECIPE

SOUL TORCH

Soul torches are a Nether-flavored variant of torches that bear a slightly less luminant blue flame instead of the traditional orange one. You can craft them in a similar way to torches, but with the addition of soul sand or soul soil. They don't generate naturally, even in the Nether.

STATS

TRANSPARENCY

LIGHT EMISSION 10

RENEWABLE

BLAST RESISTANCE 0

HARDNESS 0

FLAMMABLE

SILK TOUCH

SOUL WALL TORCH

SOFT LIGHT
Due to their lower light level, soul torches won't melt nearby snow or ice when placed, unlike stronger light sources. For some unknown reason, piglins are petrified of soul torches and will beat a hasty retreat if they see one. You can combine soul torches with 8 iron nuggets to create soul lanterns, which have a similar luminance.

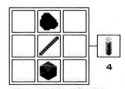

SOUL TORCH RECIPE

LANTERN

Lanterns are bright light sources that you can see illuminating snowy tundra villages and the bastion remnants of the Nether, though you can also craft them with iron nuggets and torches. Unlike most light sources, you can place lanterns on the underside of blocks as well as on top of them.

STATS

TRANSPARENCY	LIGHT EMISSION
	15

RENEWABLE	BLAST RESISTANCE	HARDNESS
	3.5	3.5

FLAMMABLE	SILK TOUCH

DANGLING ILLUMINATION

As they're made with iron, you need to mine a lantern with a pickaxe to make it drop. Lanterns combine well with chains to make dangling lights. The only light source, other than the lantern, that you can place on the underside of blocks is the End rod. Librarian villagers offer lanterns for sale.

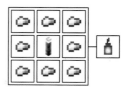

LANTERN RECIPE

SOUL LANTERN

Imbued with soul fire rather than traditional flame, soul lanterns are slightly dimmer versions of lanterns. They don't generate naturally, so you can only obtain one if you craft iron nuggets and a soul torch. Like other soul fire items, soul lanterns scare away piglins.

STATS

TRANSPARENCY	LIGHT EMISSION
	10

RENEWABLE	BLAST RESISTANCE	HARDNESS
	3.5	3.5

FLAMMABLE	SILK TOUCH

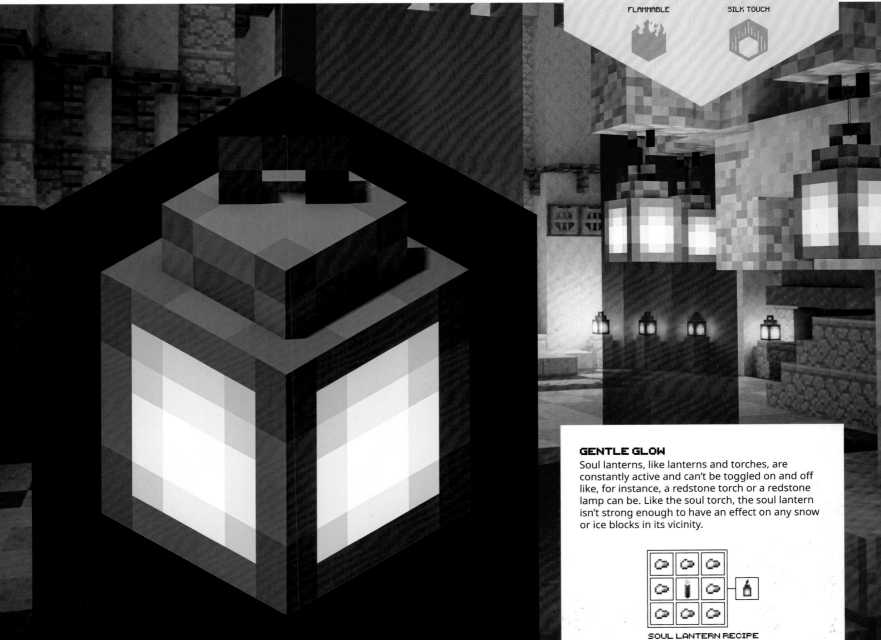

GENTLE GLOW
Soul lanterns, like lanterns and torches, are constantly active and can't be toggled on and off like, for instance, a redstone torch or a redstone lamp can be. Like the soul torch, the soul lantern isn't strong enough to have an effect on any snow or ice blocks in its vicinity.

SOUL LANTERN RECIPE

EA LANTERN

u dive down to underwater structures like ruins and ocean uments, you'll see that they're illuminated by sea lanterns. They'll prismarine crystals when you mine them unless you use a Silk Touch-hanted tool. You can use them to build the frame around a conduit.

STATS

TRANSPARENCY	LIGHT EMISSION
	15

RENEWABLE	BLAST RESISTANCE	HARDNESS
	0.3	0.3

FLAMMABLE	SILK TOUCH

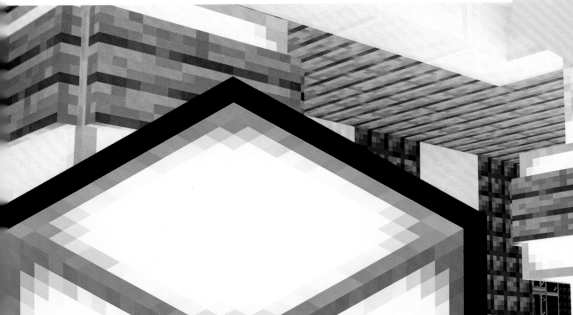

BRIGHTEN THE DEPTHS

Sea lanterns can also be crafted with 5 prismarine shards and 4 prismarine crystals, though it's more efficient to use Silk Touch. Fortune increases the number of crystals dropped to a maximum of 5. Like many semi-transparent blocks, they're fairly weak, so they're easy to mine or blow up.

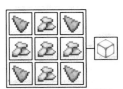

SEA LANTERN RECIPE

CAMPFIRE

Not only is the campfire one of the brightest light sources in Minecraft, but it can also cook food! You can sometimes find them in taiga and snowy taiga biomes, but it's easier to craft them, using sticks, coal and wood. Campfires damage players and mobs that step on them, so be careful!

STATS

TRANSPARENCY	LIGHT EMISSION
	15

RENEWABLE	BLAST RESISTANCE	HARDNESS
	2	2

FLAMMABLE	SILK TOUCH

UNLIT CAMPFIRE

GATHERING POINT

You can place 4 food items on a campfire at once. It cooks slower than a furnace, but doesn't need fuel. However, you can't queue food to be cooked like you can in a furnace. The smoke from a campfire can be used to calm bees if you need to remove their hive or nest. If you put a campfire on a hay bale, the smoke will rise over twice as high. The fire can be doused with a bucket of water and collected with a Silk Touch–enchanted tool.

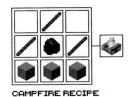

CAMPFIRE RECIPE

 50 80 156

219

SOUL CAMPFIRE

STATS

TRANSPARENCY | LIGHT EMISSION 10

RENEWABLE | BLAST RESISTANCE 2 | HARDNESS 2

FLAMMABLE | SILK TOUCH

The soul campfire employs the blue flame of soul fire to complete its cooking responsibilities. The soul campfire will be lit by default when placed, but it can be doused with water or by using a shovel on it, as for campfires. Both can be relit by flint and steel or other fiery means.

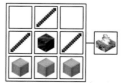

UNLIT SOUL CAMPFIRE

HOT TO THE TOUCH

Campfires and soul campfires both damage any mob or player that steps on them while they're lit, but the soul campfire is twice as harmful. You need to replace coal with soul sand or soul soil in the crafting recipe for a soul campfire; otherwise it's identical to the one for a campfire.

SOUL CAMPFIRE RECIPE

 64
 72

END ROD

STATS

TRANSPARENCY

LIGHT EMISSION — 14

RENEWABLE

BLAST RESISTANCE — 0

HARDNESS — 0

FLAMMABLE

SILK TOUCH

End rods are white, spindly light sources that you'll see around End cities. They are unique in that they can be placed on any side of a block, including underneath. They can also stack on top of each other so tall columns can be created. They always drop themselves as an item.

OMINOUS GLOW

When they're placed on the side of a block, they point directly to the side, unlike torches, which will adjust so they still point upward. You can craft End rods using a blaze rod and a popped chorus fruit. They have a light level of 14, which will melt nearby snow and ice.

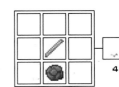

END ROD RECIPE

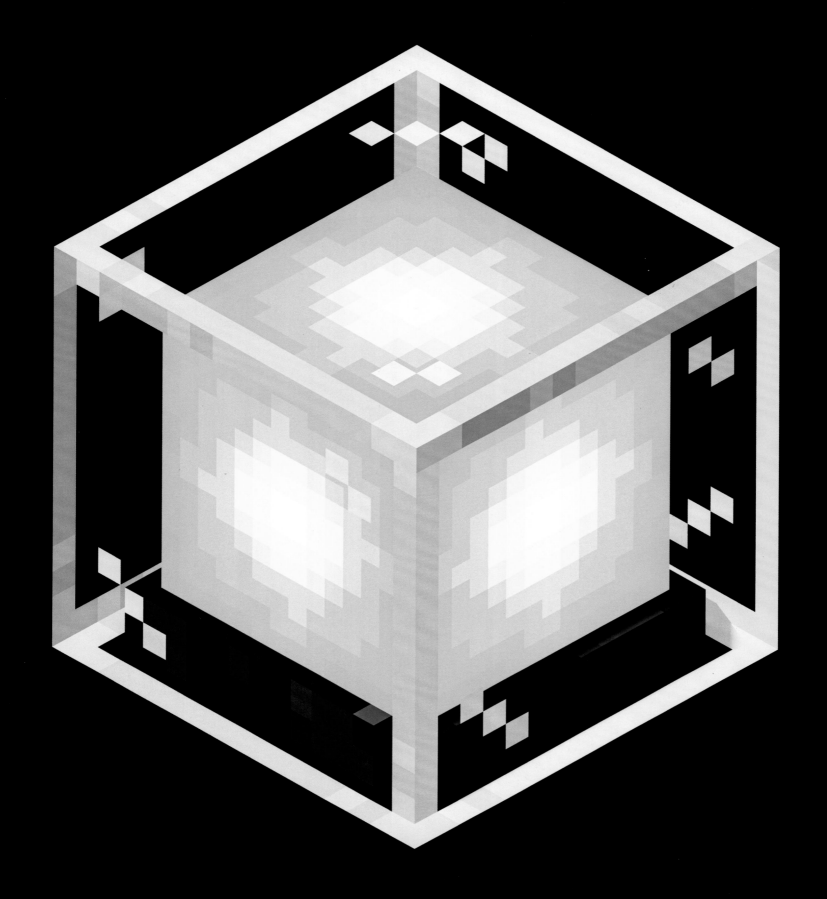

BEACON

Place a beacon on a pyramid of iron, gold, diamond, emerald or netherite and it will provide a range of buffs to aid players in the area. You must feed it with an ingot, emerald or diamond and then choose the status effect you want from a range including Haste, Jump Boost and Strength.

STATS

TRANSPARENCY	LIGHT EMISSION
	15

RENEWABLE	BLAST RESISTANCE	HARDNESS
	3	3

FLAMMABLE	SILK TOUCH

WONDROUS WAYPOINT

The platform the beacon is placed on can be built up to four tiers high to increase the range and duration of the status effects, as well as unlocking an extra buff, Regeneration. Up to 6 beacons can be placed atop a suitable pyramid so that all effects can be unlocked at once.

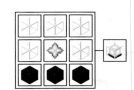

BEACON RECIPE

178 180 182 183 201

BEACON BEAM

When you activate a beacon, it creates a beam of light that shoots up into the sky. It has a luminance of 15 and can be used as a wayfinder, due to its visibility from up to 256 blocks away. It's not a block that can be added to the inventory, nor is it available in Creative mode.

STATS

TRANSPARENCY	LIGHT EMISSION
	15

RENEWABLE	BLAST RESISTANCE	HARDNESS
	0	0

FLAMMABLE	SILK TOUCH

WHITE BEACON BEAM	MAGENTA BEACON BEAM	LIGHT BLUE BEACON BEAM	YELLOW BEACON BEAM

LIME BEACON BEAM	PINK BEACON BEAM	GRAY BEACON BEAM	LIGHT GRAY BEACON BEAM

CYAN BEACON BEAM	PURPLE BEACON BEAM	BLUE BEACON BEAM	BROWN BEACON BEAM

GREEN BEACON BEAM	BLACK BEACON BEAM	RED BEACON BEAM	ORANGE BEACON BEAM

ADJUSTABLE LIGHTING

The beam color can be modified by placing stained glass blocks or panes directly above the beacon. You can combine multiple glasses to adjust the color of the beam, allowing for more than 12 million different configurations!

IRON DOOR

FOUND:
Strongholds, woodland mansions

You can only open iron doors with a mechanism, whether you've hooked it up to a redstone contraption or a simple lever. You need to mine them with a pickaxe; otherwise they'll drop nothing. They're stronger than wooden doors, resistant to mob damage and non-flammable.

STATS

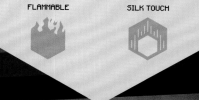

TRANSPARENCY	LIGHT EMISSION
	0

RENEWABLE	BLAST RESISTANCE	HARDNESS
	5	5

FLAMMABLE	SILK TOUCH

SAFE AS HOUSES
You can find iron doors in woodland mansion prisons and strongholds. They're crafted with iron ingots instead of planks, but in identical quantities. Some mobs are able to open iron doors if they step on pressure plates in front of the door or trip a wire linked to the door.

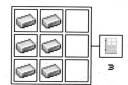

3

IRON DOOR RECIPE

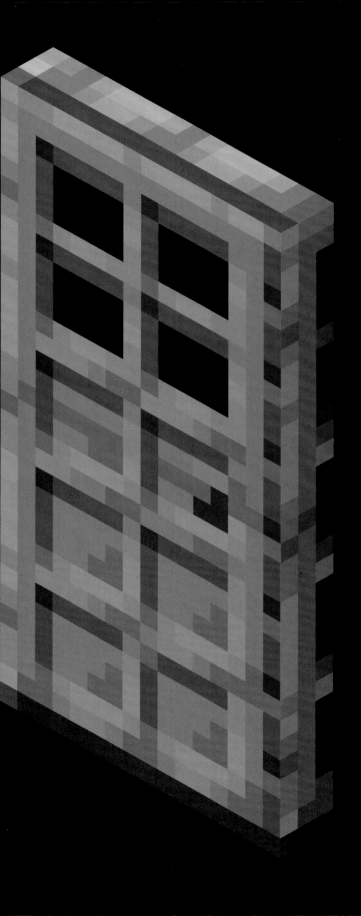

OAK DOOR

WOOD DOORS

STATS

TRANSPARENCY	LIGHT EMISSION
	0

RENEWABLE	BLAST RESISTANCE	HARDNESS
	3	3

FLAMMABLE	SILK TOUCH

To keep mobs at bay, doors are a miracle. You need to place them on top of a block and they will drop themselves if that block is destroyed, though you can also collect them with an axe easily. They can be opened only when players, villagers, wandering traders or piglins activate them.

ACACIA DOOR   BIRCH DOOR   DARK OAK DOOR   JUNGLE DOOR

SPRUCE DOOR   CRIMSON DOOR   WARPED DOOR

GENERATION
You can find all the Overworld variants of doors in the villages of several biomes. The Nether wood variants can only be crafted, using 6 Nether wood planks, and doors using Overworld wood can also be made in a similar fashion.

WARM WELCOME
Warped and crimson doors aren't flammable like their Overworld counterparts, but otherwise all doors behave identically. Mobs can only break down doors if you're playing Minecraft on Hard difficulty. Zombies, strays, husks and vindicators are all strong enough to destroy a wooden door.

3

WARPED DOOR RECIPE

TRAPDOORS

If you want an entrance in a floor or ceiling, trapdoors are perfect and come in all wood varieties and iron. The wood ones are flammable from lava, but not fire, while iron trapdoors resist both. They can all be opened with a redstone signal, but only wooden trapdoors can be opened by players.

STATS

TRANSPARENCY	LIGHT EMISSION
	0

RENEWABLE	BLAST RESISTANCE	HARDNESS
	3	3

FLAMMABLE	SILK TOUCH

JUNGLE TRAPDOOR

ACACIA TRAPDOOR	BIRCH TRAPDOOR	DARK OAK TRAPDOOR
OAK TRAPDOOR	SPRUCE TRAPDOOR	CRIMSON TRAPDOOR
WARPED TRAPDOOR	IRON TRAPDOOR	

DROPDOWN

Like their respective doors, wooden trapdoors drop quickest when you use an axe, while an iron trapdoor requires a pickaxe. You can place them at the top or bottom edge of a block, which affects the direction that the trapdoor opens. The iron variety has a slightly higher hardness and a better blast resistance.

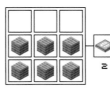
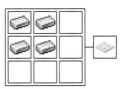

JUNGLE TRAPDOOR RECIPE

IRON TRAPDOOR RECIPE

LADDER

If stairs are taking up too much space, try swapping them out for ladders, which allow you to climb vertical walls, or slow your descent if you're falling. But watch out, because mobs can also use them! They're crafted with sticks, but aren't flammable, unlike most wooden blocks.

STATS

TRANSPARENCY	LIGHT EMISSION
	0

RENEWABLE	BLAST RESISTANCE	HARDNESS
	04	04

FLAMMABLE	SILK TOUCH

CLIMBING POPULARITY

You can place ladders on the side of any solid block and they only occupy a fraction of a block space, so they take up very little room. Players who are traveling in the direction that the ladder lies will automatically grab on and climb up. They can be stacked to make continuous ladders, as long as there's a solid block behind each one.

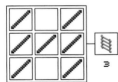

3

LADDER RECIPE

163

FENCES

STATS

TRANSPARENCY	LIGHT EMISSION
	0

RENEWABLE	BLAST RESISTANCE	HARDNESS
	3	2

FLAMMABLE	SILK TOUCH

Whether you want to keep your chickens from flying the coop or stop zombies entering your base, you need fences. No mob or player can jump over them as their collision box is higher than you can normally jump. You can find all except the Nether wood type in villages or in the Nether's fortresses.

ACACIA FENCE	DARK OAK FENCE	JUNGLE FENCE	OAK FENCE

SPRUCE FENCE	CRIMSON FENCE	WARPED FENCE	NETHER BRICK FENCE

BOUNDING BLOCK

Neither the Nether brick nor Nether wood varieties are flammable, while the former has double the blast resistance, too. You must mine Nether brick fences with a pickaxe or they drop nothing, though the others will drop with any tool. Nether brick fences won't combine directly with wood fences.

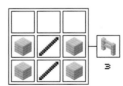

BIRCH FENCE RECIPE

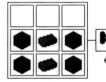

NETHER BRICK FENCE RECIPE

BIRCH FENCE

FENCE GATES

What do you get if you cross a fence with a door? The fence gate! Available in all the same flavors as a fence except Nether brick, the fence gate allows an entry point to otherwise impassable fenced areas. They join seamlessly with fences, even those made out of Nether brick.

STATS

TRANSPARENCY	LIGHT EMISSION
	0

RENEWABLE	BLAST RESISTANCE	HARDNESS
	3	2

FLAMMABLE	SILK TOUCH

ACACIA FENCE GATE

BIRCH FENCE GATE	DARK OAK FENCE GATE	JUNGLE FENCE GATE	OAK FENCE GATE

SPRUCE FENCE GATE	CRIMSON FENCE GATE	WARPED FENCE GATE

EASY ENTRANCE

Like doors and trapdoors, fence gates can be manually activated or controlled with redstone devices. You can also place them between walls, which behave in a similar way to fences. They're crafted with 4 sticks and 2 matching planks. Crimson and warped fence gates are fire-resistant.

ACACIA FENCE GATE RECIPE

COBBLESTONE WALL

Most stone walls can also be crafted using a single source block on a stonecutter, which is as efficient as crafting. These variants, including cobblestone and brick walls, can be made either way, and have the same blast resistance as their source blocks. Only the deepslate variants are harder to mine than the End stone wall.

FOUND:
Villages, woodland mansions, pillager outposts

MOSSY COBBLESTONE WALL   BRICK WALL   NETHER BRICK WALL

RED NETHER BRICK WALL   POLISHED BLACKSTONE WALL   COBBLED DEEPSLATE WALL

DEEPSLATE BRICK WALL   POLISHED DEEPSLATE WALL   DEEPSLATE TILE WALL

TRANSPARENCY	LIGHT EMISSION	RENEWABLE
	0	
BLAST RESISTANCE	HARDNESS	FLAMMABLE	SILK TOUCH
6	2		

ANDESITE WALL

This collection of walls that features andesite and blackstone varieties are weaker even than brick and cobblestone walls, though they have an identical blast resistance. As with the other walls, you can combine them with fence gates and iron bars, but not fences.

FOUND:
Some villages, bastion remnants

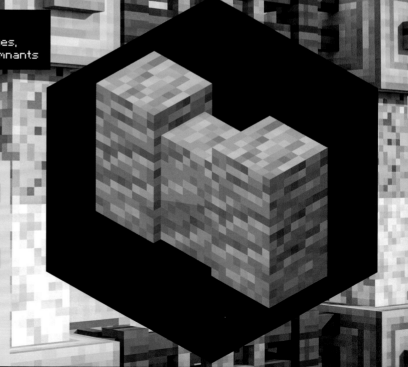

BLACKSTONE WALL   DIORITE WALL   GRANITE WALL

POLISHED BLACKSTONE BRICK WALL   PRISMARINE WALL   STONE BRICK WALL

MOSSY STONE BRICK WALL

TRANSPARENCY	LIGHT EMISSION	RENEWABLE
	0	
BLAST RESISTANCE	HARDNESS	FLAMMABLE	SILK TOUCH
6	1.5		

RED SANDSTONE WALL

FOUND:
Desert villages

The most brittle of all the available wall blocks are the sandstone variants, which have considerably worse blast resistance and hardness in comparison to even wooden fences. They are, however, among the most attractive walls on offer and are frequently used as decorations.

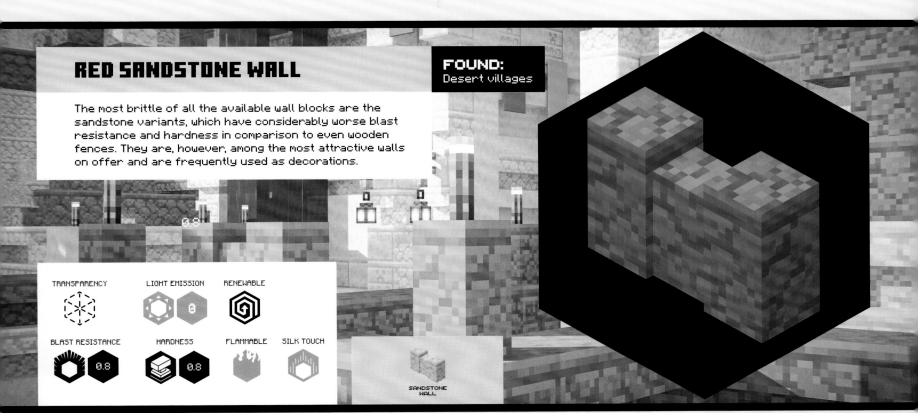

TRANSPARENCY	LIGHT EMISSION	RENEWABLE
	0	

BLAST RESISTANCE	HARDNESS	FLAMMABLE	SILK TOUCH
0.8	0.8		

SANDSTONE WALL

END STONE BRICK WALL

FOUND:
By crafting only

Walls are similar to fences in that they're impossible to jump over without aid, though most are more durable than fences. None are as strong as the End stone brick wall, which is 50% harder and more resistant to blasts than any of its counterparts. It's made from six blocks of End stone bricks.

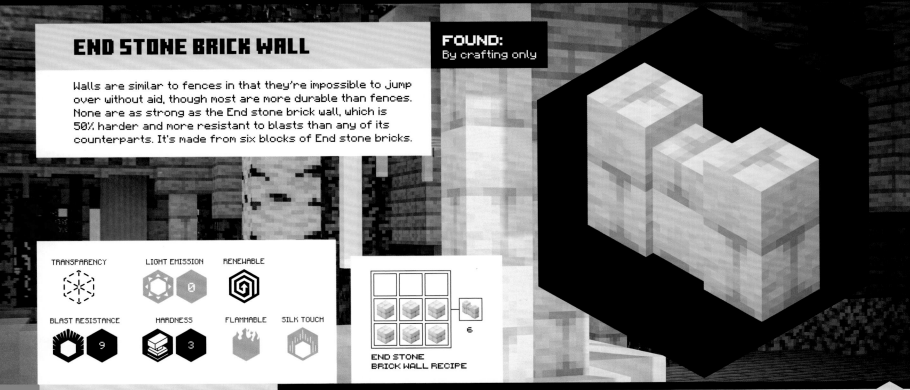

TRANSPARENCY	LIGHT EMISSION	RENEWABLE
	0	

BLAST RESISTANCE	HARDNESS	FLAMMABLE	SILK TOUCH
9	3		

6

END STONE
BRICK WALL RECIPE

IRON BARS

Rather than having an iron variant of fences, Minecraft has iron bars. They have the same bounding uses as a fence, but are perhaps more similar to glass panes in that you can join them to solid blocks or place them adjacent to other iron bars to change their configuration.

STATS

TRANSPARENCY

LIGHT EMISSION

0

RENEWABLE

BLAST RESISTANCE
6

HARDNESS
5

FLAMMABLE

SILK TOUCH

SUPER SECURITY

Most notably you'll find iron bars on the End island, where the Ender Dragon spawns. They are resistant to the Dragon's fireballs and generally have a good blast resistance and resilience, which means you must use a pickaxe to make them drop. If you look at an Enderman through the bars, they won't fly into their normal rage.

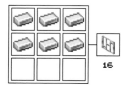

IRON BARS RECIPE

CRAFTING TABLE

FOUND:
Villages, witch huts, pillager outposts, igloos

The home of all creativity is the crafting table. Interact with this humble block to open a crafting interface that offers a whole new world of creative opportunities. You can make it with any combination of four planks, and it drops itself when destroyed with any tool or your fists.

STATS

TRANSPARENCY	LIGHT EMISSION 0
RENEWABLE	BLAST RESISTANCE 2.5	HARDNESS 2.5
FLAMMABLE	SILK TOUCH

CREATIVITY HUBS
You can find crafting tables dotted around the Overworld – in some villages, near pillager outposts and in igloo basements, for example. As well as creating new items from scratch, you can use them to repair tools and weapons if you place two identical damaged weapons or tools together in the crafting grid.

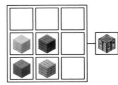

CRAFTING TABLE RECIPE

 240   244   245

FURNACE

With fuel and an item to smelt, you can use the furnace to refine base materials into more useful items. Foods can be cooked, and ores transformed into precious metals, as long as you've stocked it with fuel. It can be fueled by many items, from wooden signs to buckets of lava.

STATS

TRANSPARENCY	LIGHT EMISSION
	13

RENEWABLE	BLAST RESISTANCE	HARDNESS
	3.5	3.5

FLAMMABLE	SILK TOUCH

LIT FURNACE

FLAMES OF INDUSTRY

When you interact with a furnace, it will open a smelting interface, with slots for an item, a fuel and a product. Each fuel smelts a different number of items. You can link hoppers and chests to and from a furnace to ensure it's always fueled and its products are collected. The traditional recipe for a furnace uses cobblestone, but stone-tier blocks can be used, too.

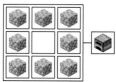

FURNACE RECIPE

BLAST FURNACE

Similar to furnaces, you can use a blast furnace to smelt items with a fuel. The blast furnace can only work with ores, metals, weapons and tools; however, it does so at twice the speed of a normal furnace, though you'll only receive half the experience for your creations.

STATS

TRANSPARENCY	LIGHT EMISSION
	13

RENEWABLE	BLAST RESISTANCE	HARDNESS
	3.5	3.5

FLAMMABLE	SILK TOUCH

UNLIT BLAST
FURNACE

ACCELERATED SMELTING

Like a furnace, blast furnaces also give off a bright light when smelting, and you can break them with any tool or your fists to collect them. If you smelt gold or iron weapons and armor in a blast furnace, they'll be transformed into iron or gold nuggets. Blast furnaces can be found in the houses of armorers in villages of every biome.

BLAST FURNACE RECIPE

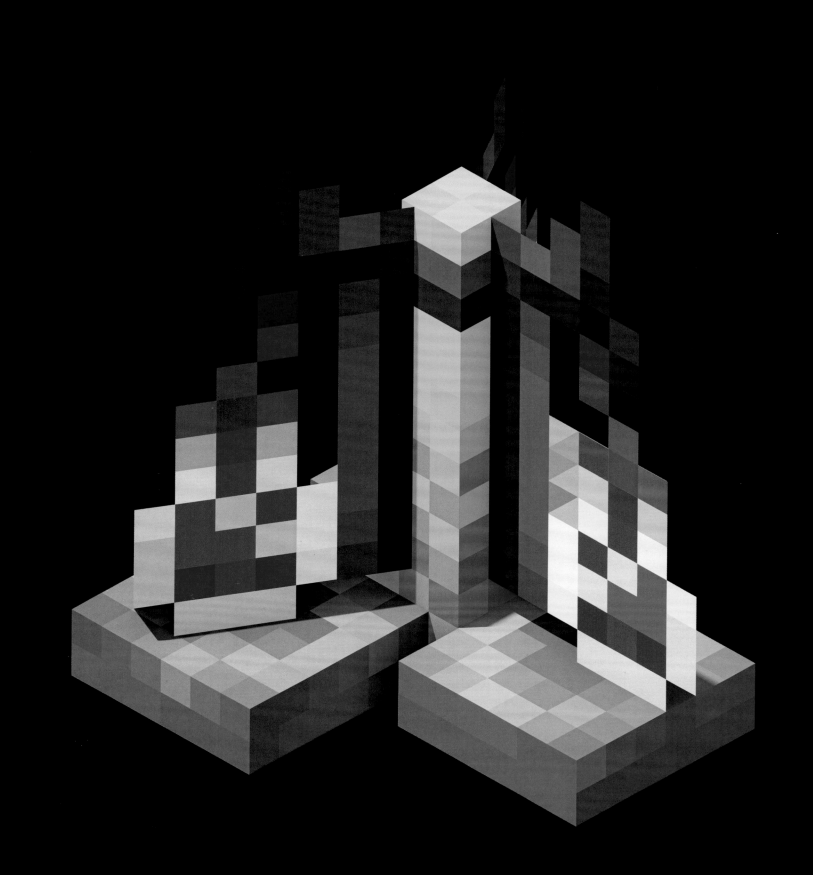

BREWING STAND

Whether it's potions or poisons you're after, the brewing stand is the block for the job. This block helps you brew all manner of concoctions, using blaze powder and ingredients to brew up to three potions at a time. It emits a faint glow at all times and must be collected with a pickaxe.

STATS

TRANSPARENCY	LIGHT EMISSION
	1

RENEWABLE	BLAST RESISTANCE	HARDNESS
	0.5	0.5

FLAMMABLE	SILK TOUCH

BEHAVIOR

Interacting with a brewing stand will bring up the brewing interface. You'll see a fuel slot for the blaze powder, an ingredient slot at the top and three potion slots that will be created. Bottles of water should be placed in potion slots to begin with, and the brewing process will begin once an ingredient, fuel and at least one bottle of water are in place.

GENERATION

Brewing stands are the job blocks of clerics, and they can be found in village temples. You may also find one in an igloo, where it'll be holding a splash Potion of Weakness, and in End ships of the End dimension, where they'll have two Instant Health Potions. You can craft them with a blaze rod and three blocks of cobblestone or blackstone.

AWKWARD START

The first thing that you should brew into water bottles is a Nether wart, which will create an Awkward Potion, the base for most other potions. Brewing in gunpowder will turn it into a splash potion, while dragon's breath will transform a potion into a lingering variant. You can add redstone dust to increase the effect duration, and glowstone dust increases its strength.

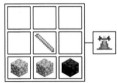

BREWING STAND RECIPE

ENCHANTING TABLE

You're clad in diamond armor and wielding a netherite sword – how could you possibly get any stronger? By enchanting your equipment on an enchanting table, of course! This block allows you to spend experience levels and lapis lazuli in exchange for a random enchantment.

STATS

TRANSPARENCY	LIGHT EMISSION
	12

RENEWABLE	BLAST RESISTANCE	HARDNESS
	1200	5

FLAMMABLE	SILK TOUCH

BEHAVIOR

When you interact with an enchanting table, it will bring up the enchantment interface, which will show up to 3 random enchantments when an item is placed in the enchantment slot. On the right, you'll see a number representing the required experience level, and on the left there's a number that shows how many levels each enchantment costs, as well as how many lapis lazuli you need.

GENERATION

Enchanting tables aren't generated anywhere in the world, so you must craft them, using 4 blocks of obsidian, 2 diamonds and a book. It has the same astronomically high blast resistance as obsidian, but a much lower hardness, so you can collect it with any pickaxe.

THE IMPORTANCE OF BOOKS

The strength of the enchantments offered to you can be increased by surrounding the enchanting table with up to 15 bookshelves a block away. The glyphs that you see representing each enchantment are from the Standard Galactic Alphabet, which was first used in the *Commander Keen* games.

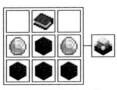

ENCHANTING TABLE RECIPE

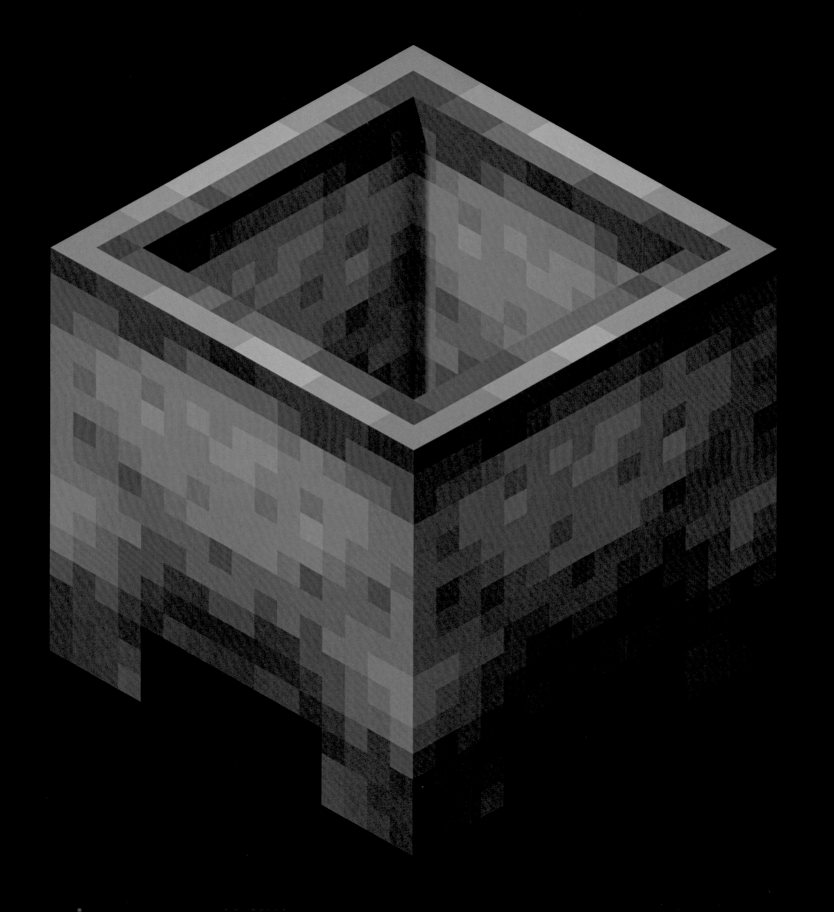

CAULDRON

Cauldrons are more multifaceted than they first appear. As well as using them to hold water, you can also dye leather armors for humans or horses in them, or leave them out in wintry weather to collect powder snow. They even turn into a light-emitting block if you fill them with lava.

STATS

TRANSPARENCY	LIGHT EMISSION 0
RENEWABLE	BLAST RESISTANCE 2	HARDNESS 2
FLAMMABLE	SILK TOUCH

| WATER CAULDRON | LAVA CAULDRON | POWDER SNOW CAULDRON |

GENERATION

Cauldrons in witch huts are sometimes filled with a potion. You'll also find them in igloo basements, woodland mansions and tanneries – where village leatherworkers live. Water can't exist in the Nether unless you place it in a cauldron. You need to mine a cauldron with a pickaxe or it drops nothing.

 16   48   74

BEHAVIOR

You can fill a cauldron with water, water bottles, lava, powder snow, and potions. A cauldron has four levels of fullness, the first of which is empty. You can use a bucket to completely empty a full cauldron of its lava or water and vice versa. Lava and water above dripstone stalactites will drip down to fill cauldrons beneath them.

DUNK AND DYE

If you use a dye on a water-filled cauldron, the water will change color. You can then use leather or horse armor on it to change the armor's color and reduce the cauldron level. You can do the same thing with potion-filled cauldrons to make tipped arrows. You can also use a water-filled cauldron to wash dye off armors.

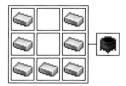

CAULDRON RECIPE

SMITHING TABLE

You can use the smithing table for a single specific function – yes, it can create tools, weapons and armor, but only by upgrading diamond versions to netherite variants. This gives them the advantage of not disintegrating in lava, as well as becoming the most powerful and durable tools in the game!

STATS

TRANSPARENCY	LIGHT EMISSION
	0

RENEWABLE	BLAST RESISTANCE	HARDNESS
	2.5	2.5

FLAMMABLE	SILK TOUCH

METALWORK MANTLE
You can find smithing tables in the houses of village toolsmiths, who use them as their job block. They're crafted with 4 planks and 2 iron ingots. It doesn't cost any experience to upgrade diamond tools to netherite, and they also retain any enchantments; however, they keep the same durability and don't get repaired.

SMITHING TABLE RECIPE

ANVIL

The sturdy anvil was made for repairing and renaming items. To repair an item, you need to combine it with another item of that type or a matching material. Anvils obey gravity and will fall when a solid block underneath is removed, damaging players or mobs beneath.

STATS

TRANSPARENCY	LIGHT EMISSION
	0

RENEWABLE	BLAST RESISTANCE	HARDNESS
	1200	5

FLAMMABLE	SILK TOUCH

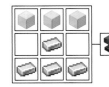

CHIPPED ANVIL	DAMAGED ANVIL

HAMMER IT OUT

You can use anvils to enchant weapons with an enchanted book, as you would on an enchanting table. You can combine enchanted books on an anvil to create stronger enchantments, as well as repair enchanted items. The anvil can also be used to create copies or zoomed-out versions of maps and include a place marker on them.

ANVIL RECIPE

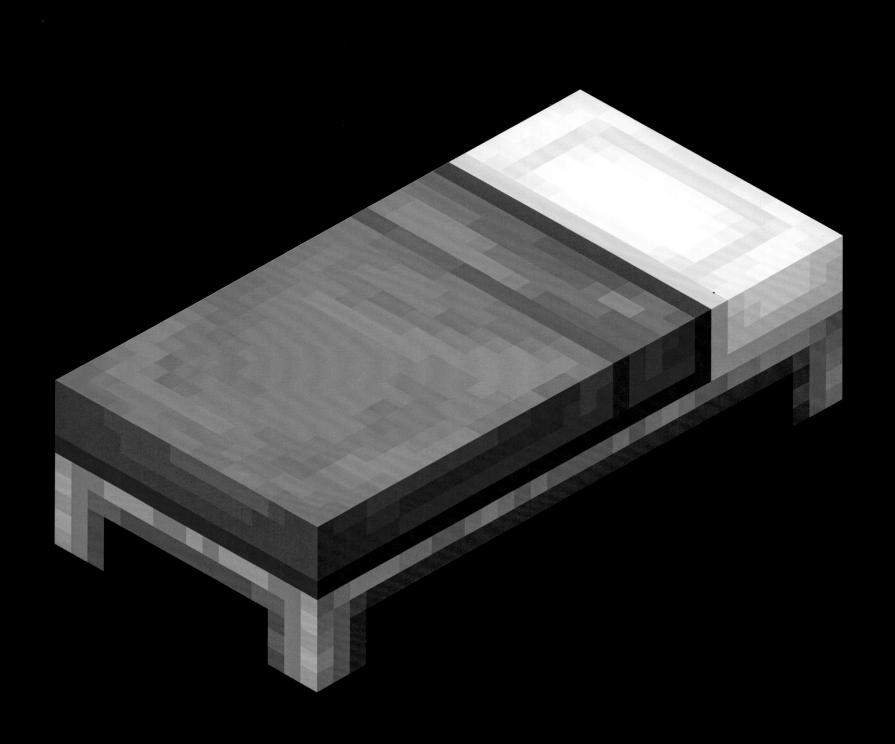

CYAN BED

BEDS

STATS

TRANSPARENCY

LIGHT EMISSION
0

RENEWABLE

BLAST RESISTANCE
0.2

HARDNESS
0.2

FLAMMABLE

SILK TOUCH

Draped in comforting colored wool, the bed is a cozy necessity for explorers in need of rest. You can only use one during the night or when storms roll in. If it's not dark or stormy, then you can just bounce on it while you wait! You can't use a bed if hostile mobs are lurking nearby.

WHITE BED	MAGENTA BED	LIGHT BLUE BED
YELLOW BED	LIME BED	PINK BED
GRAY BED	LIGHT GRAY BED	PURPLE BED
BLUE BED	BROWN BED	GREEN BED
RED BED	BLACK BED	ORANGE BED

GENERATION

The villagers of the Overworld need beds to sleep in, too, so they have at least one bed in their houses, although the color of the sheets varies between biomes. You can craft beds with 3 planks and 3 matching wools, and they occupy 2 block spaces when you place them.

BEHAVIOR

Interacting with a bed will reset your spawn point so if you're defeated, you'll respawn by the bed. You can't do this in the Nether or the End, as the bed will explode – a trait that can be utilized when battling the Ender Dragon, as the explosion is even more powerful than TNT. Trying to use a bed during the day will still reset your spawn point even though it won't let you sleep.

SLEEP HABITS 101

If you don't embrace the importance of sleep and fail to use a bed for 3 in-game days, you'll be hunted by eerie phantoms, which swoop and attack any player in need of some shut-eye.

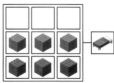

CYAN BED RECIPE

210   268

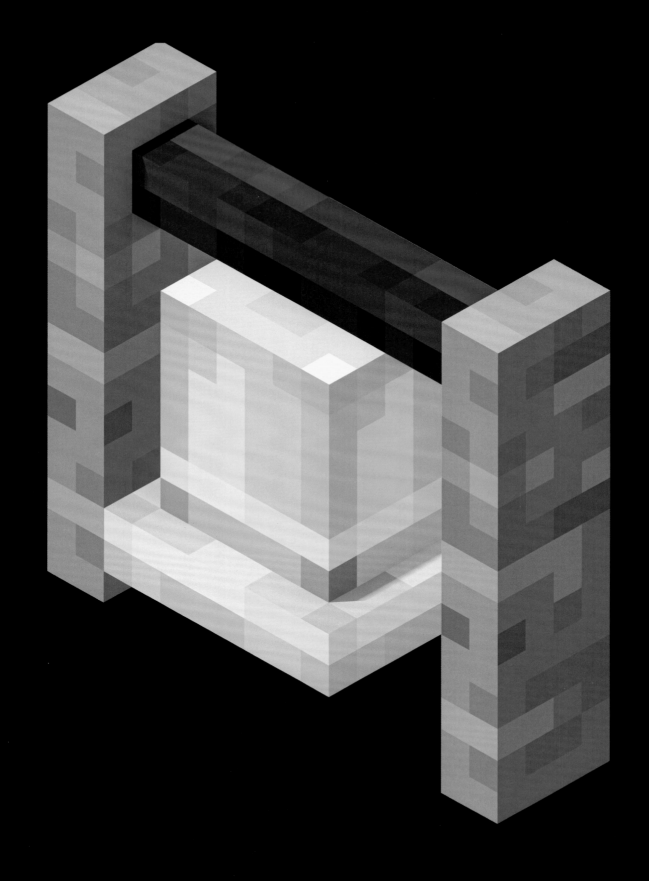

BELL

Villagers use bells to alert their people to raids from hordes of deadly pillagers. Every village has one, and they're used as a site of congregation, too. Place one on the ground and it becomes a standing bell, but you can also hang them from ceilings or attach them to the side of any solid block.

STATS

TRANSPARENCY

LIGHT EMISSION

 0

RENEWABLE

BLAST RESISTANCE

 5

HARDNESS

 5

FLAMMABLE

SILK TOUCH

HANGING BELL VARIANT

GENERATION

Bells are usually at the epicenter of a village in any biome, where most villagers will be able to hear their peals. You can trade with villagers to get your hands on a bell or find it in the Creative inventory. They can be mined with any pickaxe and always drop themselves.

BEHAVIOR

When a bell is rung, it alerts all the villagers in earshot, who will run and hide in their houses as if it was nighttime. When a pillager raid begins, the bell automatically rings to alert the townsfolk. You can ring the bell manually using a projectile like an arrow, or as part of a redstone mechanism.

FOR WHOM IT TOLLS

Armorer villagers often have a single bell available to trade, though it costs a whopping 36 emeralds. Additional bells can be placed by used beds in villages, which will move the congregation point. You'll see a flourish of green particles above the bell if you've placed it correctly.

BARREL

Commonly found in villages, barrels are simple containers that have the same 27-slot storage as a chest. They do have one advantage, however – you can access their contents even if a solid block is above them. They're the job site of fishermen, and unclaimed barrels can convert villagers to the trade.

STATS

TRANSPARENCY

LIGHT EMISSION

0

RENEWABLE   BLAST RESISTANCE   HARDNESS

2.5   2.5

FLAMMABLE   SILK TOUCH

OPEN BARREL
VARIANT

STURDY WOOD

Strangely for an item crafted with slabs and sticks, barrels are not flammable. Lava can spawn fire on flammable blocks adjacent to the barrel but the barrel will remain intact. Piglins will become infuriated with a player if they see a barrel being opened or destroyed, much as they do when someone does the same thing to a chest.

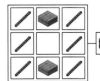

BARREL RECIPE

COMPOSTER

Recycling is really important, and composters make it super easy. They transform unwanted food and most organic items into bone meal, which you can use to fertilize crops. Each can hold seven levels of compost and you can collect bone meal from it when white circles appear on top to show it's full.

STATS

TRANSPARENCY

LIGHT EMISSION 0

RENEWABLE

BLAST RESISTANCE 0.6

HARDNESS 0.6

FLAMMABLE

SILK TOUCH

EMPTY COMPOSTER

REDUCE, REUSE, RECYCLE

Organic materials that you add to the composter have a chance to increase the compost level by 1. Cake and pumpkin pies will always add a level, while something like grass only has a 30% chance. You'll see composters in villages, where farmers use them as a job block. The fullness of a composter can also be used to produce a varying redstone signal through a redstone comparator.

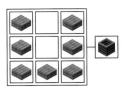

COMPOSTER RECIPE

FLETCHING TABLE

Unlike other tables in Minecraft, this one doesn't have a function for players. However, it does have some use in the world, as it attracts villagers who want to become fletchers – that's a craftsperson who creates arrows – which is why you'll see at least one in most villages.

STATS

TRANSPARENCY	LIGHT EMISSION
	0

RENEWABLE	BLAST RESISTANCE	HARDNESS
	2.5	2.5

FLAMMABLE	SILK TOUCH

STRAIGHT AS AN ARROW
Combine 4 planks with 2 pieces of flint to craft a fletching table, which is flammable from flame and lava. You can find job blocks like the fletching table throughout villages, and they're primarily used by villagers to assign themselves a profession. Only one villager can claim a job at each job block and they must already have a bed in the village.

FLETCHING
TABLE RECIPE

LECTERN

Found in librarians' houses Overworld-wide, lecterns are a handy job block that allows more than one player to read a book at a time. All you need to do is place a book on the lectern to enable a group reading session. If the block is destroyed, then any book it's holding will drop as well.

STATS

TRANSPARENCY

LIGHT EMISSION
0

RENEWABLE

BLAST RESISTANCE
2.5

HARDNESS
2.5

FLAMMABLE

SILK TOUCH

READING LEVELS

You can craft a lectern by combining a bookshelf and 4 wooden slabs. It produces a small redstone signal when a page of the book on it is turned, and a comparator can output a varying signal depending on how much is written on a page, or a maximum signal when the last page is reached.

LECTERN RECIPE

GRINDSTONE

Used by weaponsmiths, the grindstone is an important job block that can repair and disenchant items. When you interact with the grindstone, an interface with two slots will pop up. If two identical damaged items are added, they will be transformed into one item with replenished durability.

STATS

TRANSPARENCY	LIGHT EMISSION
	0

RENEWABLE	BLAST RESISTANCE	HARDNESS
	6	2

FLAMMABLE	SILK TOUCH

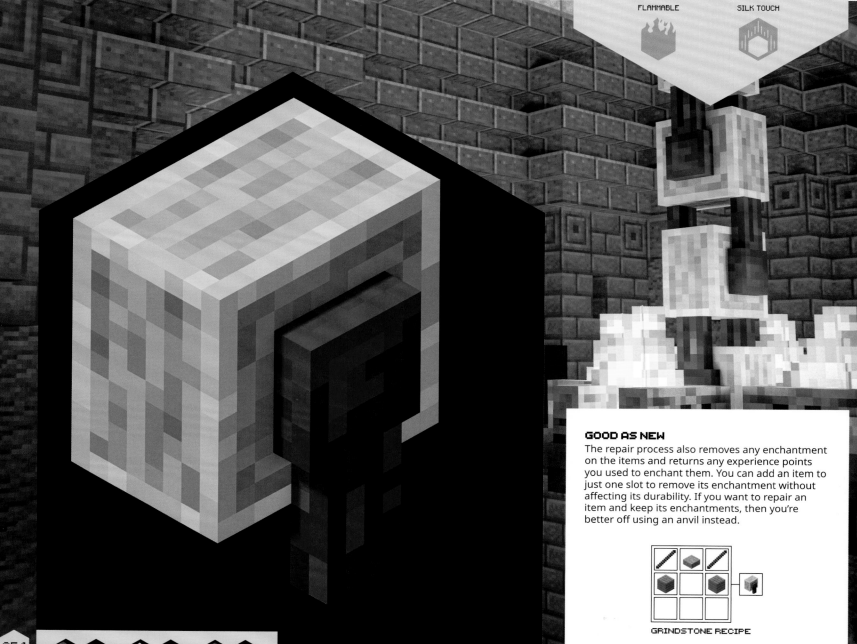

GOOD AS NEW

The repair process also removes any enchantment on the items and returns any experience points you used to enchant them. You can add an item to just one slot to remove its enchantment without affecting its durability. If you want to repair an item and keep its enchantments, then you're better off using an anvil instead.

GRINDSTONE RECIPE

STONECUTTER

You can use the versatile stonecutter to efficiently craft an array of stone blocks, from cobbled deepslate stairs to chiseled bricks. You will find them in the houses of stone masons in every village, or you can craft your own using three blocks of stone and an iron ingot.

STATS

TRANSPARENCY	LIGHT EMISSION	
	0	
RENEWABLE	BLAST RESISTANCE	HARDNESS
	3.5	3.5
FLAMMABLE	SILK TOUCH	

WORKING SMART

Stone items that you put on a stonecutter can be transformed into any of their smaller or equal-size variants, and you can usually make more items per source block than you could by crafting. For example, stone can be turned into stone stairs, slabs, bricks and walls, among others. The majority of stone blocks can be run through a stonecutter.

STONECUTTER RECIPE

SMOKER

If you need to cook a lot of food very quickly, then the smoker is your new best friend. You can only use it for food, but it works at a much faster rate than a furnace. Like most job blocks, you'll often see them in villages throughout the Overworld, being used by the town butcher.

STATS

TRANSPARENCY

LIGHT EMISSION 13

RENEWABLE

BLAST RESISTANCE 3.5

HARDNESS 3.5

FLAMMABLE

SILK TOUCH

**LIT
SMOKER**

NO SMOKE WITHOUT FIRE
Though it operates at twice the rate a furnace does, it will only reward you with half the experience for cooking and it burns fuel at twice the rate as well, so it's just as efficient as a furnace in that respect. You can't use it to cook inedible foods like the popped chorus fruit.

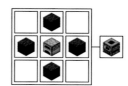

SMOKER RECIPE

LOOM

If you want to make your mark on the Minecraft world and express your personality, there's no better block than the loom. It's a job block for village shepherds, but more importantly, you can use it to customize banners by applying dyes and items to make unique patterns on them.

STATS

TRANSPARENCY

LIGHT EMISSION 0

RENEWABLE

BLAST RESISTANCE 2.5

HARDNESS 2.5

FLAMMABLE

SILK TOUCH

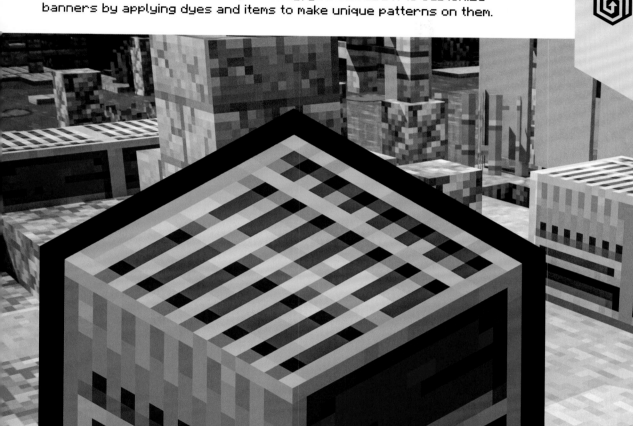

STRUNG ALONG

Interact with the loom and you'll bring up an interface that has a slot for a banner, a dye and an optional pattern. When you add at least a banner and a dye, you can select a design from a scrolling list of possible options. Then you can take the banner from the output slot to add it to your inventory, or add another dye to layer patterns.

LOOM RECIPE

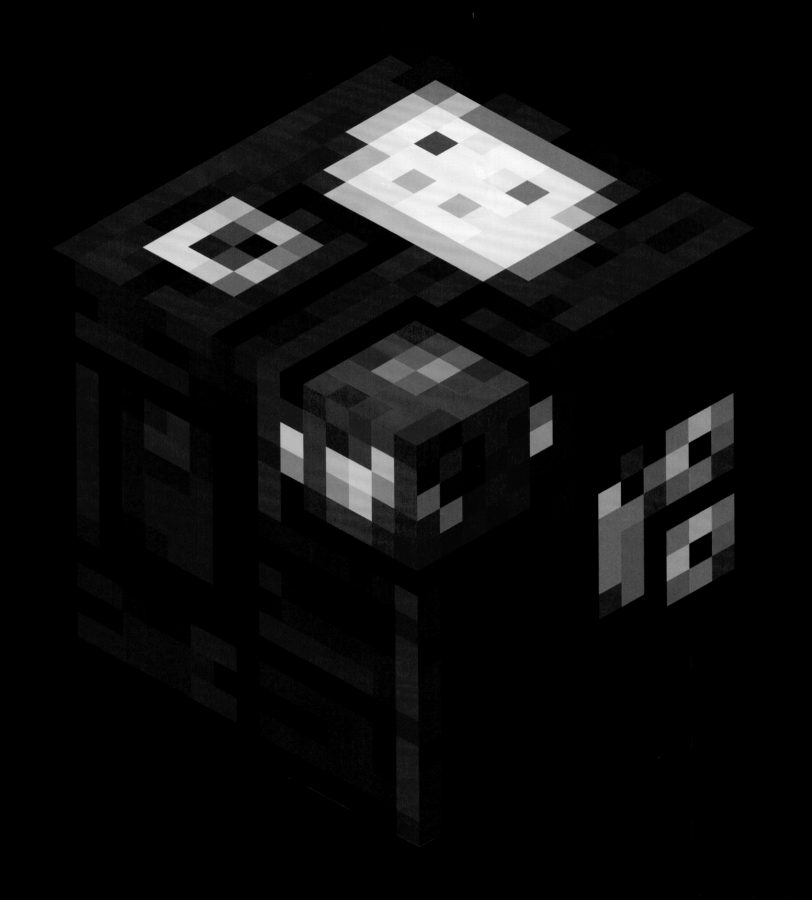

CARTOGRAPHY TABLE

If you're planning a world-spanning adventure, you may want to seek out a cartography table, where you can craft, clone and expand maps. Maps automatically chart the world as you explore, marking every land form so you can find your way in the future.

STATS

TRANSPARENCY	LIGHT EMISSION 0

RENEWABLE	BLAST RESISTANCE	HARDNESS
	2.5	2.5

FLAMMABLE	SILK TOUCH

BEHAVIOR

Interacting with the cartography table will bring up an interface that allows you to craft a few types of maps. Using paper alone will create an empty map, though combining paper with a compass will also create a locator map, which shows your current position.

GENERATION

You'll find cartography tables in villages of every biome, where cartographers use them as their job blocks. Unassigned villagers can claim unused cartography tables to become cartographers, who will be able to sell you explorer maps and banner patterns, among other useful items.

ON THE MAP

You can copy maps by combining them with an empty map on the table, or lock a map so it is no longer updated by crafting a map with a glass pane. It's also possible to rename maps on cartography tables, which is useful if you're charting several areas and need to keep track of them all.

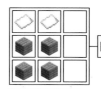

CARTOGRAPHY
TABLE RECIPE

CHEST

The ever-useful chest has 27 slots to fill with items. When you place a chest adjacent to another, they will merge together to become a double chest, which has 54 slots. You can move items to and from your inventory easily using the chest interface.

STATS

TRANSPARENCY	LIGHT EMISSION 0
RENEWABLE	BLAST RESISTANCE 2.5	HARDNESS 2.5
FLAMMABLE	SILK TOUCH

DOUBLE CHEST

PACK IT IN

Chests can be found in long-forgotten places across the Overworld, from desert temples to abandoned mine shafts, and each location yields different loot. You can use chests on llamas, donkeys and mules to turn them into transportable storage. You can also use them to craft other storage items like shulker boxes and hoppers.

CHEST RECIPE

ENDER CHEST

Like normal chests, you use Ender chests primarily for storing and retrieving items. However, they have the mysterious ability to connect with all your other Ender chests, so you can access the contents from wherever you are, no matter the dimension.

STATS

TRANSPARENCY	LIGHT EMISSION
	7

RENEWABLE	BLAST RESISTANCE	HARDNESS
	600	22.5

FLAMMABLE	SILK TOUCH

LIMITS OF MAGIC
Ender chests can't be combined, nor can they be attached to a beast of burden, which means they're slightly more limited in some respects. They also emit a light level of 7, which isn't quite enough to stop mobs spawning near them. They can only be mined with a Silk Touch–enchanted pickaxe; otherwise they will drop only 8 obsidian blocks.

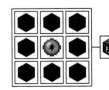

ENDER CHEST RECIPE

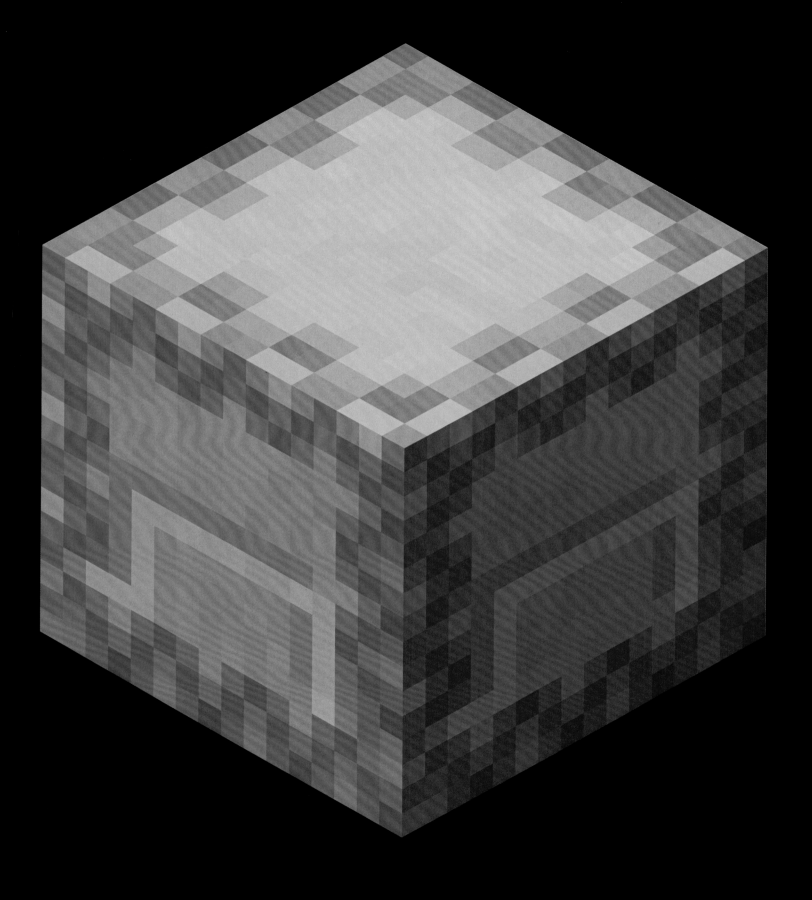

SHULKER BOX

FOUND:
By crafting only

If you need quick, portable storage on the move, look no further than the shulker box. It has the same capacity as a chest but retains its contents when you destroy it. Place it somewhere new and your inventory will be intact. You can also customize shulker boxes with any of the 16 dyes.

STATS

TRANSPARENCY

LIGHT EMISSION 0

RENEWABLE

BLAST RESISTANCE 6

HARDNESS 2

FLAMMABLE

SILK TOUCH

WHITE SHULKER BOX	MAGENTA SHULKER BOX	LIGHT BLUE SHULKER BOX	YELLOW SHULKER BOX
LIME SHULKER BOX	PINK SHULKER BOX	GRAY SHULKER BOX	LIGHT GRAY SHULKER BOX
CYAN SHULKER BOX	PURPLE SHULKER BOX	BLUE SHULKER BOX	BROWN SHULKER BOX
GREEN SHULKER BOX	RED SHULKER BOX	BLACK SHULKER BOX	ORANGE SHULKER BOX

GENERATION

Shulker boxes don't generate naturally, so you will need to defeat shulkers and craft two of their shells with a chest to make one. You can craft a shulker box with a dye to alter its color, and you can also rinse the dye off by using the dyed shulker box on a cauldron filled with water.

BEHAVIOR

You don't need a tool to collect the shulker box, so it's easy to destroy and move quickly and often. Its contents will remain inside, so you're able to store thousands of items at once in your inventory or in storage items like chests. You can even see the contents in the item description when you hover over a shulker box in your inventory.

AMBIDEXTERITY

You can place a shulker box on any surface, including walls and ceilings; however, you won't be able to open them if they have a solid block above their top face, just like chests. As with chests, piglins will be enraged if you open or destroy a shulker box and will start to attack you!

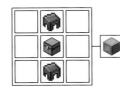

SHULKER BOX RECIPE

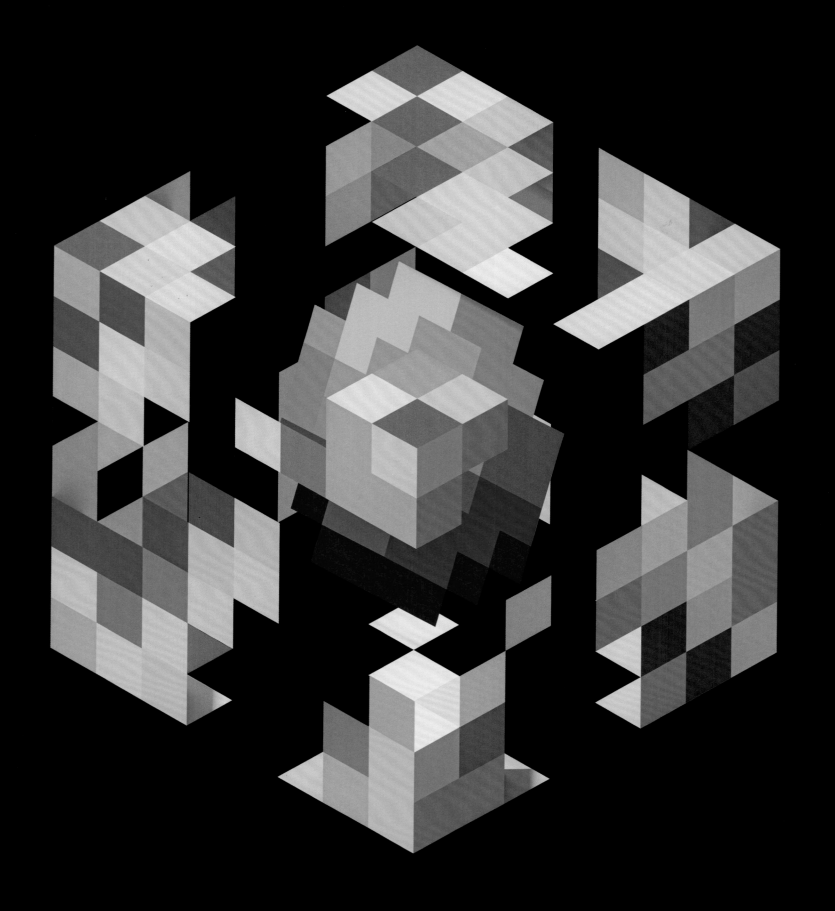

CONDUIT

Crafted from extremely rare marine materials, the conduit is similar to a beacon in that it provides buffs to players in its vicinity, though these buffs are most useful underwater. You must place the conduit within a specific construction to activate it.

CLOSED
CONDUIT

CONDUIT
STRUCTURE
CONFIGURATION

GENERATION

You won't find the conduit anywhere in the naturally generated world. Instead, you'll need to craft it using 8 nautilus shells and a heart of the sea. The shells are found in fishing, dropped by defeated drowned or offered by wandering traders, while the heart of the sea can only be collected from buried treasure on beaches and the ocean floor.

 45   218   222

BEHAVIOR

When activated within a frame made from any prismarine block or sea lanterns, the conduit bestows the Conduit Power buff to any players within at least 32 blocks. This gives players the Water Breathing, Haste and Night Vision effects. The buff area can be increased by adding blocks to the frame: one that consists of 42 blocks will have a maximum effect radius of 96 blocks.

WAVE POWER

Conduits brightly light up the area around them and damage any hostile mobs within an 8-block radius. They can be built on land, too, but as the buffs are primarily to improve performance underwater, they're largely redundant.

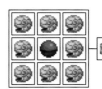

CONDUIT RECIPE

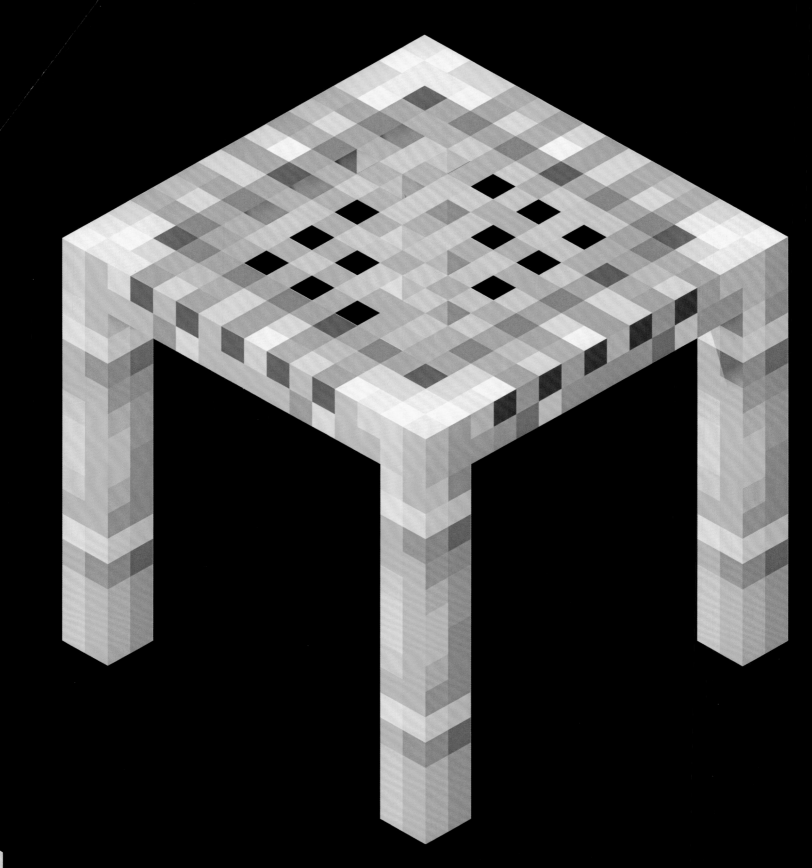

SCAFFOLDING

FOUND:
By crafting only

Making grand builds in Survival mode can be a perilous endeavor, but not if you rig up a bunch of scaffolding to support you! It's a temporary build block intended to make it easier and safer to scale up and descend from great heights, preventing workers from plummeting to their doom.

STATS

TRANSPARENCY

LIGHT EMISSION — 0

RENEWABLE

BLAST RESISTANCE — 0

HARDNESS — 0

FLAMMABLE

SILK TOUCH

BEHAVIOR

Players can move up and down through scaffolding by jumping and sneaking, making it easy to reach heights and drop from them quickly. Attempting to place a scaffolding block too far from a supporting tower will cause the block to drop and be placed on the first solid block it hits.

EASY REMOVALS

You can destroy scaffolding instantly by hand and it will drop itself as an item, which makes it very easy to bring down scaffolding when a build is completed. Any scaffolding block above a destroyed block will also drop, as well any blocks that were being supported horizontally, unless they're within 6 blocks of a different support.

GENERATION

You can craft 6 blocks of scaffolding with 6 pieces of bamboo and a single piece of string. When you place a scaffolding block, it will become part of a support scaffold, which can be stacked as high as required. Scaffolding blocks that you place on the side of a support tower have a slightly different appearance and can only be placed a maximum of 6 blocks away from any support.

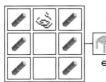

SCAFFOLDING RECIPE

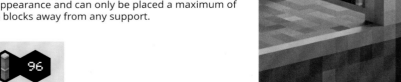

RESPAWN ANCHOR

The Nether's dangers will defeat even the bravest warriors, and because you can't place a bed there, you'll be thrown back to the Overworld, far from your gear. The solution: a respawn anchor. You can charge it with glowstone to save your respawn point in the Nether!

STATS

TRANSPARENCY	LIGHT EMISSION
	0-15

RENEWABLE	BLAST RESISTANCE	HARDNESS
	1200	50

FLAMMABLE	SILK TOUCH

FULLY-CHARGED VARIANT

MEETING POINT

Every respawn reduces the number of charges by 1. The respawns can be shared between players, so a whole team will respawn at the same place, but each person will expend a charge. When you use glowstone on a respawn anchor placed in the Overworld or End, it will explode, like a bed does in any dimension except the Overworld.

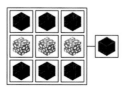

RESPAWN ANCHOR RECIPE

LODESTONE

STATS

TRANSPARENCY	LIGHT EMISSION
	0

RENEWABLE	BLAST RESISTANCE	HARDNESS
	3.5	3.5

FLAMMABLE	SILK TOUCH

Altering where a compass points to is handy if you want to find your way back to a spot – enter the lodestone. When you place the block and link it to a compass, the compass will point to the lodestone. You can place it in any dimension, but compasses will go wild if in a different dimension from the block.

LEAD THE WAY

To assign a compass to a lodestone, you must use it on a placed lodestone, at which point the compass will be covered in a cyan sheen. You can often find lodestones in chests of bastion remnant structures in the Nether. You need to mine them with a pickaxe to make them drop themselves.

LODESTONE RECIPE

BEEHIVE

While bees naturally craft bee nests, any player can craft beehives. To the bees, they're the same. Bees will buzz off and pollinate flowers, bring pollen back and stack up the honey inside, which you can collect with a glass bottle. If the hive is sheared, honeycomb will drop instead.

STATS

TRANSPARENCY	LIGHT EMISSION
	0

RENEWABLE	BLAST RESISTANCE	HARDNESS
	0.6	0.6

FLAMMABLE	SILK TOUCH

BEEWARE

Bees will become angry when a beehive is destroyed without a Silk Touch–enchanted tool – though you don't need a tool to collect a hive. You'll also anger bees if you put their honey into bottles, or if you shear the beehive for honeycomb. You can calm bees in all these situations if there's smoke from a campfire nearby.

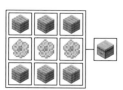

BEEHIVE RECIPE

 152 207 208

JUKEBOX

Playing music is simple if you have a jukebox and a music disc. Jukeboxes are crafted with eight wood planks and a diamond, so they're relatively expensive, but music can be heard up to 65 blocks away. There are 13 different discs that you can find across the Overworld and the Nether.

STATS

TRANSPARENCY

LIGHT EMISSION
  0

RENEWABLE

BLAST RESISTANCE
 6

HARDNESS
 2

FLAMMABLE

SILK TOUCH

DISC JOCKEY

Music discs will play once before they're ejected and won't play again until someone inserts another, whether by hand or by using a hopper. When a jukebox plays a music disc, it emits a redstone signal that changes strength depending on which disc is being played.

JUKEBOX RECIPE

CHAIN

STATS

TRANSPARENCY	LIGHT EMISSION
	0

RENEWABLE	BLAST RESISTANCE	HARDNESS
	6	5

FLAMMABLE	SILK TOUCH

Chains are decorative blocks that can suspend light blocks, such as lanterns, horizontally and vertically. They have similar properties to other iron blocks, so you must collect them with a pickaxe. You might spot them in Nether structures like bastion remnants and ruined portals.

IN SUSPENSE
You can hang chains from ceilings or attach them to walls and extend their length by connecting their ends together. You can combine chains seamlessly with some utility items like lanterns, soul lanterns and bells to suspend them in midair and create dangling features in your builds.

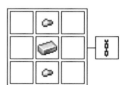

CHAIN RECIPE

SLIME BLOCK

It can be tricky to tell the slime block from slime mob, especially as you craft the block with slimeballs that the mob drops! A slime block will bounce players, mobs and items up in the air and stick to adjacent blocks, moving them with it as it's pushed and pulled.

STATS

TRANSPARENCY	LIGHT EMISSION
	0

RENEWABLE	BLAST RESISTANCE	HARDNESS
	0	0

FLAMMABLE	SILK TOUCH

GREENSTONE MECHS

You can use the sticky properties of slime with pistons in redstone mechanisms. Slime drags adjacent blocks with it to create moving parts, as long as no more than 12 blocks are connected to any single slime block. Unlike the honey block, which is also sticky, items will bounce off slime, rather than stick to it.

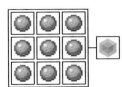

SLIME BLOCK RECIPE

 207   302

273

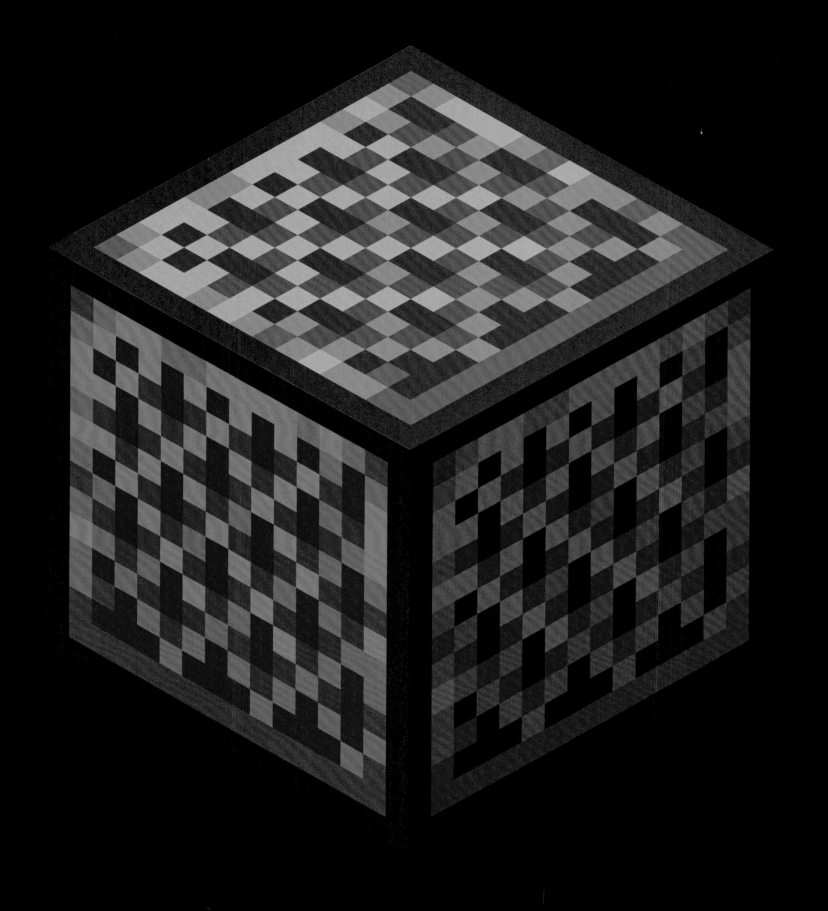

NOTE BLOCK

FOUND:
By crafting only

If you prefer a more customized playlist than a jukebox offers, use note blocks to make your own tunes. You can interact with a note block to alter its pitch, and it will play the note you set when it receives a redstone signal. The instrument that it plays the note on depends on the block beneath it.

STATS

TRANSPARENCY

LIGHT EMISSION

RENEWABLE

BLAST RESISTANCE 0.8

HARDNESS 0.8

FLAMMABLE

SILK TOUCH

BEHAVIOR

A note block upon a bone block will play a xylophone, a didgeridoo note will play if it's on a pumpkin and if honeycomb is underneath, the note will sound like it comes from a flute. If the block a note block sits on doesn't have one of 16 special instrument sounds assigned to it, the note block will play the note on a piano by default.

HOLDING A TUNE

If you interact with a note block, it will alter the pitch that the block plays and will change the color of the symbol it produces. Note blocks are powered by a redstone signal passing over or beside it. If you arrange a long series of note blocks beside a continuous redstone circuit, it's possible to create whole songs.

GENERATION

Note blocks are wooden blocks that you can craft with a combination of 8 planks, including Nether wood versions, and a single piece of redstone dust. They won't burn when coming into contact with fire, but they will when exposed to lava.

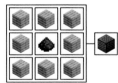

NOTE BLOCK RECIPE

TNT

One of the most explosive blocks in Minecraft, and the only one purpose-built for the job, TNT should be handled with care. Once you've placed it, it can be easily destroyed with any tool; however, if it has been activated you won't be able to collect it – just run away as quickly as you can!

STATS

TRANSPARENCY	LIGHT EMISSION
	0

RENEWABLE	BLAST RESISTANCE	HARDNESS
	0	0

FLAMMABLE	SILK TOUCH

BEHAVIOR

When you place a TNT block, you can ignite it in various ways, including with a flint and steel, by exposing it to fire, or by activating it with a redstone signal. The blast radius is relatively small, but you can create a huge explosion by combining more than one block. You can easily work it into redstone circuits to create bespoke traps.

EXPLOSIVE NATURE

The blast from TNT damages any player, mob or block in range, unless it detonates underwater, in which case it won't damage blocks. It can move players, mobs and dropped items, some of which can come in handy. For example, dropped arrows can be fired by the blast of TNT.

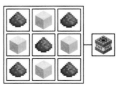

TNT RECIPE

GENERATION

You can create TNT with a combination of 4 sand – either variant will do – and 5 pieces of gunpowder. You might also find it in structures as part of ingenious traps, like the ones that have been laid in woodland mansions and desert temples, and you can also collect TNT from loot chests in underwater ruins and shipwrecks.

 26 246 268

SIGNS

You can add text to signs to create warnings, signposts and more. You can also use them in your builds to create patterns of differing depths. You can attach signs – which are available in all varieties of wood – to walls or place them in the ground to create a standing sign.

STATS

TRANSPARENCY

LIGHT EMISSION 0

RENEWABLE

BLAST RESISTANCE 1

HARDNESS 1

FLAMMABLE

SILK TOUCH

JUNGLE STANDING SIGN

ACACIA STANDING SIGN

BIRCH STANDING SIGN

DARK OAK STANDING SIGN

OAK STANDING SIGN

SPRUCE STANDING SIGN

CRIMSON STANDING SIGN

WARPED STANDING SIGN

ACACIA WALL SIGN

BIRCH WALL SIGN

DARK OAK WALL SIGN

JUNGLE WALL SIGN

OAK WALL SIGN

SPRUCE WALL SIGN

CRIMSON WALL SIGN

WARPED WALL SIGN

SHOW THE WAY

You can find signs in the Overworld, either in igloo basements or taiga villages, where they're used to build chairs! You can use a dye on a sign to change the color of text, or apply a glow ink sac to make the text glow – very useful in dark areas. You can make them drop without a tool.

 159

LIGHTNING ROD

FOUND:
By crafting only

Lightning will strike twice — and many more times after that — with the lightning rod. This useful device, crafted from copper ingots, will attract bolts of lightning within a 32-block radius and convert it into a redstone signal, which will save flammable buildings nearby from being destroyed.

STATS

TRANSPARENCY

LIGHT EMISSION — 0

RENEWABLE

BLAST RESISTANCE — 6

HARDNESS — 3

FLAMMABLE

SILK TOUCH

ALMIGHTY ROD
Lightning rods can be placed on any side of a block, making it easy to redirect the created signal into a mechanism. The lightning called by a trident enchanted with Channeling can also be redirected with the lightning rod, so be careful where you're throwing your trident!

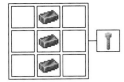

LIGHTNING ROD RECIPE

REDSTONE BLOCKS

REDSTONE DUST

FOUND:
Jungle pyramids,
woodland mansions

The magical conducting element for redstone signals is redstone dust. You can mine it from redstone ore and place it on most blocks to begin a circuit. When you place it adjacent to other redstone dusts, it will join to create wires that curve and create crossroads in circuits.

STATS

TRANSPARENCY

LIGHT EMISSION
  0

RENEWABLE

BLAST RESISTANCE
 0

HARDNESS
 0

FLAMMABLE

SILK TOUCH

UNLIT REDSTONE
DUST

BEGIN TRANSMISSION

Redstone dust can carry a signal from power sources like redstone torches to other redstone components like comparators. The maximum signal strength is 15, but that weakens by 1 for every block it travels. You can use redstone dust in recipes for most redstone components, or to increase the length of a potion's effect in brewing.

REDSTONE TORCH

As well as providing a medium light, the redstone torch is a source of power for circuits and mechanisms, which you can place on the top or side of blocks. It puts out the maximum possible redstone signal of 15 when active, but it can be toggled off if it receives a redstone signal.

STATS

TRANSPARENCY	LIGHT EMISSION
	7

RENEWABLE	BLAST RESISTANCE	HARDNESS
	0	0

FLAMMABLE	SILK TOUCH

UNLIT REDSTONE TORCH	REDSTONE TORCH WALL FIXTURE	LIT REDSTONE TORCH WALL FIXTURE

LIGHT SWITCH

Redstone torches will turn off if they're attached to a block that receives another redstone signal. When on, they will power adjacent redstone dust, or activate pistons, lamps, dispensers and other mechanisms, and send a signal through comparators and repeaters facing away from the torch.

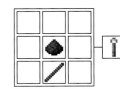

REDSTONE TORCH RECIPE

 181   298   300

283

BUTTONS

You can use the humble button to power mechanism blocks that it is attached or adjacent to, though it will automatically turn off after a short period of time. You can place buttons on all sides of a block, so they can be used to send a redstone signal from any direction.

STATS

TRANSPARENCY

LIGHT EMISSION
0

RENEWABLE

BLAST RESISTANCE

0.5

HARDNESS

0.5

FLAMMABLE

SILK TOUCH

ACACIA
BUTTON

BIRCH
BUTTON

DARK OAK
BUTTON

JUNGLE
BUTTON

SPRUCE
BUTTON

CRIMSON
BUTTON

WARPED
BUTTON

STONE
BUTTON

POLISHED BLACKSTONE
BUTTON

PULSATING

A button also provides the maximum possible redstone signal and powers the same range of mechanisms as a redstone torch, though only for a short period of time. You can craft buttons from any wood planks, stone or polished blackstone, so they can blend in with their surroundings better.

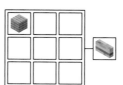

OAK BUTTON RECIPE

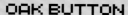
OAK BUTTON

LEVER

Sometimes you don't want a brief signal, like a button produces. Often you'll want a switch to turn on and off for as long as is necessary. For this, you need a lever. You can switch it between inactive and active states and pass a redstone signal of 15 into the block it's attached to.

STATS

TRANSPARENCY	LIGHT EMISSION
	0

RENEWABLE	BLAST RESISTANCE	HARDNESS
	0.5	0.5

FLAMMABLE	SILK TOUCH

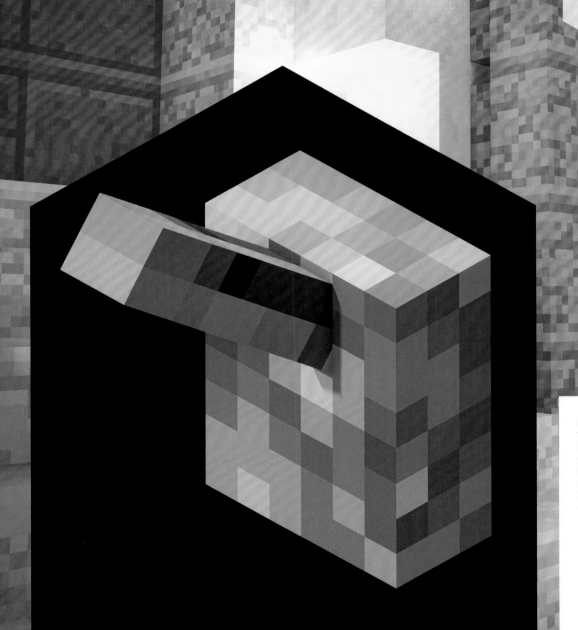

MULTI-TALENTED
You can attach levers to any face of a block, just like buttons, and power any redstone components adjacent to the block they're attached to in a similar fashion. When you place it vertically, if the lever is down, that means it's active. If placed horizontally, it's active when the lever points north or west.

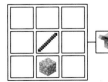

LEVER RECIPE

285

TRAPPED CHEST

FOUND:
Woodland mansions

At first glance, you may not see a difference between a normal and a trapped chest. However, look closely at the clasp and you'll see a reddish ring of redstone power. You can use trapped chests for storage and combine them into doubles, like chests, but they also output a redstone signal when opened.

STATS

TRANSPARENCY	LIGHT EMISSION
	0

RENEWABLE	BLAST RESISTANCE	HARDNESS
	2.5	2.5

FLAMMABLE	SILK TOUCH

DOUBLE TRAPPED CHEST

TRAP OUTPUT
The strength of the signal the trapped chest produces is determined by how many people are accessing it at once. It transmits a signal through most redstone components except a comparator, which only measures fullness of the chest. You may find a trapped chest in a woodland mansion, but be careful when you open it, as it's attached to TNT!

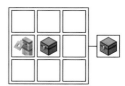

TRAPPED CHEST RECIPE

TRIPWIRE HOOK

FOUND:
Jungle temples

Tripwire hooks produce a redstone signal when the tripwire lying between them is snagged. You need to use two tripwire hooks on opposite blocks and run tripwire between them. Like buttons, tripwire hooks produce a redstone signal that turns off after half a second, but the tripwire can be repeatedly triggered.

TRANSPARENCY	LIGHT EMISSION	RENEWABLE
	0	

BLAST RESISTANCE	HARDNESS	FLAMMABLE	SILK TOUCH
0	0		

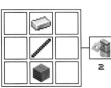

TRIPWIRE HOOK
RECIPE

TRIPWIRE

FOUND:
Only by placing string

Tripwire is actually just string that's placed between tripwire hooks. It has no redstone ability on its own, but you can use it to create a tripwire up to 40 blocks long. A tripwire will trigger whenever players or mobs pass through it. Perhaps you could rig it to a bell to warn you that you have visitors...

TRANSPARENCY	LIGHT EMISSION	RENEWABLE
	0	

BLAST RESISTANCE	HARDNESS	FLAMMABLE	SILK TOUCH
0	0		

WOODEN PRESSURE PLATE

FOUND:
Some villages

The wooden pressure plate, which you can craft with two matching planks, mimics the texture of its component blocks so it can blend in as a trap. It's the most sensitive of the pressure plates and will even produce a maximum redstone signal when an item is on top of it.

ACACIA PRESSURE PLATE

TRANSPARENCY	LIGHT EMISSION	RENEWABLE

BLAST RESISTANCE	HARDNESS	FLAMMABLE	SILK TOUCH
0.5	0.5		

BIRCH PRESSURE PLATE DARK OAK PRESSURE PLATE JUNGLE PRESSURE PLATE

OAK PRESSURE PLATE SPRUCE PRESSURE PLATE CRIMSON PRESSURE PLATE

WARPED PRESSURE PLATE

STONE PRESSURE PLATE

FOUND:
Desert pyramids

The pressure plates made from stone and polished blackstone are slightly less sensitive than wooden ones, as they can only detect the presence of mobs and players on top of them, not items. They won't catch fire, unlike wooden pressure plates. Lava and water will flow around all types of pressure plate.

TRANSPARENCY	LIGHT EMISSION	RENEWABLE
	0	

BLAST RESISTANCE	HARDNESS	FLAMMABLE	SILK TOUCH
0.5	0.5		

POLISHED BLACKSTONE PRESSURE PLATE

LIGHT WEIGHTED PRESSURE PLATE

FOUND:
By crafting only

Made from gold ingots, the light weighted pressure plate gives out a variable redstone signal based on the quantity of mobs, items and players on the pressure plate. If you place one item atop this plate, it would give a signal of 1, and 15 items would output the maximum signal to adjacent blocks.

TRANSPARENCY

LIGHT EMISSION 0

RENEWABLE

BLAST RESISTANCE 0.5

HARDNESS 0.5

FLAMMABLE

SILK TOUCH

HEAVY WEIGHTED PRESSURE PLATE

FOUND:
By crafting only

The heavy weighted pressure plate takes the greatest number of entities to power. It has a variable output like the light weighted variant, but the power increases by a single level for every ten mobs, players or items on top of it. You need at least 141 such entities to create the maximum signal.

TRANSPARENCY

LIGHT EMISSION 0

RENEWABLE

BLAST RESISTANCE 0.5

HARDNESS 0.5

FLAMMABLE

SILK TOUCH

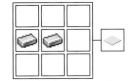

HEAVY WEIGHTED
PRESSURE PLATE RECIPE

 225 284 285

OBSERVER

FOUND:
By crafting only

The friendly face of the observer is always checking for changes to blocks that it's looking at. When it observes a change in the block directly in front of it, it will output a signal behind it, which is transmitted at the maximum strength and powers adjacent redstone components.

STATS

TRANSPARENCY

LIGHT EMISSION 0

RENEWABLE

BLAST RESISTANCE 3.5

HARDNESS 3.5

FLAMMABLE

SILK TOUCH

UPDATE LOG

The range of block updates the observer can detect is wide. It can tell when snow forms on grass or melts away, or when sugar cane grows, as well as when doors are opened or droppers and dispensers are activated. It's one of the most versatile power sources because of the quantity of events it can detect.

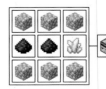

OBSERVER RECIPE

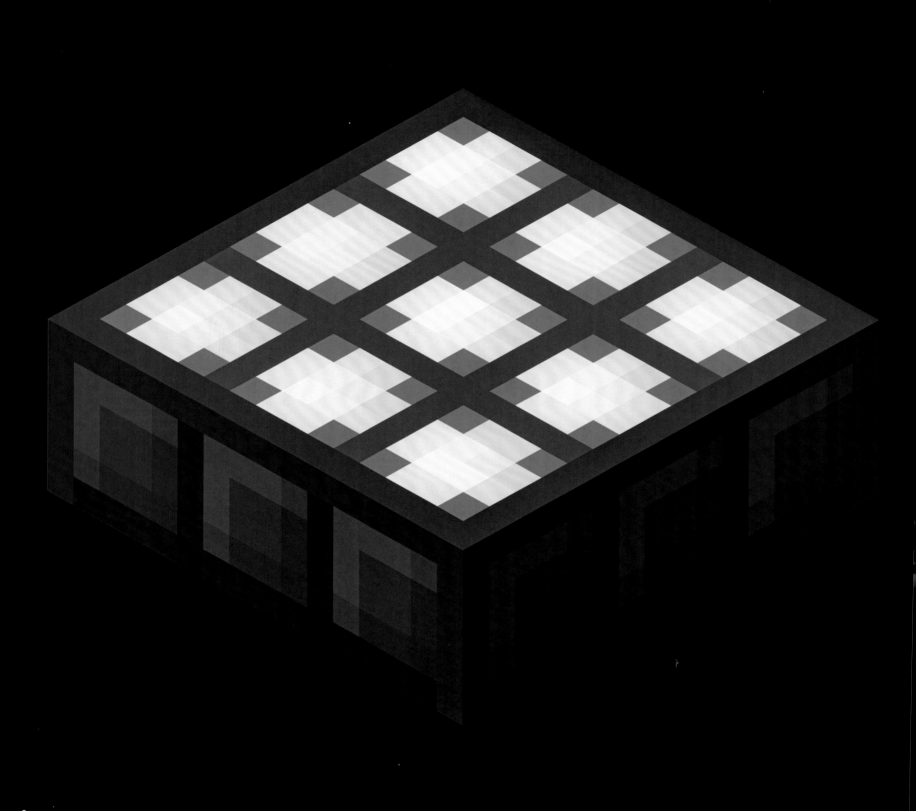

DAYLIGHT DETECTOR

FOUND:
By crafting only

Able to output variable strengths of redstone signal, the daylight detector is powered by natural sunlight. If sun shines brightly on the detector, it will output a maximum signal, but at nighttime, it produces nothing. Other light sources have no effect on the light detection.

STATS

TRANSPARENCY	LIGHT EMISSION
	0

RENEWABLE	BLAST RESISTANCE	HARDNESS
	0.2	0.2

FLAMMABLE	SILK TOUCH

INVERTED
DAYLIGHT
DETECTOR

TEMPERAMENTAL
You can interact with a daylight detector to invert it and produce a maximum signal when there's no light. Weather can also affect its output. When it's powered, it will transmit a signal through adjacent redstone components, so you could link a daylight detector up to redstone lamps, ensuring they turn on as soon as the sun goes down.

DAYLIGHT
DETECTOR RECIPE

293

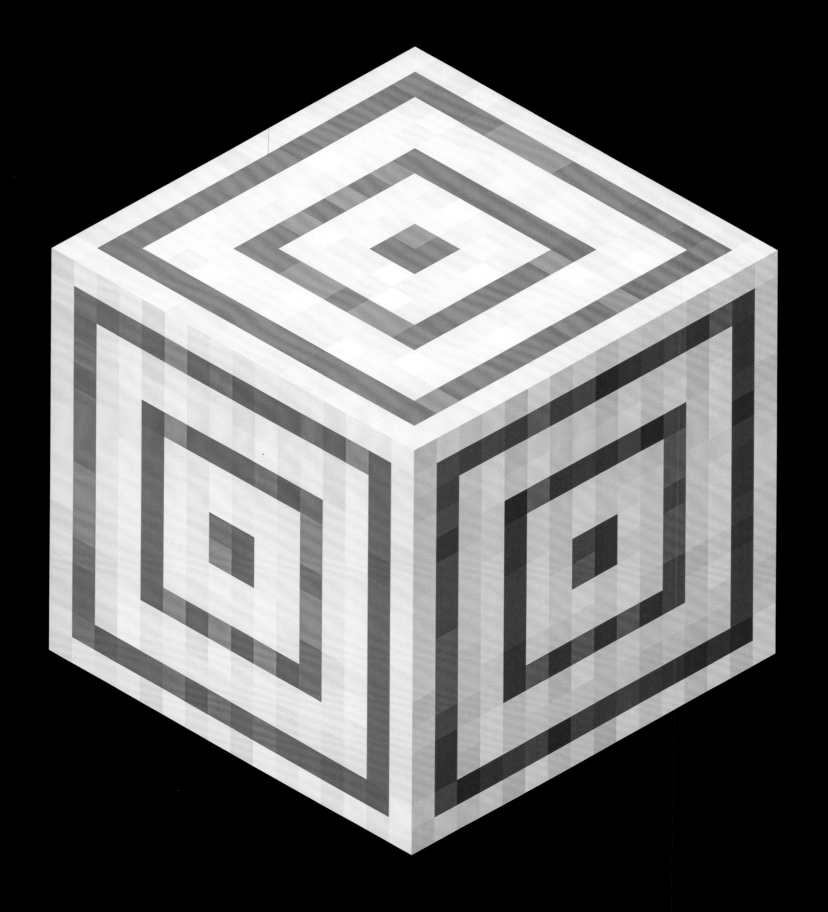

TARGET

FOUND:
By crafting only

If you want to keep your archery skills as sharp as an arrowhead, then the target block is exactly what you need. It outputs a signal when you hit it with projectiles like arrows, tridents and eggs! The closer the projectile is to the bull's-eye, the more powerful the signal it produces.

STATS

TRANSPARENCY	LIGHT EMISSION
	0

RENEWABLE	BLAST RESISTANCE	HARDNESS
	0.5	0.5

FLAMMABLE	SILK TOUCH

GENERATION
You can craft a target block with 4 pieces of redstone dust and a hay bale, which lends its flammable quality to the target. They don't naturally generate in the world so you will need to craft a target block to get your hands on one.

BEHAVIOR
When hit by a projectile, the target will output a redstone signal for a short period of time before switching off again. You can't power it with redstone and it acts unusually in circuits, so it's best used purely as a power source.

BULL'S-EYE
The target block can be activated by arrows, tridents, eggs, snowballs, splash potions, fire charges, lingering potions and even llama spit! Tridents and arrows will make the target produce a signal for one second, over twice as long as any other projectile.

TARGET RECIPE

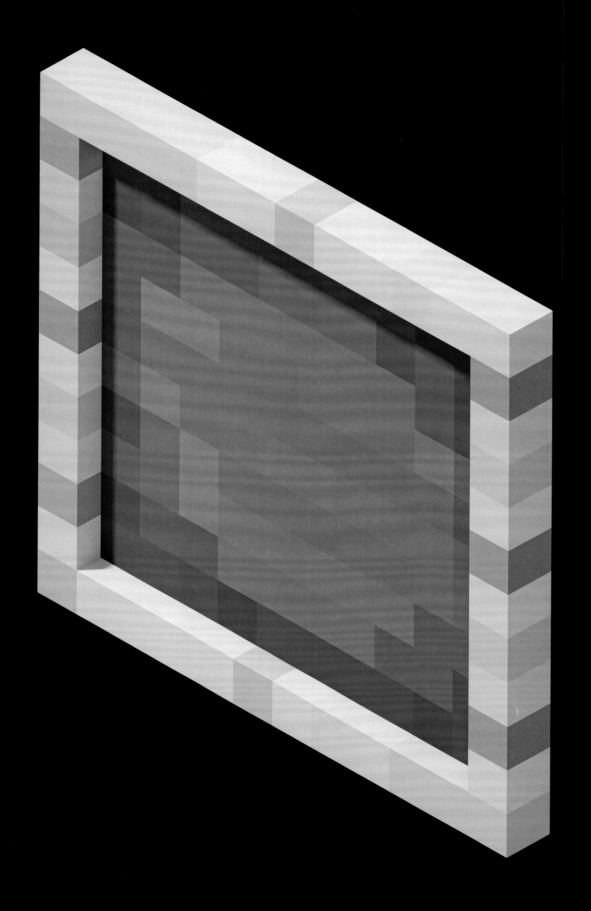

ITEM FRAME

FOUND:
End ships

More commonly thought of as a decorative block that can showcase items and create unique ornaments, the item frame is also a versatile redstone source. You can place items in the frame and rotate them, which a comparator can measure and turn into a redstone signal.

STATS

TRANSPARENCY	LIGHT EMISSION
	0

RENEWABLE	BLAST RESISTANCE	HARDNESS
	0	0

FLAMMABLE	SILK TOUCH

GLOW ITEM FRAME

GENERATION
You'll find one item frame in each End ship, where it houses a pair of elytra. The glow item frame has a similar set of functions to the normal version, but it illuminates its contents. You can combine an item frame with a glow ink sac to craft one.

BEHAVIOR
You can display item frames on all faces of blocks, including some you wouldn't expect to support a frame, like pressure plates and slabs. If you place a map in an item frame, it will show the frame's location on the map in green, which can be handy for finding bases and points of interest.

MASTERPIECE
You can rotate most items in an item frame to 8 positions, allowing for 8 signal strengths, though you can only rotate a map 4 times. The most useful item you can place is an arrow, which acts as a dial to the different redstone signal strengths.

ITEM FRAME RECIPE

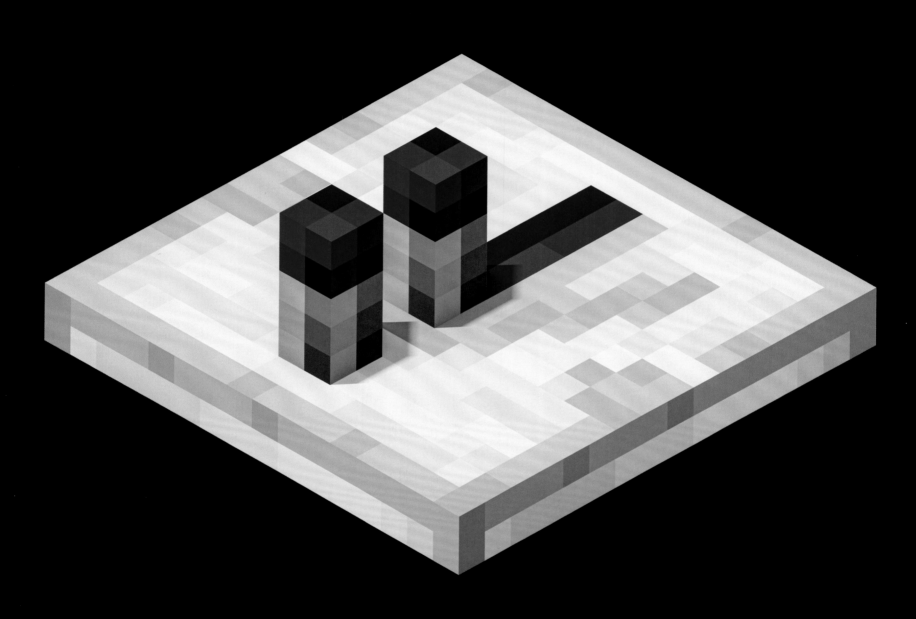

REDSTONE REPEATER

FOUND:
Jungle temples

One of the most important blocks in the transmission of redstone is the redstone repeater, the main function of which is to amplify a weakened signal back to full strength. If you interact with the repeater, you can add a delay of up to 4 redstone ticks to any signal passing through it.

STATS

TRANSPARENCY	LIGHT EMISSION 0
RENEWABLE	BLAST RESISTANCE 0
	HARDNESS 0
FLAMMABLE	SILK TOUCH

BEHAVIOR

Repeaters only transmit signals they receive from behind in a single direction, which allows you to control the signal direction in circuits. If it receives a signal from the side via another repeater or a redstone comparator, it will lock, preventing any signal from passing from the front of the block.

GO AGAIN

You can tell what delay a repeater has been set to by looking at how close the mini-torches are. When you place one, it's automatically set to a single tick delay. When powered, the two torches on the repeater will be lit. When the repeater is locked, a bar will appear across the repeater.

ACTIVE
REDSTONE
REPEATER

LOCKED
REDSTONE
REPEATER

GENERATION

There's only one place you can find repeaters in the wild: tucked away in the hidden room of a jungle temple. It's likely that budding redstone engineers will need more, so, thankfully, you can also craft them with 3 pieces of stone, 2 redstone torches and a single piece of redstone dust.

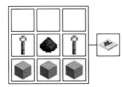

REDSTONE
REPEATER RECIPE

 282   300

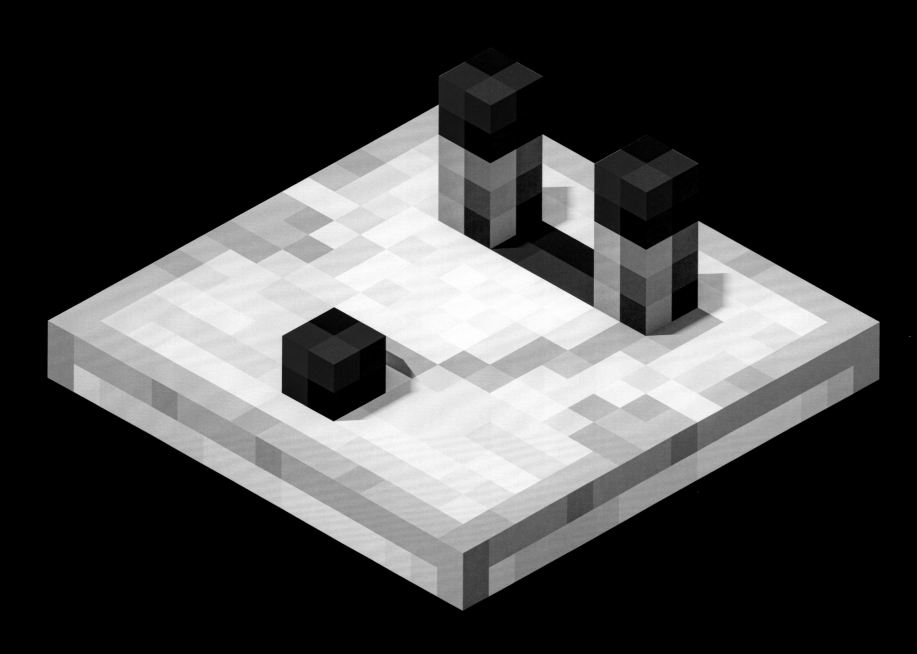

REDSTONE COMPARATOR

FOUND:
By crafting only

Like the redstone repeater, the comparator is an important component in redstone circuits. It's most commonly used to measure, compare or subtract multiple signals, as well as to control the direction of a signal. You can switch between comparison and subtraction modes by interacting with it.

STATS

TRANSPARENCY

LIGHT EMISSION
0

RENEWABLE

BLAST RESISTANCE
0

HARDNESS
0

FLAMMABLE

SILK TOUCH

ACTIVE REDSTONE COMPARATOR

SUBTRACTION MODE

BEHAVIOR

In comparison mode, the comparator will only pass a signal forward if the signal it receives from behind is greater than the one it receives in the side. In subtraction mode, it will reduce the signal it receives in the back by the one it receives in the side. If the signal strength entering the back of a comparator is 10, and the signal strength in the side is 4, a signal of 6 will be output.

FAVORABLE COMPARISON

Unlike a repeater, the comparator will only maintain a signal, not increase it to full strength as it passes through. The comparator can output a signal based on the fullness of storage or other state, for instance, how full a chest is, or how much of a cake you've eaten.

GENERATION

You won't find comparators generating naturally in the world, so they must be crafted. The recipe you need to use includes 3 pieces of stone, 3 redstone torches and a single piece of Nether quartz, which means you'll need to take a trip to the Nether if you want to make one!

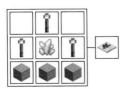

REDSTONE COMPARATOR RECIPE

PISTON

FOUND:
By crafting only

When you power it with a redstone signal, a piston will extend its head and push a block in front of it. Not all blocks are moveable – obsidian is a notable exception – but those that are will be moved forward a block space. If any blocks are stuck to that block, like slime or honey, they will also be pushed.

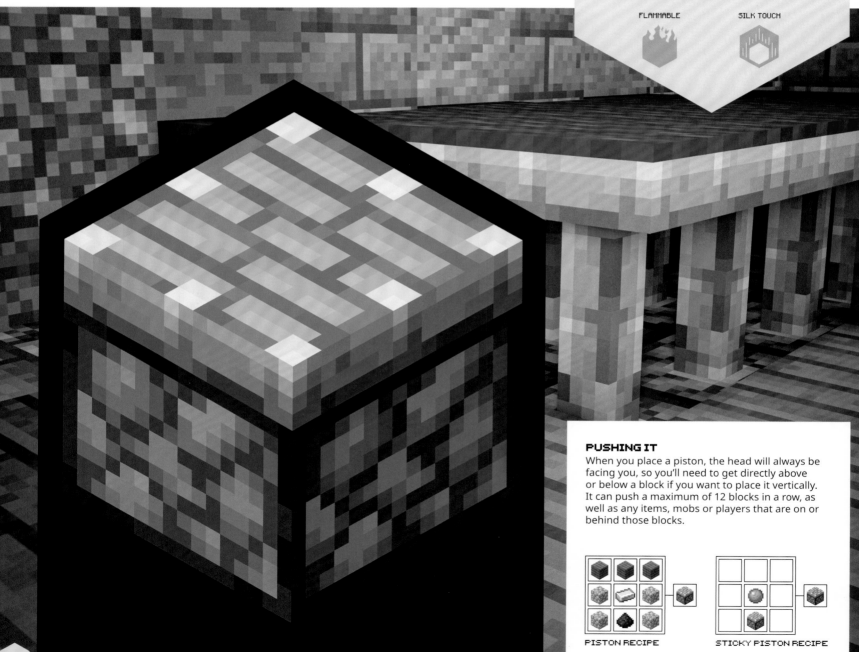

STATS

TRANSPARENCY

LIGHT EMISSION 0

RENEWABLE

BLAST RESISTANCE 0.5

HARDNESS 1.5

FLAMMABLE

SILK TOUCH

PUSHING IT
When you place a piston, the head will always be facing you, so you'll need to get directly above or below a block if you want to place it vertically. It can push a maximum of 12 blocks in a row, as well as any items, mobs or players that are on or behind those blocks.

PISTON RECIPE

STICKY PISTON RECIPE

302

STICKY PISTON

FOUND:
Jungle temple

The sticky piston has the additional advantage of being able to pull moveable blocks as well as push them. You can craft one by combining a piston with a slimeball, which lends a sticky quality. It's no more powerful than the piston, so it's unable to push blocks like obsidian, droppers and chests.

TRANSPARENCY	LIGHT EMISSION	RENEWABLE
	0	

BLAST RESISTANCE	HARDNESS	FLAMMABLE	SILK TOUCH
0.5	1.5		

PISTON HEAD

FOUND:
Connected to
either piston

The piston head, or sticky piston variant, is a technical block that occupies the space of a block that has just been pushed. The piston heads only exist when they're part of a piston, so you can't collect them as an item, nor can you find them in the Creative inventory.

STICKY
PISTON HEAD

TRANSPARENCY	LIGHT EMISSION	RENEWABLE
	0	

BLAST RESISTANCE	HARDNESS	FLAMMABLE	SILK TOUCH
0.5	1.5		

DISPENSER

The dispenser is an item-ejecting storage block often used in traps. It can hold up to nine stacks of items and will emit an item through the side with a hole when it receives a redstone signal. It also has the ability to use certain items, such as splash potions, as it ejects them.

STATS

TRANSPARENCY	LIGHT EMISSION
	0

RENEWABLE	BLAST RESISTANCE	HARDNESS
	3.5	3.5

FLAMMABLE	SILK TOUCH

ACTIVATED EJECTION
You can interact with a dispenser to move items in from your inventory. When you activate it, some items will be dropped as an item, but it can fire arrows, launch eggs and even set off fireworks. A powered dispenser can also transmit a signal to adjacent blocks.

DISPENSER RECIPE

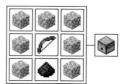

DROPPER

Like the dispenser, the dropper can also manipulate and move items; however, it doesn't activate them, so the dropper can move items between storage blocks like chests or other manipulation blocks like the hopper or dispenser. Similar to the dispenser, it has nine inventory slots.

STATS

TRANSPARENCY	LIGHT EMISSION
	0
RENEWABLE	BLAST RESISTANCE	HARDNESS
	3.5	3.5
FLAMMABLE	SILK TOUCH

DROPOUT

When you power it with a redstone signal, the dropper will eject a block from its inventory. It's good for moving items vertically and also creating item-sorting contraptions. The dropper has a cool-down period of a single redstone tick, so it can't be activated constantly.

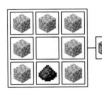

DROPPER RECIPE

HOPPER

With a wide-open top, the hopper is able to catch items and store them in its inventory or pass them on to another block through its output tube. You can throw items into a hopper, or it can suck items out of storage blocks above it, which makes it great for collecting items.

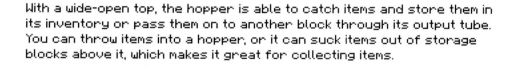

STATS

TRANSPARENCY	LIGHT EMISSION
	0

RENEWABLE	BLAST RESISTANCE	HARDNESS
	4.8	3

FLAMMABLE	SILK TOUCH

SIDE-FACING VARIANT

PASSING THE BLOCK

By default, the output tube of a hopper faces directly down, which means items will flow into a storage block beneath it. However, if you sneak while placing the hopper on a side of the block, the input tube will bend and the hopper will be placed beside the storage block, and items will flow into it horizontally.

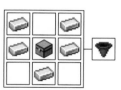

HOPPER RECIPE

REDSTONE LAMP

You can craft a redstone lamp with a glowstone and four pieces of redstone dust. It's a shining light source that requires a constant redstone signal to remain lit. When powered, it always produces the brightest light, no matter the power of the signal it receives.

STATS

TRANSPARENCY	LIGHT EMISSION
	15

RENEWABLE	BLAST RESISTANCE	HARDNESS
	0.3	0.3

FLAMMABLE	SILK TOUCH

LIT REDSTONE LAMP

BY LAMPLIGHT

You can power redstone lamps with any normal method of redstone signal. You can attach redstone torches to a lamp, but it won't be powered by them as they face away from it. You can attach levers to redstone lamps to make a switchable light, or link one to a daylight detector to make an automatic lighting system.

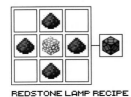

REDSTONE LAMP RECIPE

RAIL

To get around the Minecraft world quickly, you can start building a network of rails, which will allow you to whiz around in mine carts. They will curve to connect two rails on the ground that are diagonally adjacent, or form ramps to climb single blocks. If you create a T-junction, you can use an adjacent redstone signal to switch the track's direction.

CURVED VARIANT

TRANSPARENCY	LIGHT EMISSION	RENEWABLE	

BLAST RESISTANCE	HARDNESS	FLAMMABLE	SILK TOUCH
0.7	0.7		

RAIL RECIPE   16

DETECTOR RAIL

If any mine cart rolls over a detector rail, it will output a signal that can power any adjacent redstone components. When a mine cart with a chest rolls over a detector rail, it will output a signal depending on how full the chest is, so you can create systems that send empty chests to the mine and full ones back to your base.

LIT DETECTOR RAIL

TRANSPARENCY	LIGHT EMISSION	RENEWABLE	
	0		

BLAST RESISTANCE	HARDNESS	FLAMMABLE	SILK TOUCH
0.7	0.7		

DETECTOR RAIL RECIPE   6

POWERED RAIL

Use powered rails to control the speed of your mine carts, which otherwise need you to ride them in order to move. If the powered rail is activated, the velocity of a mine cart will increase, allowing it to climb steep slopes, but if inactive, the powered rail will have the opposite effect and slow the mine cart to a halt.

LIT POWERED RAIL

TRANSPARENCY

LIGHT EMISSION 0

RENEWABLE

BLAST RESISTANCE 0.7

HARDNESS 0.7

FLAMMABLE

SILK TOUCH

POWERED RAIL RECIPE

6

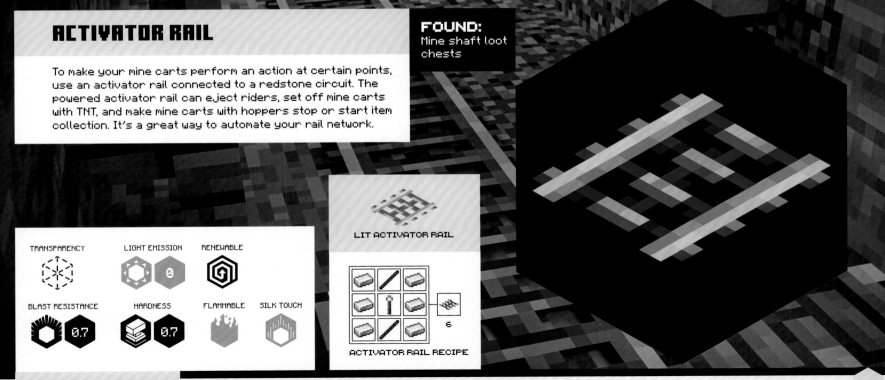

ACTIVATOR RAIL

FOUND:
Mine shaft loot chests

To make your mine carts perform an action at certain points, use an activator rail connected to a redstone circuit. The powered activator rail can eject riders, set off mine carts with TNT, and make mine carts with hoppers stop or start item collection. It's a great way to automate your rail network.

LIT ACTIVATOR RAIL

TRANSPARENCY

LIGHT EMISSION 0

RENEWABLE

BLAST RESISTANCE 0.7

HARDNESS 0.7

FLAMMABLE

SILK TOUCH

ACTIVATOR RAIL RECIPE

6

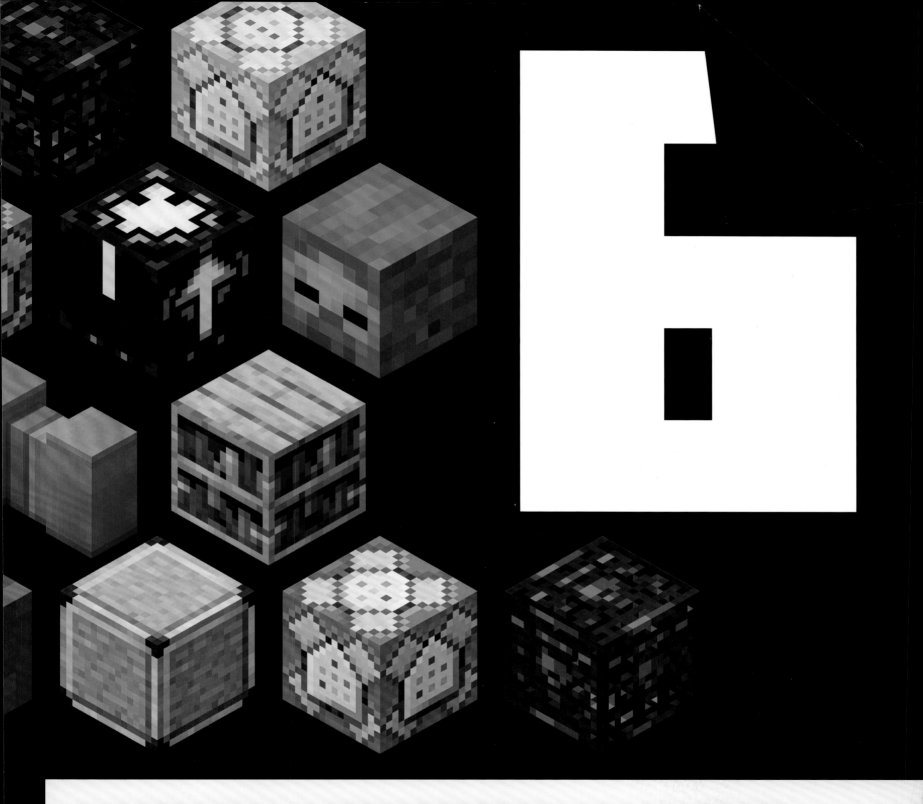

6

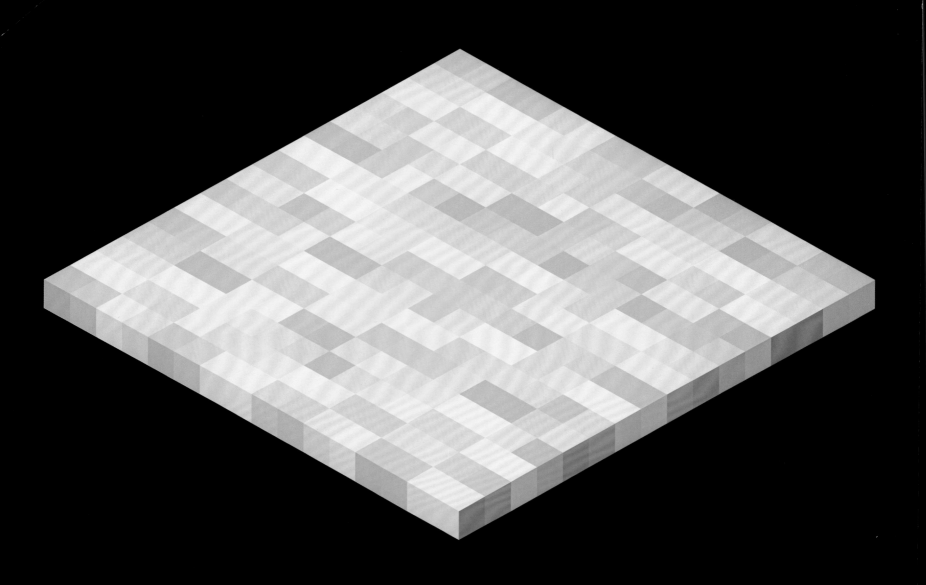

PINK CARPET

CARPETS

Thin, flat and colorful, the carpet block is a useful decoration block crafted from wool, which has a fluffy, comfy texture. You can collect carpets in all 16 colors, either by dying a white carpet or by crafting them from a colored wool block. Like wool, carpets are extremely flammable.

STATS

TRANSPARENCY	LIGHT EMISSION
	0

RENEWABLE	BLAST RESISTANCE	HARDNESS
	0.1	0.1

FLAMMABLE	SILK TOUCH

WHITE CARPET · MAGENTA CARPET · LIGHT BLUE CARPET

YELLOW CARPET · LIME CARPET · GRAY CARPET

LIGHT GRAY CARPET · CYAN CARPET · PURPLE CARPET

BLUE CARPET · BROWN CARPET · GREEN CARPET

RED CARPET · BLACK CARPET · ORANGE CARPET

GENERATION

You'll come across carpets in villages throughout the world, but nowhere more so than woodland mansions, where you'll see all but the orange carpet. You can craft 3 carpets with any 2 matching wool blocks, though white carpets can be colored with a dye ingredient as well.

BEHAVIOR

You can place carpet on top of almost any block – even non-solid ones, with the exception of item frames and paintings. They also let light through, allowing you to hide light sources while still brightening your rooms.

COLORFUL COVER

Village shepherds often have carpets of all colors to sell. When you use a carpet on a llama, it will change the color of its saddle. You can place carpets on top of fences to make the un-jumpable block surmountable. They can also cover the top of hoppers without interfering with their function.

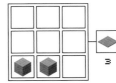

CARPET RECIPE

210

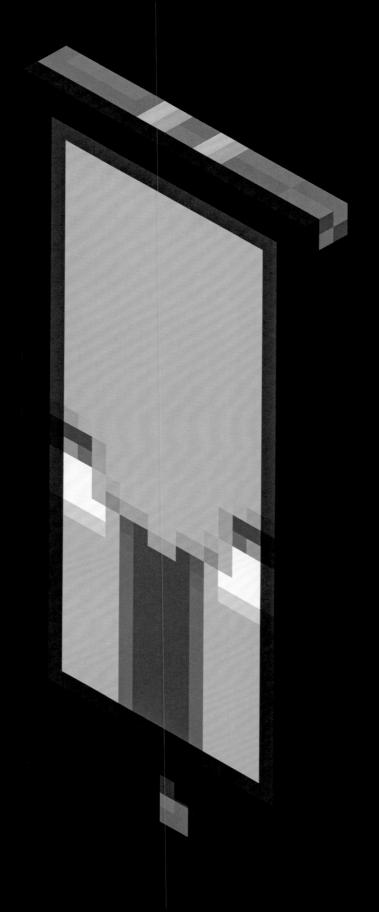

ILLAGER BANNER

BANNERS

Possibly the most customizable block in all of Minecraft, the banner is an item of expression. You can use dyes to alter the primary and pattern colors - stacking up to six different patterns to make unique designs, then place them freely or attach them to the side of other blocks.

STATS

TRANSPARENCY

LIGHT EMISSION

0

RENEWABLE

BLAST RESISTANCE

1

HARDNESS

1

FLAMMABLE

SILK TOUCH

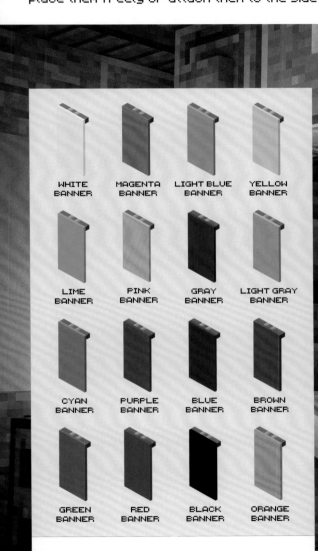

WHITE BANNER | MAGENTA BANNER | LIGHT BLUE BANNER | YELLOW BANNER

LIME BANNER | PINK BANNER | GRAY BANNER | LIGHT GRAY BANNER

CYAN BANNER | PURPLE BANNER | BLUE BANNER | BROWN BANNER

GREEN BANNER | RED BANNER | BLACK BANNER | ORANGE BANNER

BEHAVIOR
Patterns can be added by using the banner and a dye on a loom. Using a banner on a cauldron filled with water will wash off the last pattern you applied. They stand two blocks tall, but have no collision box, so players and mobs can move through them. You can also place a block on one half of a banner to obscure it and further allow for customization in the form of half-banners.

UNDER THE BANNER
Both shepherds and cartographer villagers will offer you banners as part of a trade. The illager banner is only dropped by illagers during raids, though it's also available in the Creative inventory.

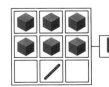

BANNER RECIPE

GENERATION
You craft banners with 6 pieces of matching wool and a stick. The color of wool used will determine the primary color of the banner. You'll also spot them throughout the world in villages, woodland mansions and End cities, while pillager raiders carry the illager banner into raids.

 210
 242
 257

FLOWER POT

A plant placed in a flower pot is sure to brighten up any base. Though the name suggests otherwise, flower pots can hold more than flowers – you can also plant cacti, fungi, bamboo and saplings in them. You must place them on a full-height block before planting anything, though.

STATS

TRANSPARENCY	LIGHT EMISSION
	0

RENEWABLE	BLAST RESISTANCE	HARDNESS
	0	0

FLAMMABLE	SILK TOUCH

POT LUCK
You can remove plants from a flower pot directly to your inventory by interacting with it. If you destroy it, the pot will drop itself and the plant within it separately as items. You can find flower pots in igloos, witch huts, villages and some other locations, with a range of contents.

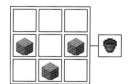

FLOWER POT RECIPE

BOOKSHELF

Crafted with books and wooden planks, the bookshelf is the perfect decorative block for your libraries and reading rooms. You can also use it to boost the power of enchantments! Silk Touch is required to collect the block itself; otherwise it will only drop the three books used to craft it.

STATS

TRANSPARENCY	LIGHT EMISSION
	0

RENEWABLE	BLAST RESISTANCE	HARDNESS
	1.5	1.5

FLAMMABLE	SILK TOUCH

MAGIC AMPLIFIER

You can use bookshelves to unlock the most powerful enchantments. To do this, you'll need to place 15 bookshelves a block space away from an enchanting table. You can even place them diagonally from the table, by stacking bookshelves on top of each other.

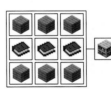

BOOKSHELF RECIPE

CAKE

The only placeable foodstuff in the game, cakes are a delicious, if not nutritious, feast. Cakes have seven slices, each of which replenishes two hunger points. It's also the best composting component you can use as it will automatically increase the compost level by one.

STATS

TRANSPARENCY	LIGHT EMISSION
	0

RENEWABLE	BLAST RESISTANCE	HARDNESS
	0.5	0.5

FLAMMABLE	SILK TOUCH

HAVE IT AND EAT IT

Cake is good for sharing with others, but be wary of placing a cake in an awkward spot: once it's down, you can't pick it up again. Some pandas are cake-lovers and will eat any placed cake they find. Comparators can also measure how much cake is left and output a variable redstone signal!

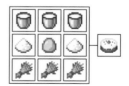

CAKE RECIPE

TURTLE EGG

When turtles travel to their home beach and breed, they lay a number of turtle eggs. The eggs nestle on sand and go through three stages of growth before hatching into baby turtles. You can only collect them with Silk Touch, or the eggs will be destroyed.

STATS

TRANSPARENCY	LIGHT EMISSION
	0

RENEWABLE	BLAST RESISTANCE	HARDNESS
	0.5	0.5

FLAMMABLE	SILK TOUCH

WALKING ON EGGSHELLS

Sea turtle eggs are understandably delicate – even standing on them for too long can break them. Zombies will go out of their way to trample all over turtle eggs, so you should protect them if you can. They can take days to hatch, but the process speeds up during the night.

VARIOUS TURTLE EGG CONFIGURATIONS

DRAGON EGG

Your solitary prize for defeating the Ender Dragon is this gigantic egg. It teleports if you try to mine it directly, and you should instead push it with a piston, or drop it on a half-height block such as a torch, to make it drop as an item. It also adheres to the laws of gravity.

STATS

TRANSPARENCY	LIGHT EMISSION
	1

RENEWABLE	BLAST RESISTANCE	HARDNESS
	9	3

FLAMMABLE	SILK TOUCH

NEST EGG

When you finally vanquish the Ender Dragon, the dragon egg spawns on top of the exit portal in the End. Unlike other falling blocks, the dragon egg won't suffocate you if it falls on your head as it's transparent. It also gives off a level 1 light, which makes it glow ominously in the dark of the End.

MOB HEADS

These decorative blocks are macabre shows of a player's skill. You can wear them as helmets, which reduces the risk that a corresponding enemy will notice you. As blocks, only the Wither skeleton skull has a function – you can combine it with soul sand or soul soil to summon the feared Wither.

STATS

TRANSPARENCY	LIGHT EMISSION
	0

RENEWABLE	BLAST RESISTANCE	HARDNESS
	1	1

FLAMMABLE	SILK TOUCH

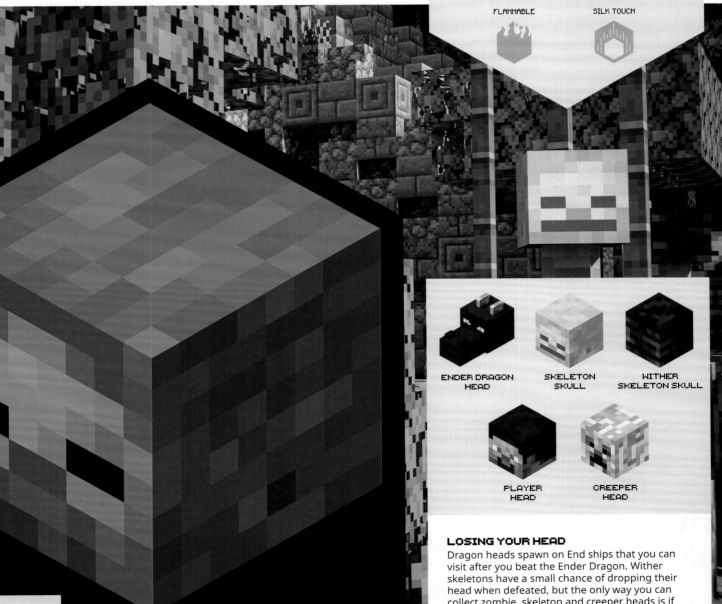

ZOMBIE HEAD

 64   65

ENDER DRAGON HEAD	SKELETON SKULL	WITHER SKELETON SKULL
PLAYER HEAD	CREEPER HEAD	

LOSING YOUR HEAD

Dragon heads spawn on End ships that you can visit after you beat the Ender Dragon. Wither skeletons have a small chance of dropping their head when defeated, but the only way you can collect zombie, skeleton and creeper heads is if those mobs are obliterated by a charged creeper's explosion. You can only get your hands on player heads in Creative mode.

321

MOB SPAWNER

The bane of adventurers all over the world, mob spawners are factories of terror that churn out endless streams of mobs. Each spawns a specific mob: through the cage exterior, you'll see a representation of which one it is. You can most easily destroy them with a pickaxe but you can also disable them by placing torches on all visible faces.

STATS

TRANSPARENCY	LIGHT EMISSION
	3

RENEWABLE	BLAST RESISTANCE	HARDNESS
	5	5

FLAMMABLE	SILK TOUCH

BEHAVIOR
Spawners only begin to create hostile mobs when you get within a 16-block distance of the spawner, including through walls. It will attempt to spawn up to 4 of its particular mob and will wait up to 40 seconds before it tries again. Normal mob-spawning conditions apply, so you can also disable them with light sources.

GENERATION
You'll find mob spawners in any hostile environment, from dungeons and mine shafts to strongholds and Nether fortresses. Their potential spawns are determined by the structure they're in – dungeons have a chance to host spider, zombie and skeleton mob spawners, while Nether fortresses have at least one that spawns blazes.

SOURCE OF EVIL
Though they have a transparent appearance, the block is actually treated as opaque, allowing blocks to be placed on all its faces. They have a relatively low blast resistance and hardness, but you can't move them with pistons or sticky pistons. TNT should allow you to get rid of one easily, though...

IMPULSE COMMAND BLOCK

FOUND:
By command only

Obtainable only with the pick block tool or by using commands, and intended for those building multiplayer games or maps on servers, the impulse command block executes a series of commands when it receives a redstone signal. It can hold up to 35,000 characters, so you can add many commands to a single block.

STATS

TRANSPARENCY	LIGHT EMISSION
RENEWABLE	BLAST RESISTANCE	HARDNESS
	3.6m	∞
FLAMMABLE	SILK TOUCH

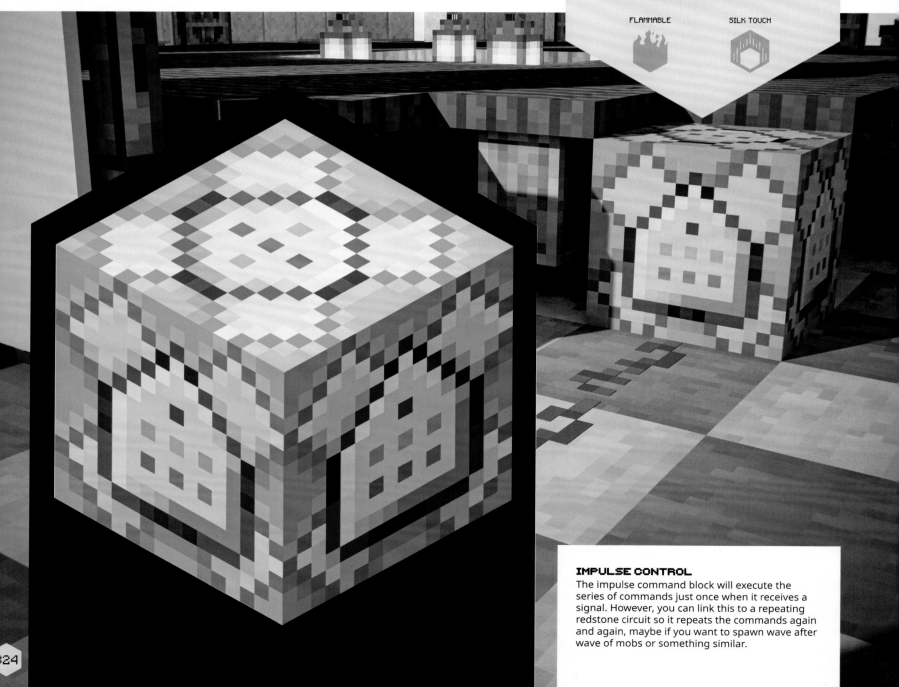

IMPULSE CONTROL

The impulse command block will execute the series of commands just once when it receives a signal. However, you can link this to a repeating redstone circuit so it repeats the commands again and again, maybe if you want to spawn wave after wave of mobs or something similar.

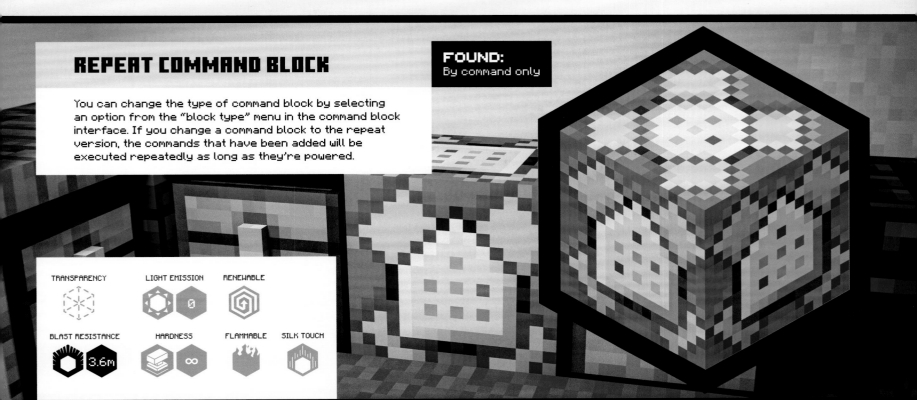

REPEAT COMMAND BLOCK

You can change the type of command block by selecting an option from the "block type" menu in the command block interface. If you change a command block to the repeat version, the commands that have been added will be executed repeatedly as long as they're powered.

TRANSPARENCY	LIGHT EMISSION	RENEWABLE	
	0		

BLAST RESISTANCE	HARDNESS	FLAMMABLE	SILK TOUCH
3.6m	∞		

CHAIN COMMAND BLOCK

The final type of command block is the chain variant, which only triggers if a command block facing into it has triggered. Command blocks are directional, signified by the direction the arrows on its side point. They can be switched between conditional and unconditional modes to determine whether or not they need an action to happen in order to trigger the next command block.

TRANSPARENCY	LIGHT EMISSION	RENEWABLE	
	0		

BLAST RESISTANCE	HARDNESS	FLAMMABLE	SILK TOUCH
3.6m	∞		

BARRIER

The barrier block is the secret weapon of adventure map-makers, as it allows them to control where players can and can't go. It looks invisible when viewed in Adventure mode, but will show a barred circle in Creative in order to make it easy to visibly block off areas.

STATS

TRANSPARENCY	LIGHT EMISSION
	0

RENEWABLE	BLAST RESISTANCE	HARDNESS
	3.6m	∞

FLAMMABLE	SILK TOUCH

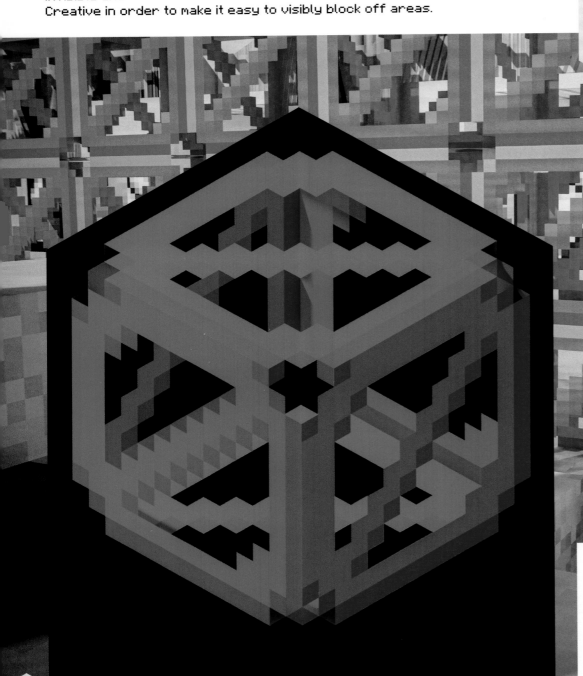

VISIBILITY MODE

If you run into or along a barrier block, the icon will appear as a particle effect. It's completely indestructible, and acts as a solid block, so you can place other blocks on top of it. They're mostly used to control the flow of a map, or to keep players away from important pieces like command blocks, but you can also create cool effects, like making players think they're walking on air!

BORDER

Available only by using commands or the pick block function, border blocks are similar to the barrier as they create invisible, impassable walls; however, the boundaries they create are not limited to the block space it inhabits, but includes any that are vertically aligned.

STATS

TRANSPARENCY	LIGHT EMISSION
	0

RENEWABLE	BLAST RESISTANCE	HARDNESS
	3.6m	∞

FLAMMABLE	SILK TOUCH

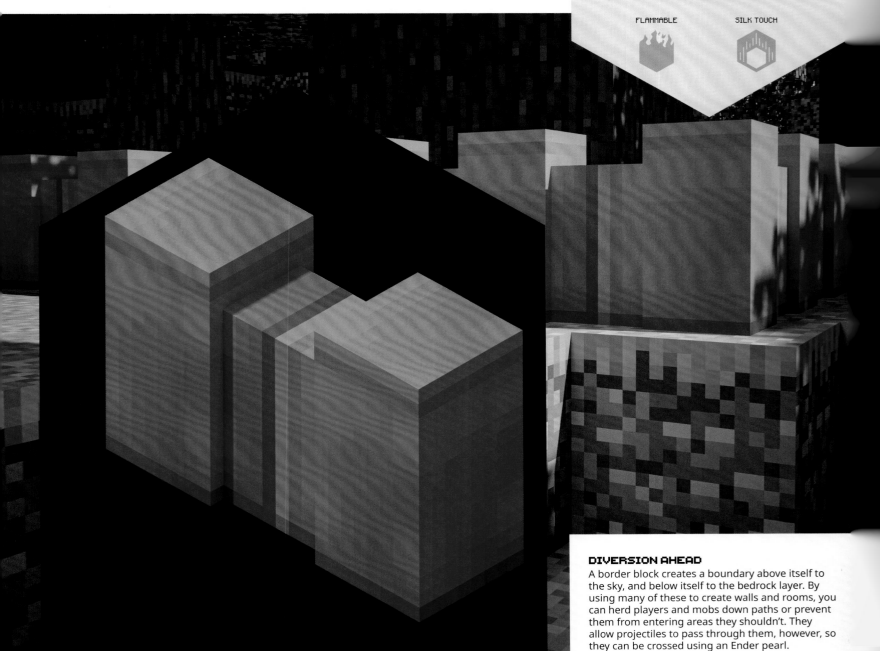

DIVERSION AHEAD

A border block creates a boundary above itself to the sky, and below itself to the bedrock layer. By using many of these to create walls and rooms, you can herd players and mobs down paths or prevent them from entering areas they shouldn't. They allow projectiles to pass through them, however, so they can be crossed using an Ender pearl.

JIGSAW

You can use this powerful technical block in Creative mode to spawn naturally generated locations such as pillager outposts, villages and bastion remnants. The jigsaw block is only obtainable through commands or the pick block tool.

STATS

TRANSPARENCY	LIGHT EMISSION 0
RENEWABLE	BLAST RESISTANCE 3.6m	HARDNESS ∞
FLAMMABLE	SILK TOUCH

STRUCTURE SEED

When you place and interact with a jigsaw block, it will bring up many parameters that you can play around with to dictate how a structure should generate. When "generate" is pressed, it will choose a random template for the structure and begin creating it according to the set parameters.

328

STRUCTURE BLOCK

FOUND:
By command only

You can only obtain it with commands and use it in Creative mode, but the structure block allows you to save or load a structure and generate it in a world. It has additional modes that allow users to look at a structure's data or even export a structure as a 3D model.

STATS

TRANSPARENCY	LIGHT EMISSION 0
RENEWABLE	BLAST RESISTANCE 3.6m	HARDNESS ∞
FLAMMABLE	SILK TOUCH

CREATION CAPABILITIES

When you use the structure block in save mode, you can set the position and dimensions of the structure you want to save and name it. Loading works in a similar way, except you must use a file path leading to where the structure is saved instead, as well as setting the position, rotation and various other parameters.

ALLOW

If you want to control what players can do in your world, use the allow block and its sibling, the deny block, to restrict and open their ability to place blocks in specific areas. The blocks have no effect on players that have the "World Builder" status within a world.

STATS

TRANSPARENCY

LIGHT EMISSION   0

RENEWABLE

BLAST RESISTANCE   3.6m

HARDNESS   ∞

FLAMMABLE

SILK TOUCH

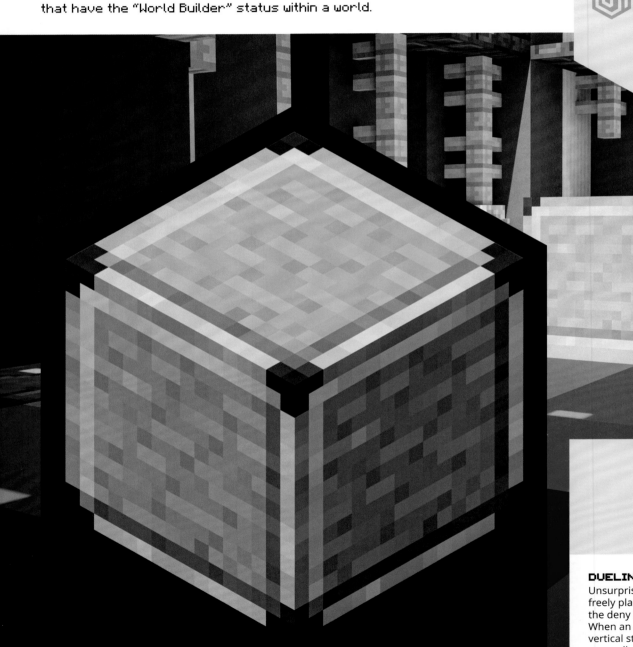

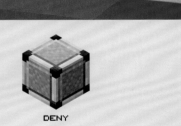

DENY

DUELING BLOCKS

Unsurprisingly, the allow block will let players freely place blocks in an area above them, while the deny block prevents blocks from being placed. When an allow and deny block appear in the same vertical stack, the topmost one takes precedence, so an allow block above a deny one would mean you can build directly above both.

LIGHT BLOCK

Most similar in its properties to air, the light block is an invisible, untouchable, unobtainable block that determines the light level of an area. You can only obtain them with commands, and they're mostly used by map- and minigame-makers to illuminate certain areas.

STATS

TRANSPARENCY		LIGHT EMISSION 0-15
RENEWABLE	BLAST RESISTANCE 3.6m	HARDNESS ∞
	FLAMMABLE	SILK TOUCH

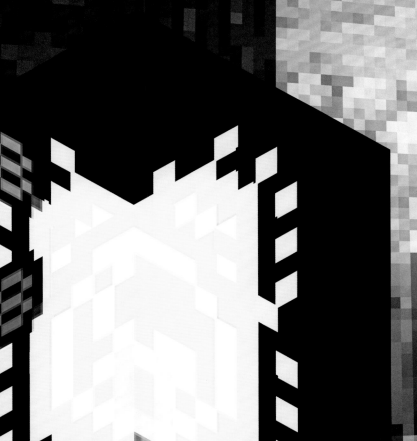

DIMMER SWITCH

Each light block has a corresponding light level, which can be as low as 0 and as high as 15 – the same bright light level that lava or glowstone produces. When you place them in the world, they generate their light level from that block space without the need for a light source.

INDEX